Perspectives in Law, Business and Innovation

Over the last three decades, interconnected processes of globalization and rapid technological change—particularly, the emergence of networked technologies—have profoundly disrupted traditional models of business organization. This economic transformation has created multiple new opportunities for the emergence of alternate business forms, and disruptive innovation has become one of the major driving forces in the contemporary economy. Moreover, in the context of globalization, the innovation space increasingly takes on a global character. The main stakeholders—innovators, entrepreneurs and investors—now have an unprecedented degree of mobility in pursuing economic opportunities wherever they arise. As such, frictionless movement of goods, workers, services, and capital is becoming the "new normal".

This new economic and social reality has created multiple regulatory challenges for policymakers as they struggle to come to terms with the rapid pace of these social and economic changes. Moreover, these challenges impact across multiple fields of both public and private law. Nevertheless, existing approaches within legal science often struggle to deal with innovation and its effects.

Paralleling this shift in the economy, we can, therefore, see a similar process of disruption occurring within contemporary academia, as traditional approaches and disciplinary boundaries—both within and between disciplines—are being re-configured. Conventional notions of legal science are becoming increasingly obsolete or, at least, there is a need to develop alternative perspectives on the various regulatory challenges that are currently being created by the new innovation-driven global economy.

The aim of this series is to provide a forum for the publication of cutting-edge research in the fields of innovation and the law from a Japanese and Asian perspective. The series will cut across the traditional sub-disciplines of legal studies but will be tied together by a focus on contemporary developments in an innovation-driven economy and will deepen our understanding of the various regulatory responses to these economic and social changes.

The series editor and editorial board carefully assess each book proposal and sample chapters in terms of their relevance to law, business, and innovative technological change. Each proposal is evaluated on the basis of its academic value and distinctive contribution to the fast-moving debate in these fields.

All books and chapters in the Perspectives in Law, Business and Innovation book series are indexed in Scopus.

Mateo Aboy · Marcelo Corrales Compagnucci ·
Timo Minssen
Editors

Quantum Technology Governance II

Frameworks, Standards and Ethics

Springer

Editors
Mateo Aboy
Centre for Law, Medicine and Life Sciences (LML) and Centre for Intellectual Property and Information Law (CIPIL)
University of Cambridge
Cambridge, UK

Marcelo Corrales Compagnucci
Center for Advanced Studies in Bioscience Innovation Law (CeBIL), Faculty of Law
University of Copenhagen
Copenhagen, Denmark

Timo Minssen
Center for Advanced Studies in Bioscience Innovation Law (CeBIL), Faculty of Law
University of Copenhagen
Copenhagen, Denmark

ISSN 2520-1875 ISSN 2520-1883 (electronic)
Perspectives in Law, Business and Innovation
ISBN 978-981-92-3767-8 ISBN 978-981-92-3768-5 (eBook)
https://doi.org/10.1007/978-981-92-3768-5

This work was supported by Centre for Advanced Studies in Bioscience Innovation Law (CeBIL), Faculty of Law, University of Copenhagen.

This Springer imprint is published by the registered company Springer Nature Singapore Pte Ltd.
The registered company address is: 152 Beach Road, #21-01/04 Gateway East, Singapore 189721, Singapore

Preface

Quantum technologies are transitioning from experimental prototypes to deployable systems with direct implications for scientific research, life sciences, high-tech companies, security, and industry ranging from drug discovery to materials sciences and drug discovery. As quantum computing, quantum information processing, and related applications mature, questions of technology governance increasingly extend beyond formal law and regulation to include international standards-setting, governance frameworks, ethical principles, and fundamental rights considerations. These governance considerations and instruments operate upstream of legislation, shaping technological trajectories, interoperability, legitimacy, and trust at early stages of development.

This multiple-volume series offers a systematic and interdisciplinary examination of the legal, regulatory, standard, framework, and ethical dimensions of quantum technologies, advancing original and timely contributions to the emerging discourse on quantum technology governance. As the first comprehensive anthology to integrate these domains, it provides a scholarly collection that captures the global scope of recent developments in quantum governance, law, standards, ethics, and policy.

Quantum Technology Governance II: Frameworks, Standards & Ethics, the second volume of the Quantum Technology Governance series, builds and expands on the legal and regulatory foundations established in *Volume I* by examining how governance is constructed through frameworks, standards, and ethical analysis. Together, the two volumes offer a comprehensive and interdisciplinary analysis of how quantum technologies are (or could be) governed across their life cycle. While *Volume I* focuses on legal and regulatory mechanisms, *Volume II* addresses the softer yet equally important and structurally decisive layers of governance that influence overall quality management systems (QMS), design choices, risk management, organizational and technical controls, implementation and deployment pathways, and societal integration, adoption and trust.

The present volume explores how international consensus standards can function as *de facto* governance tools, why they matter for emerging quantum applications, and how governance frameworks and ethical reflection can be operationalized without resorting to technological exceptionalism. The contributions examine governance as a layered and dynamic process, spanning technical and organizational architectures, institutional governance and coordination, and normative commitments.

The chapters in this volume address, *inter alia*:

- The strategic role of *standards* in shaping quantum technology governance.
- The institutional and political dynamics of *standards development*, highlighting why standards matter for overall governance and consensus expectations, coordination, interoperability, and global alignment in quantum innovation.
- A *governance-stack framework* for quantum technology applications in the *life sciences*, examining ontological challenges, integration frictions, and cross-layer dependencies between technical and normative systems.
- *Ethical frameworks* for quantum information technologies, offering a roadmap that connects high-level principles to concrete governance practices.
- *Critical reflections on claims of ethical exceptionalism* in quantum computing, drawing lessons from classical computing to avoid overstated novelty while remaining attentive to genuine risks.
- An analysis of quantum computing through the lens of the *right to science*, using it both as a stress-test for existing human rights frameworks and as a test case for future-oriented governance.

Collectively, these contributions suggest that effective quantum governance does not (and likely could not rely) on law and regulation alone. Instead, it requires a broader but coherent governance stack in which international consensus standards, ethical analysis and reflection, and institutional frameworks interact with legal rules to help guide responsible innovation. By foregrounding these dimensions, *Volume II* provides scholars, practitioners, policymakers, standard-setters, and technologists with analysis and conceptual frameworks to navigate the normative and organizational challenges posed by quantum technologies as they move toward real-world deployment and required fit-for-purpose governance systems (e.g., Quantum Technology Management Systems or QT-QMS) similar to those employed in other areas such as medical devices (MD-QMS).

Taken together, *Quantum Technology Governance I* and *II* are designed to serve both as an accessible entry point and as an advanced reference work for those engaged in shaping the future of quantum technologies. With contributions from leading experts across disciplines (including engineering, law and ethics) and various jurisdictions, the series advances a general (and nuanced) understanding of how governance can respond to the technical, legal, and ethical demands of the quantum era.

This publication was made possible by the generous support of a Novo Nordisk Foundation (NNF) grant for a scientifically independent Collaborative Research Program in Bioscience Innovation Law (Inter-CeBIL Program—grant no. NNF23SA0087056). In the preparation of their contribution, the authors acknowledge that "any use of generative AI in this manuscript adheres to ethical guidelines for use and acknowledgement of generative AI in academic research. Each author has made a substantial contribution to the work, which has been thoroughly vetted for accuracy, and assumes responsibility for the integrity of their contributions" in accordance with the ethical guidance on AI use and disclosure set out by Porsdam Mann et al. in *Nature Machine Intelligence, Vol 6, 2024, 1272–1274.*

Cambridge, UK Mateo Aboy
Copenhagen, Denmark Marcelo Corrales Compagnucci
Copenhagen, Denmark Timo Minssen

Contents

Editors and Contributors

About the Editors

Mateo Aboy is Director of Research in Technology & Law (Biomedical Innovation, AI, QT & Law) at the Faculty of Law, University of Cambridge. He is a member of the Centre for Law, Medicine & Life Sciences (LML) and the Centre for IP & Information Law (CIPIL) at the University of Cambridge. His multidisciplinary background includes a combination of law, engineering, regulatory science, and management experience. He holds degrees in electrical & computer engineering (BS, BSEE, MSECE, MPhil/DEA, PhD ECE), law (SJD/PhD/LLD), and international management (MBA), as well as professional registrations as a Professional Chartered Engineer (CEng, EU/ES COIT), Certified Licensing Professional (CLP), Patent Practitioner with a Bar Admission/License to practice in patent cases before the United States Patent Office (USPTO), Fellow of Information Privacy (FIP, IAPP), Certified Privacy Information Professional (CIPP/E), Certified Privacy Manager (CIPM), Lead Implementer of Information Security Management Systems-ISMS (ISO 27001), Lead Auditor of Medical Device Quality Management Systems (ISO 13485), Lead Implementer of Privacy Information Management Systems—PIMS (ISO 27701), and Certified Data Protection Officer (C-DPO). Mateo's research seeks to understand the drivers of technology-based innovation, IP incentives, and the determinants of how emergent technologies are protected, regulated, funded, developed, adopted and used in practice. He is the author of more than 200 scholarly articles published in leading scientific, engineering and legal journals. His professional experience includes work in various senior roles both in private sector and in academia. He holds over 20 patents as an inventor.

Marcelo Corrales Compagnucci is Associate Professor and Associate Director at the Center for Advanced Studies in Bioscience Innovation Law (CeBIL), Faculty of Law, University of Copenhagen in Denmark. He is also Inter-CeBIL Research Affiliate at the Petrie-Flom Center for Health Law Policy, Biotechnology, and Bioethics at Harvard Law School. He specializes in information technology, AI governance, privacy, data protection, and data security law. His research interests are the legal issues involved in disruptive innovation technologies and biomedicine. He is the founder of CORCOM IT Law Consulting. His past activities have included working as a consultant and lawyer for law firms and IT companies. He was also a research associate with the Institute for Legal Informatics (IRI) at Leibniz Universität Hannover in Germany, and a visiting research fellow in various research centers around the world, including Harvard Law School, Cambridge University, the Max Planck Institute, University of Edinburgh, Turin University, and the Academia Sinica in Taiwan. He has a Doctor of Laws (LL.D.) degree from Kyushu University in Japan. He also holds a Master of Laws (LL.M.) in international economics and business law from Kyushu University, and an LL.M. in law and information technology and an LL.M. in European intellectual property law, both from the University of Stockholm in Sweden. He has several publications in the field of IT Law. His most recent book collections co-edited with various authors include *Generative AI, Contracts, Law and Design* (Springer, 2025), *International Transfers of Health Data: A Global Perspective* (Springer, 2024); *AI in eHealth: Human Autonomy, Data Governance and Privacy in Healthcare* (Cambridge University Press, 2022), *Smart Contracts: Technological, Business and Legal Perspectives* (Hart Publishing, 2021); *Legal Design: Integrating Business, Design and Legal Thinking with Technology* (Edward Elgar Publishing, 2021).

Timo Minssen is Professor of Law at the University of Copenhagen (UCPH). He is Director of UCPH's Center for Advanced Studies in Bioscience Innovation Law (CeBIL), Faculty of Law and holds the UNESCO Co-Chair in the Right to Science. Timo is also an Inter-CeBIL Research Affiliate at Harvard Law School and at the University of Cambridge, as well as Associate Member of the Centre of Genomics and Policy at McGill University. His research and practice concentrates on IP-, Competition & Regulatory Law in emerging technologies, including the law and ethics of AI, quantum technologies, and health & life science innovation. Timo holds a German law degree from the University of Göttingen, and biotech and IP-related LL.M. M.I.C.L., LL.Lic., and LL.D. degrees from Lund and Uppsala University. Previously, he was an Epigenetics fellow at the Pufendorf Institute for Advanced Studies and Visiting Professor at the Technical University of Munich, the Universities of Cambridge and Oxford, Waseda Law School, Harvard Law School, and the Max Planck Institute for Innovation and Competition. In 2007, he also held the position of Associate Professor at the Chicago-Kent College of Law, teaching a course in comparative European and US patent law. Moreover, he was trained in the German Court system, the European Patent Office, law firms, and start-ups. Timo is Scientific Advisory Board Member of the Munich Intellectual Property Law Centre (MIPLC). He also serves as an advisor to the WHO, WIPO, OECD, the EU Commission, companies, national governments, and law firms. At UCPH he leads several interdisciplinary research projects on legal issues in emerging biotechnologies, precision medicine, ATMPs, antimicrobial resistance, pandemic preparedness, advanced medical computing, medical devices, and in sustainable innovation. He is the PI and grant holder of a large research program in bioscience innovation law, funded by the

Novo Nordisk Foundation and involving international core partners, such as Harvard, DTU, and the Universities of Cambridge and Michigan. His research comprises 8 books and 260+ publications in leading law and science journals. It is frequently featured in international media, such as The Economist, Financial Times, El Mundo, Politico, Times of India, WHO Bulletin, and Times Higher Education.

List of Contributors

Mateo Aboy Centre for Law, Medicine and Life Sciences (LML) and Centre for Intellectual Property and Information Law (CIPIL), University of Cambridge, Cambridge, United Kingdom

Marcelo Corrales Compagnucci Center for Advanced Studies in Bioscience Innovation Law (CeBIL), Faculty of Law, University of Copenhagen, Copenhagen, Denmark;
Inter-CeBIL Research Affiliate at the Petrie-Flom Center for Health Law Policy, Biotechnology, and Bioethics, Havard Law School, Cambridge, MA, US

Peter Alexander Earls Davis Centre for Advanced Studies in Bioscience Innovation Law (CeBIL), Faculty of Law, University of Copenhagen, Copenhagen, Denmark

Brian D. Earp Center for Biomedical Ethics, Yong Loo Lin School of Medicine, National University of Singapore, Singapore, Singapore

Gabriela Lenarczyk Center for Advanced Studies in Bioscience Innovation Law (CeBIL), Faculty of Law, University of Copenhagen, Copenhagen, Denmark

Timo Minssen Center for Advanced Studies in Bioscience Innovation Law (CeBIL), Faculty of Law, University of Copenhagen, Copenhagen, Denmark;
LML Research Affiliate at the University of Cambridge, Cambridge, UK;
Inter-CeBIL Research Affiliate at the Petrie-Flom Center for Health Law Policy, Biotechnology, and Bioethics, Havard Law School, Cambridge, MA, US;
Associate Member of McGill University's Centre of Genomics and Policy, Quebec, Canada

Elija Perrier Centre for Quantum Software and Information, University of Technology, Sydney, Australia;
Centre for Law, Medicine and Life Sciences (LML), University of Cambridge, Cambridge, UK

Sebastian Porsdam Mann Center for Advanced Studies in Bioscience Innovation Law (CeBIL), Faculty of Law, University of Copenhagen, Copenhagen, Denmark;
Center for Biomedical Ethics, Yong Loo Lin School of Medicine, National University of Singapore, Singapore, Singapore

Hannah Louise Smith Centre for Advanced Studies in Bioscience Innovation Law (CeBIL), Faculty of Law, University of Copenhagen, Copenhagen, Denmark

Chapter 1
Governing Quantum Technology Upstream: Frameworks, Standards and Ethics

Mateo Aboy, Marcelo Corrales Compagnucci, and Timo Minssen

1.1 Introduction: From Regulation to Upstream Governance

Quantum technologies are transitioning from experimental prototypes to actually deployable systems with real-world implications for scientific discovery, drug development, national security and competitive positioning, healthcare, and technology-based innovation across sectors. As an example, quantum computing promises breakthroughs in cryptanalysis, life science R&D, and complex optimization in several application domains. As these technologies mature, governance questions increasingly arise at early stages preceding formal legislation.[1,2]

The first volume of this series shows that quantum technologies are already indirectly regulated through export controls,[3] cybersecurity[4] and intellectual property frameworks,[5] semiconductor policy, and sector-specific safety regimes. Yet, as Smith et al.[6] observe, quantum technologies largely remain in a pre-legislative phase, where dedicated statutory regimes are sparse and governance is instead exercised

[1] Aboy et al. (2022).

[2] Aboy et al. (2025).

[3] Davis et al. (2026).

[4] Davis et al. (2026).

[5] Lenarczyk et al. (2026).

[6] Smith et al. (2026).

M. Aboy (✉)
Centre for Law, Medicine and Life Sciences (LML) and Centre for Intellectual Property and Information Law (CIPIL), University of Cambridge, Cambridge, United Kingdom

M. C. Compagnucci · T. Minssen
Center for Advanced Studies in Bioscience Innovation Law (CeBIL), Faculty of Law, University of Copenhagen, Copenhagen, Denmark

M. Aboy et al. (eds.), *Quantum Technology Governance II*, Perspectives in Law, Business and Innovation, https://doi.org/10.1007/978-981-92-3768-5_1

through softer mechanisms (e.g., international standards) that shape technological development indirectly.[7,8]

Drawing on concepts like the SEA (safeguarding, engaging, advancing)[9] framework and governance-stack model[10] which aligns regulatory instruments with quantum information technologies (QIT)'s technical layers from hardware to algorithms, this volume explores how existing technology governance frameworks can be applied or adapted to quantum technologies. As was the case with the first volume, several contributions in this volume underscore the need for sensible technology governance to ensure that quantum technologies continue to advance and benefit humanity (*advancement*) while mitigating potential downside risks and harms (*safeguarding*)[11].

This observation motivates one of the central themes of this chapter: quantum governance must be understood as layered and dynamic. It unfolds not only through binding rules but through international standards, institutional coordination, governance frameworks, ethical reflection, funding strategies, and strategic industrial policy. These instruments collectively form what we describe as a governance stack, that is a configuration of interlocking layers that operate at different levels in the stack (and different level of abstraction) yet mutually interact one another.[12]

1.2 The Governance Stack as Analytical Framework

The governance stack model responds to the Collingridge dilemma identified in emerging technology governance. Regulate too early, and one risks locking in assumptions that later prove misguided; regulate too late, and technological infrastructures become entrenched and resistant to reform. Smith et al.[13] situate quantum standardization precisely within this dilemma, arguing that standards provide an anticipatory mechanism capable of influencing technological trajectories without imposing rigid statutory or regulatory constraints. Within the governance stack, international consensus standards such as the ISO/IEC operate as pragmatic coordination tools. Developed through international consensus-based organizations, they supply shared terminology, testing protocols, interoperability criteria, and quality benchmarks.[2] Their best-practice international consensus character often results in normative influence, that is, international standards typically become *de facto* requirements through market pressure, procurement or vendor qualification rules and expectations, or incorporation into legislation or regulation by reference. As Smith

[7] Kop et al. (2024a).

[8] Aboy et al. (2022).

[9] Kop et al. (2024a).

[10] Perrier and Aboy (2026a, b, c).

[11] Kop et al. (2024a, b).

[12] Perrier and Aboy (2026a, c).

[13] Smith et al. (2026).

et al.[14] notes, standard-setting bodies such as ISO/IEC and other regional organizations can shape quantum development and technology governance through technical committees, subcommittees, and harmonized outputs that influence how quantum systems are evaluated and integrated. This not only includes technical standards focused on interoperability or cryptography standards but also broader standards defining the requirements for quality management systems (QMS) for the development and deployment of quantum systems (e.g., QT-QMS) similarly to the ISO standards currently required for the development and deployment of medical devices (MD-QMS).

Ethical analysis forms a complementary layer within the governance stack. Rather than replacing law, regulation or international standards, it helps provide a normative orientation and often clarifies the values at stake. Porsdam Mann et al.[15] frame the debate as one of "ethical exceptionalism", that is, whether or to what extent quantum computing introduces fundamentally novel ethical challenges or whether its dilemmas are similar in kind to those of classical computing, perhaps in a transformed or amplified form in certain specific applications (e.g., decryption). Drawing on historical case studies from computer ethics, the authors argue that while quantum technologies may shift ethical issues to deeper infrastructural layers (such as cryptographic vulnerability) the underlying concerns of security, justice, governance, and human agency remain recognizable in their essence. The implication is not complacency, but careful learning and adaptation of existing ethical frameworks from classical computer ethics to quantum-specific contexts, especially in quantum computing.

Sector-specific governance frameworks and sectoral governance mechanisms constitute another layer. Perrier and Aboy[16] illustrate this in the life sciences context, where very early-stage quantum technologies confront mature governance and regulatory regimes in pharmaceuticals, medical devices, and biotechnology. The contribution identifies two central dilemmas: (1) a technical dilemma arising from the ontological differences between quantum and classical information processing, and (2) an integration dilemma concerning the harmonization of nascent QIT oversight with established life sciences regulation. Accordingly, the proposed governance stack model analysis for quantum in the life sciences maps quantum interventions across a hierarchical life sciences "stack", from atomic-level simulations to population-level analytics, illustrating how governance obligations or considerations attach differently at each level. One of the findings is that the existing and matured governance frameworks employed in regulated life sciences contexts such as drug discovery, drug development and medical devices are already likely well suited to accommodate the introduction of quantum-based technologies (e.g., for aiding the various phases in drug discovery and development) while adequately managing the overall risk of these programs (e.g, without the novel quantum technology introduced and employed for

[14] Smith et al. (2026).

[15] Porsdam Mann et al. (2026a).

[16] Perrier and Aboy (2026c).

particular tasks in the drug development life cycle materially increasing the aggregate risk of the program) due to the overarching risk-management controls already surrounding the regulated activity (e.g., drug development).

Finally, formal law and human rights norms can provide insights as well as overarching constraints and guiding principles. Porsdam Mann et al.[17] argue that the human right to science enshrined in the Universal Declaration of Human Rights offers an underutilized yet powerful normative framework for quantum governance.

1.3 International Quantum Standards as Governance Tools

International consensus standards occupy a distinctive position within the governance stack. Although formally voluntary, they frequently function as quasi-legal or quasi-norm instruments when incorporated into regulatory frameworks. One example for this are quality management systems (QMS) in medical devices which are required under US FDA and EU MDR laws (and the associated notified bodies or accredited third parties audits often based on the ISO 13485 QMS standard for medical devices). Thus, Smith et al.[18] describe how harmonized standards can result in something akin to legal effects when linked to legislative or regulatory instruments, blurring the distinction between soft and hard law.

This hybrid character reflects the evolving distribution of governance authority between states and non-state actors. That said, standard-setting organizations may be formally recognized by governments or operate through quasi-formal associations with national standard setting bodies. In either case, they represent a partial externalization of regulatory functions. Accordingly, their legitimacy derives not from electoral representation (at least directly) but from technical expertise, stakeholder input (including leading technical entities), consensus processes, transnational coordination, and global harmonization.

In the quantum domain, the diversity of applications (e.g., from sensing to communication to computing) creates a complex governance landscape. Overall, standards are helping at this early stage of the development process. For instance, terminology standards facilitate research and development collaboration at early stages, while quality management systems and interoperability standards become more salient as technologies approach commercialization based on similar frameworks already well-known in other areas such as medical devices. A standards-first approach thus reflects both the stage of technological development and governance prudence.

---

[17] Porsdam Mann et al. (2026b).

[18] Smith et al. (2026).

1.4 A Sectoral Illustration: Quantum in the Life Sciences

The life sciences provide a concrete illustration of the governance stack in operation within a particular high-stakes regulated sector. Perrier and Aboy[19] emphasize that quantum technologies are informational in character, since their primary effects are mediated through information processing, simulation, sensing, and communication rather than direct physical intervention. Nevertheless, their outputs influence decision-making at multiple levels of the life sciences hierarchy, from atomic modelling in drug discovery to macro-level simulation.

The ontological features of quantum systems (e.g., superposition, entanglement, no-cloning, probabilistic nature) appear to challenge classical regulatory assumptions that rely on deterministic reproducibility and stable validation metrics. That said, this is an area where governance models (including risk-management controls in pharmaceutical drug development and medical device authorizations) are quite robust and the overall QMS routinely employed to meet regulatory requirements are capable of (and used to) dealing with high-risk technological and scientific developments and novel tools. In pharmaceutical innovation, for example, quantum simulations may generate probabilistic outputs that require hybrid validation strategies combining classical and quantum benchmarking. However, rather than mandating wholesale regulatory reinvention, the chapter argues for targeted guidance layered onto existing regulatory frameworks to accommodate quantum-specific effects while preserving institutional continuity with existing QMS practices and know-how.

This approach reinforces a broader lesson of the *governance stack* model, namely that governance need not begin from scratch with each technological shift. Instead, existing frameworks often possess adaptive capacity and flexibility, provided they are supplemented with technical precision and informed by technical, legal, regulatory, standard-setting, and ethical reflection.

1.5 Ethical Continuity and Layer Shifts

The ethical debate surrounding quantum computing echoes earlier controversies in classical computing. Porsdam Mann et al. argue that concerns about encryption vulnerability, dual-use potential, digital divides, and governance opacity are not completely unprecedented. Some of these concerns parallel those already encountered in earlier technological developments, such as classical computing and the development of the internet (and more recently AI). In classical computing, issues of opacity often arose at the software or algorithmic layer. In quantum computing, they may also arise at the hardware or ontological level, where quantum processes are inherently inaccessible to direct classical observation. Yet there is nevertheless a level of continuity and usefulness associated with the technology ethics reflections from previous computing advances.

[19] Perrier and Aboy (2026c).

The concept of “layer shifts” thus complements the governance stack model. As ethical challenges migrate across technical layers, governance instruments must recalibrate accordingly. For instance, international consensus standards may embed QMS and technical requirements into hardware development and evaluation protocols; institutional governance frameworks and notified bodies may mandate reporting or auditing mechanisms based on such standards; and human rights norms may impose access and non-discrimination obligations. Ethical exceptionalism might therefore neither be completely warranted nor entirely misguided. In that regard, Porsdam et al. further find that quantum technologies demand adaptation, not wholesale ethical reinvention.

Similarly, the human right to science situates quantum governance within a global normative framework that transcends national security and industrial competition. Porsdam Mann et al. identify a number of potential challenges to reconciling quantum development with this right. These include geopolitical access controls, corporate knowledge concentration, economic exclusion and the quantum divide, tensions between participation and scientific freedom, and restrictive definitions of science that marginalize ethical and social inquiry. Quantum computing thus functions both as a “stress-test” for the right to science and as a potential “opportunity” to operationalize it. By embedding quantum governance within a human-rights framework, policymakers can move beyond narrowly focused security logics toward a more comprehensive vision of equitable technological development (which includes security as well as other broader ethical considerations).

1.6 Conclusion

Quantum governance is not reducible only to regulatory export controls or prospective quantum-specific regulatory regimes such as the potential EU Quantum Act. Rather it is a layered, dynamic process in which international consensus standards help coordinate practice and real-world governance implementations, ethical reflection clarifies values and objectives, institutional frameworks mediate integration and practical risk-management, and human rights norms anchor overall legitimacy. The governance stack model provides a conceptual lens for understanding how these instruments interact across technical and organizational levels.

International standards offer flexibility and global harmonization at a stage when legislative rigidity would be premature. Ethical analysis, informed by historical lessons from classical computing, helps ensure a degree of continuity without complacency. Sectoral case studies in key areas (e.g., life science R&D) demonstrate the latent and adaptive capacity of existing regulatory systems when supplemented with quantum-specific guidance. And the right to science situates quantum development within a broader commitment to shared benefit, democratic participation, and global justice.

As quantum technologies advance from laboratory experimentation to societal infrastructure, governance must evolve in tandem. The task is not simply to regulate quantum systems, especially during the very early stages of technology development and market introduction (which is still arguably quite limited). Rather the challenge lies in designing a coherent governance ecosystem, which is effective, adaptive, inclusive, and normatively grounded, and that can promote and steer this transformative innovation *(advancement)* with high potential for important sectors such as the life sciences and healthcare (Kop et al. 2024a, b). Overall, the various contributions across both volumes suggest that quantum technologies can be guided through coordinated, adaptive integration of international standards, ethical reflection, institutional oversight, and human rights norms upstream of regulation (*safeguarding*) (Kop et al. 2024a, b). This would make prudent consensus-standards and regulatory evolution the appropriate path for responsible quantum governance as opposed to entirely novel legal regimes (Aboy et al. 2025).

Acknowledgments This work was made possible through the generous support of the Novo Nordisk Foundation (NNF) via a grant for the scientifically independent Collaborative Research Program in Bioscience Innovation Law (Inter-CeBIL Program—Grant No. NNF23SA0087056). Any use of AI in this manuscript adheres to ethical guidelines for use and acknowledgement of AI in academic research. Each author has made a substantial contribution to the work, which has been thoroughly vetted for accuracy, and assumes responsibility for the integrity of their contributions in accordance with the ethical guidance on AI use and disclosure set out by Porsdam Mann et al.[20]

References

Aboy, M., Minssen, T., Kop, M. (2022) Mapping the Patent Landscape of Quantum Technologies: Patenting Trends, Innovation and Policy Implications. *IIC* 53: 853-882.

Aboy, M., et al. (2025) Quantum technology governance: A standards-first approach. *Science* 380(6760): 575-578.

Aboy, M., Crespo, C., Minssen, T., (2026) Mapping the Patent Landscape of Quantum Technologies: Evolving Patenting Trends and Policy Implications, in: Aboy M., Corrales Compagnucci, M. and Minssen, T. (eds) *Quantum Technology Governance I: Law & Regulation*, Perspectives in Law, Business and Innovation (Springer Nature, Singapore). ahead-of-print.

Davis, P. et al. (2026b) EU Cybersecurity Regulation in the Quantum Age, in: Aboy M., Corrales Compagnucci, M. and Minssen, T. (eds) *Quantum Technology Governance I: Law & Regulation*, Perspectives in Law, Business and Innovation (Springer Nature, Singapore). ahead-of-print.

Davis, P., Aboy, M., Minssen, T. (2026a) Regulatory Challenges and Opportinuties of Export Controls on Quantum Computing, in: Aboy M., Corrales Compagnucci, M. and Minssen, T. (eds) *Quantum Technology Governance I: Law & Regulation*, Perspectives in Law, Business and Innovation (Springer Nature, Singapore). ahead-of-print.

Kop, M., et al. (2024a) Towards responsible quantum technology: safeguarding, engaging and advancing quantum R&D. *UC Law Science & Technology Journal* 15(1): 63-94.

Kop, M. et al. (2024b) Ten principles for responsible quantum innovation. *Quantum Science and Technology* 9(3): 035013.

Lenarczyk, G., Minssen, T., Aboy, M., (2026) IP in Superposition: Patents, Trade Secrets, and Open Innovation in Quantum Information Technology, in: Aboy M., Corrales Compagnucci, M. and

[20] Porsdam Mann et al. (2024).

Minssen, T. (eds) *Quantum Technology Governance I: Law & Regulation*, Perspectives in Law, Business and Innovation (Springer Nature, Singapore). ahead-of-print.

Perrier, E., Aboy, M. (2026a) Quantum Information Technology & the Law, in: Aboy M., Corrales Compagnucci, M. and Minssen, T. (eds) *Quantum Technology Governance I: Law & Regulation*, Perspectives in Law, Business and Innovation (Springer Nature, Singapore). ahead-of-print.

Perrier, E., Aboy, M. (2026b) Quantum Information Technologies and Public International: Strategic, Legal, And Geopolitical Dimensions, in: Aboy M., Corrales Compagnucci, M. and Minssen, T. (eds) *Quantum Technology Governance I: Law & Regulation*, Perspectives in Law, Business and Innovation (Springer Nature, Singapore). ahead-of-print.

Perrier, E., Aboy, M. (2026c) A Governance Stack Framework for Quantum Technology Applications in Life Sciences: Examining Ontological and Integration Challenges, in: Aboy M., Corrales Compagnucci, M. and Minssen, T. (eds) *Quantum Technology Governance II: Frameworks, Standards & Ethics*, Perspectives in Law, Business and Innovation (Springer Nature, Singapore). ahead-of-print.

Porsdam Mann, S., et al. (2024). Guidelines for Ethical Use and Acknowledgment of Large Language Models in Academic Writing. *Nature Machine Intelligence* 6: 1272-1274.

Porsdam Mann, S., et al. (2026a) Quantum Computing and Ethical Exceptionalism: Lessons from Classical Computing, in: Aboy M., Corrales Compagnucci, M. and Minssen, T. (eds) *Quantum Technology Governance II: Frameworks, Standards & Ethics*, Perspectives in Law, Business and Innovation (Springer Nature, Singapore). ahead-of-print.

Porsdam Mann, S., et al. (2026b) Quantum Computing and the Right to Science: A Stress-Test and Test Case, in: Aboy M., Corrales Compagnucci, M. and Minssen, T. (eds) *Quantum Technology Governance II: Frameworks, Standards & Ethics*, Perspectives in Law, Business and Innovation (Springer Nature, Singapore). ahead-of-print.

Smith, H.L., et al. (2026) Quantum Governance in the Making: Why Standards Matter, in: Aboy M., Corrales Compagnucci, M. and Minssen, T. (eds) *Quantum Technology Governance II: Frameworks, Standards & Ethics*, Perspectives in Law, Business and Innovation (Springer Nature, Singapore). ahead-of-print.

Chapter 2
Quantum Governance in the Making: Why Standards Matter

Hannah Louise Smith, Mateo Aboy, Peter Alexander Earls Davis, and Timo Minssen

2.1 Introduction

Quantum Technologies (QTs) promise to revolutionize information processing, communication, and sensing by capitalizing on the unique properties of quantum systems, such as entanglement and superposition. Currently, there are three main types of QT that are being developed and deployed[1]; quantum sensing technologies such as atomic clocks and inertial sensors that attain unparalleled accuracy, quantum computing technologies such as universal quantum computers that operate with quantum gates that enable them to potentially solve problems that are intractable for classical computers, and quantum communication technologies such as quantum key distribution technologies that encode cryptographic keys in qubits, exploiting their tendency to decohere when observed as a means to strengthen digital security.

The range of quantum technologies means they have the potential to impact upon many sectors and industries within society. Quantum sensing technologies have shown great promise concerning improving the outputs of medical imaging devices and other diagnostic devices,[2] quantum computing is a promising prospect for the energy sector with potential applications including quantum simulations to discover more energy efficient material and processes and improve energy forecasting,[3] and research into quantum key distribution technologies has explored its

H. L. Smith (✉) · P. A. E. Davis · T. Minssen
Center for Advanced Studies in Bioscience Innovation Law (CeBIL), Faculty of Law, University of Copenhagen, Copenhagen, Denmark

M. Aboy
Centre for Law, Medicine and Life Sciences, (LML) and Centre for Intellectual Property and Information Law (CIPIL), University of Cambridge, Cambridge, UK

[1] CEN-CENELEC (2023), European Commission (2025).

[2] Wu and Weil (2022).

[3] Ajagekar and You (2022).

M. Aboy et al. (eds.), *Quantum Technology Governance II*, Perspectives in Law, Business and Innovation, https://doi.org/10.1007/978-981-92-3768-5_2

potential for improving the security of critical infrastructure.[4] This great array of technologies has the potential to secure significant benefits, particularly in the fields of healthcare, the energy sector, and communications, but also poses great risks to a range of interests and societal values.[5] In particular, there are fears about the ability of quantum computers to break existing cryptographic methods, undermining the security of global data transmissions and quantum sensors being used to facilitate advanced levels of surveillance. Quantum technologies vary significantly in their maturity levels, with some technologies reaching the point of commercialization, such as certain quantum sensing applications, and others only displaying early experimental proof of concept.[6]

The increasing maturity of quantum technologies and their attendant scope for enabling the shift from *potential* to *actual* benefits and risks, raises questions as to the governance of these technologies.[7] In the absence of much law specifically governing quantum technologies, this chapter explores the potential role of standards as one of the available mechanisms for governing the development of a range of quantum technologies. To do so, it explores potential reasons for why quantum technologies have largely remained untouched by legislation, in contrast to the EU's extensive legislative response to artificial intelligence, and the potential role of standards as a means for shaping the current development of quantum technologies.[8] It then analyses the potential strengths and weaknesses of relying upon standards, before discussing what role states are currently playing in quantum technologies instead of legislators. Where relevant, the chapter draws upon the unfolding regulation of other emerging, yet more mature, technologies, such as AI to see what, if any, lessons may be learned from their governance trajectory.

2.2 Current State of Regulating Quantum Technologies

Novel technologies have always posed challenges for regulators. One of the more notable challenges is the Collingridge dilemma, which highlights the difficulties in determining the best time to regulate. It posits that the early regulation of technologies risks introducing legislation that constrains and promotes certain behaviors that may prove to not align with how the regulated technology actually develops. Equally, waiting to understand better how a given technology may impact on society increases the risk of attitudes, applications, and infrastructure being entrenched within society.

---

[4] Swayne (2025a).

[5] Danish Business Authority and Danish Quantum Community (2024).

[6] Aboy et al. (2023).

[7] Kop et al. (2024a).

[8] The current EU Executive Vice-President for Tech Sovereignty, Security, and Democracy referenced a potential EU Quantum Act during her confirmation hearing and the EU Commission's 2025 Work Programme references plans to create a Quantum Act after it has published its EU Quantum Strategy. Nevertheless, this legislation is not guaranteed and will not enter into force until 2026 at the earliest even if the legislative process goes smoothly.

This undermines the ability of laws to influence change in a meaningful and cost-effective way. These two outcomes thus create a dilemma for regulators trying to decide when best to respond to novel technologies so that they act upon a solid foundation of knowledge but don't face an uphill battle trying to use laws to change norms, practices, or institutions that have become entrenched over time. Accordingly, non-legislative forms of governance have gained prominence,[9] sometimes described as "anticipatory governance"[10] or "upstream governance" to denote the efforts to shape and guide technologies prior to the law becoming an appropriate means of governance.[11]

This does not mean there are no laws that govern QTs, nor that the development of QTs has gone unnoticed by regulators. In the EU, the European Chips Act,[12] which entered into force in September 2023, aims to accelerate innovation in the field of semiconductor technologies, including quantum chips by establishing design libraries for quantum chips, developing pilot lines for the integration of quantum circuits and control electronics for building quantum, chips, and supporting the development of facilities for testing and validating advanced quantum components. In the US, the National Quantum Initiative Act[13] was signed into law in 2018 that aimed to accelerate the development of quantum information science and technology applications in the US by strengthening and coordinating research and development activities across government departments and agencies, industry, and the academic community. The National Quantum Initiative Act was amended by the CHIPS and Science Act of 2022[14] to further enhance efforts to innovate QT. The legislation encourages further research and coordination efforts by allocating funding for different programs related to QT and supporting the development of a quantum-aware workforce.

Therefore, it is a misnomer to state that QTs are completely unregulated but, so far, the focus is less upon QTs or their uses and more upon creating an innovation-friendly regulatory ecosystem. There are also laws that regulate the export of QTs with the US Department of Commerce's Bureau of Industry and Security implementing controls through Export Control Classification Numbers and licensing requirements and the EU governing the export of certain QTs under its own Dual-Use Regulation and licensing requirements for exporting QTs to non-EU countries. These efforts are fairly nascent and, at least in principle, are directed towards the protection of interests such as national security rather than comprising a fully-fledged regulatory regime.[15] Instead, standards are starting to play a role in influencing QT development and dissemination.

---

[9] Kop et al. (2024b).

[10] Perrier (2022).

[11] Hagemann et al. (2018).

[12] Regulation (EU) 2023/1781 of the European Parliament and of the Council of 13 September 2023 establishing a framework of measures for strengthening Europe's semiconductor ecosystem and amending Regulation (EU) 2021/694 (Chips Act) (Text with EEA relevance).

[13] National Quantum Initiative Act (2018).

[14] CHIPS and Science Act (2022).

[15] CEN-CENELEC (2023), Davis et al. (2025b).

It thus appears that, drawing upon the ideas articulated by the Collingridge dilemma, that legislation is not the most appropriate regulatory option for securing the technology's benefits and constraining its risks. The purpose of this paper is not to assess the wisdom of this decision, but rather to explore what governs the development of QTs when legislators decide it is not an appropriate time to legislate via traditional laws and the respective strengths and weaknesses of a governance approach that relies on alternative mechanisms to laws. An expansionist approach to quantum governance, which goes beyond legislation, adds nuance to the initial starkness of the Collingridge dilemma. First, it highlights the range of ways in which QTs can be governed and moves away from the implied assumption that legislation provides a "one shot" opportunity, and binary choice, to currently regulate. Second, it expands the range of actors that are relevant to the governance of QTs beyond legislators. Third, it reduces the risks associated with considering QTs in isolation or only having a select and potentially homogenous set of voices feed into regulatory conversations, which may overlook how QTs are predicted to impact society and societal values.

2.3 The Importance of Standards

In general, standards are a means for "guiding and judging behavior".[16] In this context, the International Organization for Standardization (ISO) and the International Electrotechnical Commission (IEC), two of the most significant international standards organizations, define a standard as a "*document, established by consensus and approved by a recognized body that provides for common and repeated use, rules, guidelines or characteristics for activities or their results, aimed at the achievement of the optimum degree of order in a given context. Standards should be based on consolidated results of science, technology, and experience, and aimed at the promotion of optimum community benefits*".[17] This definition is largely echoed by Regulation (EU) No 1025/2012, which also emphasizes the voluntary nature of standards.[18] This section provides a primer on standards before contextualizing them to the governance of QTs.

---

[16] Cihon (2019).

[17] ISO and IEC (2024a).

[18] Regulation (EU) No 1025/2012 of the European Parliament and of the Council of 25 October 2012 on European standardisation, amending Council Directives 89/686/EEC and 93/15/EEC and Directives 94/9/EC, 94/25/EC, 95/16/EC, 97/23/EC, 98/34/EC, 2004/22/EC, 2007/23/EC, 2009/23/EC and 2009/105/EC of the European Parliament and of the Council and repealing Council Decision 87/95/EEC and Decision No 1673/2006/EC of the European Parliament and of the Council Text with EEA relevance.

2.3.1 A Primer on Standards

The definition of a standard highlights certain characteristics that shed light on its purpose. The requirements of a consensus signify how standards foster the efficient development of a technology by providing a shared understanding that should reduce international barriers to trade, increase interoperability, and eliminate duplicative governance efforts.[19] For researchers and scientists involved in the development of technologies, the ability of standards to develop a consensus on terminology and activities enables better communication and the ability to compare results that can enable and enhance collaboration.[20] For industry, standards can assist with getting products to market as the resulting coordination reduces uncertainty, builds trust between the product and consumer, and lower transaction costs. For States, standards can be a foundation for their own rules to foster a more effective and cost-efficient development of regulation by relying upon pre-existing and, to some extent, already tested technical approaches.

2.3.2 Standards in Quantum Technologies

Standards have many uses relevant to the development of QTs, including providing common terminology, creating quality control processes, and establishing performance metrics and interoperability requirements. The relevance of different types of standards partially depends upon the maturity of a technology.[21] For example, QTs at an early stage of development would benefit from standards that seek to create common terminologies, whereas more mature QTs will benefit from standards that help technologies enter the market[22] Underlying the production of standards is the idea that these should facilitate trade, boost the quality of products, and incentivize actors to adopt these rules by facilitating trade and meaningful oversight by providing a set of shared terminology and common standards. An up-to-date compilation of the various standardization initiatives and current developments related to standardization efforts in quantum technology is available in a recent article advocating for a "standards-first" approach for quantum technology governance.[23]

---

[19] Cihon (2019).

[20] CEN-CENELEC (2023).

[21] Aboy et al. (2025).

[22] Aboy et al. (2025).

[23] Aboy et al. (2025).

2.3.3 The Role of Standards Within Legal Systems

One way to explore the character of standards as a governance mechanism is to compare them to, and contrast them with, traditional forms of legislation. Law-making is traditionally conceived as the product of politically legitimized bodies, from which the legitimacy of their outputs arises.[24] By contrast, the outputs of standards setting organizations rely upon their knowledge and expertise to justify the legitimacy of their outputs.

As discussed in further detail in Sect. 2.4, standards are created by a variety of bodies that have differing levels of influence on the development of technologies. Some standards are set by industry consortia that are not formal Standards Setting Organizations, but rather alliances of industry actors. These seek to exchange information or generate their own standards and have greater freedom over the design of their rules and processes such as the terms of collaboration and the process for introducing new members.[25] These bodies, and the standards that they promulgate, are not the focus of this chapter. Instead, this chapter focusses on the more formal Standards Setting Organizations that can be categorized into quasi-formal groups, such as the IEEE Standards Association, which are typically well-organized and respected but lack official government recognition, and Standards Setting Organizations that are formally recognized by governments, such as ETSI and CEN, which are the focus of this chapter.[26]

ETSI has over 900 member organizations, including private companies, research entities and academia, and government and public organizations from 60 different countries, including the US, UK, and China.[27] The UK has 118 member organizations registered as part of ETSI, including manufacturers, universities, and governmental bodies.[28] Under Regulation 1025/2012, it is described as a based upon "direct participation" by stakeholders in contrast to other bodies such as CEN, which is described as being based upon "national representation".[29] CEN is an association that brings together the National Standardization Bodies of 34 different European countries.[30] The National Standardization Bodies are the foremost standards bodies within each represented country and can be public or private sector organizations, or even a combination of the two. Dansk Standard, that represents Denmark in CEN, is a commercial

[24] Fosch Villaronga and Golia (2019).

[25] Keil (2002), Teubner et al. (2021).

[26] Contreras (2017).

[27] ETSI (n.d.(a)).

[28] ETSI (n.d.(a)).

[29] Regulation (EU) No 1025/2012 of the European Parliament and of the Council of 25 October 2012 on European standardisation, amending Council Directives 89/686/EEC and 93/15/EEC and Directives 94/9/EC, 94/25/EC, 95/16/EC, 97/23/EC, 98/34/EC, 2004/22/EC, 2007/23/EC, 2009/23/EC and 2009/105/EC of the European Parliament and of the Council and repealing Council Decision 87/95/EEC and Decision No 1673/2006/EC of the European Parliament and of the Council Text with EEA relevance.

[30] European Committee for Standardization (n.d.).

foundation that channels any profits into beneficial societal activities,[31] the Estonian Centre for Standardization and Accreditation is a non-profit association that is supported by the State,[32] and the British Standards Institute, as the UK National Standards Body, is a private company that is incorporated by a Royal Charter[33] and has a Memorandum of Understanding with the UK Government regarding its activities.[34]

Standards can thus be conceived as an example of the, at least, partial externalization of a function once solely held by States. This can reduce pressure on States to reach the required political consensus to regulate and reduce the risk of such legislative outputs potentially introducing significant regulatory burdens for industry and economically unattractive market fragmentation. Standards are traditionally conceived as a form of "soft law", an amorphous concept that describes a plethora of regulatory techniques that are not directly enforceable or demand compulsory compliance, as opposed to "hard law", which impose binding obligations on parties that can be judicially enforced and are created through standardized governmental procedures.[35] Whilst not enforceable, standards such as ISO 13485, that defines international consensus standards for medical device quality management system (QMS), facilitates international harmonization and auditing across multiple jurisdictions including the USE, EU, UK, and China. There is an added incentive for those who must abide by the EU's Medical Device Regulation as this legislation requires a QMS but compliance with its provisions is assumed where companies adhere to ISO 13485. This harmonization simplifies the regulatory process for manufacturers, as compliance with a globally recognized standard like ISO 13485 can simultaneously meet the requirements of multiple regulatory authorities, thereby easing market access across different regions. This opportunity for streamlined regulatory compliance makes abiding by ISO 13485 a highly logical choice and one probably made by most of those who must have a medical device QMS in place, but it does not prevent a company using alternate means and nor is a failure to abide by ISO 13485 a source of illegality. Nevertheless, it remains highly influential and a useful example in showing how standards can steer the development of a technology and its governance towards a harmonized path.

In this sense, many have acknowledged the blurring of the terms "hard" and "soft" law and their existence as upon a spectrum, rather than as a mutually exclusive dichotomy.[36] In the context of standards, they can exhibit some "hard law" tendencies in the EU where they are in the form of harmonized standard developed by a recognized European Standards Organization in response to a request from the European Commission. Compliance with these standards is deemed to demonstrate compliance with the relevant EU legislation, a link that the ECJ found to give such standards "legal effects" in the context of EU law and thus form part of the EU

---

[31] Dansk Standard (2025).

[32] ISO (n.d.(a)).

[33] British Standards Institution (2025).

[34] The UK Government and British Standards Institution (2024).

[35] Hagemann et al. (2018).

[36] Karlsson-Vinkhuyzen and Vihma (2009).

law corpus.[37] These legislative references to standards that are to be subsequently created leads Cantero Gamito to describe standards as having a "post law" function.[38] Beyond the EU, the World Trade Organization (WTO) relies upon internationally recognized standards in the Technical Barriers to Trade Agreement (TBT) whereby States must justify any deviations from such standards as reasonable to prevent being found in contravention of the Agreement. Where States thus choose to adopt voluntary standards into law, one can describe standards as having a "para law" function that sees their character shift into the territory of a mandatory benchmark, rather than voluntary.[39]

Alongside the character of standards, the institutional underpinnings of their creation demonstrate they are not a governance tool that is completely free from State influence. A more accurate description of many standards is that they are a form of hybrid governance as States can and do influence standard-setting developments. As a result, certain standards are not politically neutral and, upon publication, can then propagate through later regulatory and policy choices, further entwining the public and private modes of regulation.[40]

2.4 Standardization Organizations

QTs describe a vast field of technologies at different stages of maturity and with many different applications, such as quantum computing, quantum sensing, and quantum communications. This means there are a great number of bodies that create standards for QTs that exist at a national, regional, and international level, making the standardization landscape complex. The importance of QTs mean that many States have established bodies to create QT standards or have ensured existing standards bodies focus on QTs. This section will outline some of the main standardization bodies, including the key stakeholders and some of their key outputs.

2.4.1 International Bodies

At an international level, the International Organization for Standardization (ISO) and International Electrotechnical Commission (IEC) work together to produce standards relevant to QTs. These organizations are a network of national standards bodies, with countries either being full, correspondent, or subscriber members with different levels

---

[37] Case C-588/21, Public.Resource.Org, Inc. and Right to Know CLG v European Commission Judgment of the Court (Grand Chamber) of 5 March 2024.

[38] Cantero Gamito (2021).

[39] Kamara (2024).

[40] Cantero Gamito (2021).

of influence over the bodies' work.[41] It is only full members that can participate in developing standards, developing policy, selling ISO standards and publications, and participating in the governance of ISO as the other types of memberships have fewer benefits.[42]

Currently, the ISO membership comprises 174 national standards bodies. These national standards bodies are at the forefront of national standards developments and can be public or private entities, or a combination of the two and can be part of several standardization organizations e.g. at an international level and a European level. For example, the British Standards Institution represents the UK at both ISO and CEN.[43] The process of producing standards within ISO is the responsibility of technical committees (TCs) and joint technical committees (JTCs) where the latter refers to committees with representatives from different Standards Development Organizations. For example, ISO/IEC JTC 1 is a JTC of the ISO and IEC and is the JTC responsible for developing, maintaining, and promoting standards in the field of information and communications technology. These committees have subcommittees that specialize in a particular area. All draft standards that are proposed by the appropriate JTC or its relevant subcommittee are sent to participating national standardization bodies for ballot, comments, and contributions. A standard can only be published where not more than one-quarter of the total votes oppose the final draft.

ISO/IEC JTC 1/SC 27, a subcommittee of the Joint Technical Committee ISO/IEC JTC 1, develops international standards within the field of information security, cybersecurity, and privacy protection. The subcommittee was established in 1989 and currently has 54 participating members and 37 observing members.[44] As part of its remit it has turned its attention to post-quantum cryptography (PQC) as an urgent priority, specifically focusing on encryption, key establishment, and digital signatures.[45] PQC does not necessarily exploit quantum phenomena, in contrast to quantum key distribution, which does leverage principles such as quantum superposition and entanglement to achieve certain information-theoretic security advantages.[46] Nevertheless, given that PQC and QKD are often regulated in tandem, and both are clearly linked to the development of QTs, both are relevant in discussing the standards-making efforts within the QT space. In 2023, it published ISO/IEC 23837-1:2023 that specifies a "general framework for the security evaluation of quantum key distribution (QKD) according to the ISO/IEC 15408 series",[47] ISO/

[41] ISO (n.d.(b)).

[42] ISO (2015).

[43] See ISO/IEC (2024) *ISO/IEC Directives, Part 1 Procedures for the technical work*, 2.7.3 available at https://iso.org/sites/directives/current/consolidated/index.html#_Toc165305001.

[44] ISO (n.d.(c)).

[45] Chen et al. (2023).

[46] Davis et al. (2025a).

[47] ISO/IEC JTC 1/SC 27.

IEC 23837-2:2023 that specifies test and evaluation methods for the security evaluation of QKD,[48] and is currently developing a standard concerned with the effect of different transmission media on the security evaluation of QKD.[49]

ISO/IEC JTC 3 is a Joint Technical Committee specifically concerned with standardization in the field of QTs. It has 28 participating members and 10 observing members and published ISO/IEC 4879:2024 in 2024, which provides definitions for terms common in the field of quantum computing to provide a shared vocabulary between commercial enterprises, government agencies, research institutions, and other entities.[50]

In addition to the work of the ISO/IEC Joint Technical Committees, the ITU-T (International Telecommunication Union Standardization Sector) has published several standards related to quantum technologies as relevant to the telecommunications sector. ITU is the UN specialized agency in the field of telecommunications, information and communication technologies, with members comprising of companies from UN Member States, representatives from academia, and other regional and international organizations such as the African Union, the EU, and IEEE. ITU-T publishes recommendations, that are its equivalent to standards including ITU-T Y.3800,[51] which gives an overview of networks that support QKD to support the design, deployment, operation and maintenance for the implementation of QKD networks. ITU-T has published 26 recommendations relating to QKD networks on topics including functional architecture and resilience.[52] These are issued by ITU-T Study Group 13, which develops recommendations within the scope of future networks and emerging network technologies.

Finally, there is the IEEE Quantum Technical Community that was launched in 2019 and develops formal standards in response to a Project Authorization Request (PAR) from an individual or company working within an area. Several PARs have been submitted, prompting a project to create a standard. Active projects include P1943 titled Standard for a Post-Quantum Network Security[53] and P3172, which is a request for a new IEEE Standard on Recommended Practice for Post-Quantum Cryptography Migration, among others.

---

[48] ISO/IEC JTC 1/SC 27.

[49] ISO/IEC JTC 1/SC 27, 25544.

[50] IEC/ISO JTC 3.

[51] ITU Telecommunication Standardization Sector (2020).

[52] ITU-T (2025).

[53] IEEE (2022).

2.4.2 European Bodies

Alongside international bodies, that are several European bodies involved in developing standards relating to QTs. This section will focus on the 3 SDOs, the European Committee for Standardization (CEN), the European Committee for Electrotechnical Standardization (CENELEC) and the European Telecommunications Standards Institute (ETSI), which are recognized European Standards Organizations under Regulation 1025/2012 on European Standardization[54] and are able to develop harmonized standards and European standards. Harmonized standards are developed following a request from the European Commission and compliance with these standards is treated as a means to demonstrate compliance with the relevant EU legislation. Harmonized standards are technically voluntary but are usually adopted by relevant stakeholders as an efficient means of demonstrating compliance. The bodies can also issue European standards that are not requested by the European Commission, but these do not provide the same presumption of conformity with relevant EU legislation.

CEN and CENELEC memberships are based upon the National Standardization Bodies and National Committees within EU Member States or based in other European countries that are part of the European Single Market. However, Art 5 of the Standards Regulation requires the European Standardization Organizations to "encourage and facilitate an appropriate representation and effective participation of all relevant stakeholders, including SMEs, consumer organizations and environmental and social stakeholders."[55] Alongside these stakeholders, businesses and industry members also can feed into the process of developing standards. CEN/CENELEC established a Joint Technical Committee, CEN/CLC/JTC 22 on Quantum Technologies that focuses upon developing standards for quantum metrology, sensing, computing, communication, and cryptography. It consists of a plenary and four Working Groups. It has yet to produce any standards but has issued a Standardization Roadmap to identify standardization needs and opportunities.[56]

In contrast to CEN and CENELEC, ETSI membership is mostly comprised of representatives from industry, with some members coming from the public sector and research institutions. It has over 900 member organizations from over 60 countries

---

[54] Regulation (EU) No 1025/2012 of the European Parliament and of the Council of 25 October 2012 on European standardisation, amending Council Directives 89/686/EEC and 93/15/EEC and Directives 94/9/EC, 94/25/EC, 95/16/EC, 97/23/EC, 98/34/EC, 2004/22/EC, 2007/23/EC, 2009/23/EC and 2009/105/EC of the European Parliament and of the Council and repealing Council Decision 87/95/EEC and Decision No 1673/2006/EC of the European Parliament and of the Council Text with EEA relevance.

[55] Regulation(EU) No 1025/2012 of the European Parliament and of the Council of 25 October 2012 on European standardisation, amending Council Directives 89/686/EEC and 93/15/EEC and Directives 94/9/EC, 94/25/EC, 95/16/EC, 97/23/EC, 98/34/EC, 2004/22/EC, 2007/23/EC, 2009/23/EC and 2009/105/EC of the European Parliament and of the Council and repealing Council Decision 87/95/EEC and Decision No 1673/2006/EC of the European Parliament and of the Council.

[56] CEN-CENELEC (2023).

so whilst it serves European needs, it does this through a "global perspective".[57] This alternative structure has led to criticisms that ETSI is too driven by industry needs and, in particular, commercial entities that are not based in Europe.[58] For example, despite ETSI's strong history of producing standards in the field of AI, in the final version of the EU's AI Act, it was excluded from the standardization request issued by the European Commission. Nevertheless, ETSI has been highly productive in the field of QTs, though no harmonized standards have been issued and many of ETSI's outputs are General Specifications, such as ETSI GS QKD 002 that outlines use cases relating to Quantum Key Distribution.

2.4.3 National Bodies

Alongside international and regional bodies, many countries have national bodies involved in the creation of standards. In the US, the National Institute of Standards and Technology (NIST) is a federal agency heavily involved in standards development, in addition to other tasks to promote innovation and industrial competitiveness.[59] The NIST Standards Coordination Office is specifically concerned with developing standards and encouraging their adoption and use. NIST is heavily involved in the development of standards in relation to PQC, finalizing a set of Federal Information Processing Standards (FIPS) post-quantum encryption standards in 2024, including algorithms like CRYSTALS-Kyber for encryption and CRYSTALS-Dilithium for digital signatures, designed to secure electronic information against quantum computer attacks.[60] The current Trump administration has emphasized the importance of QTs for national security and ensuring the US remains economically competitive.

The China National Institute of Standardization plays a central role in developing and promoting standards within China,[61] but it is the Chinese Cryptography Standardization Technical Committee that has considered quantum resistant encryption and is currently soliciting proposals for post-quantum cryptographic algorithms to establish national standards for encryption that can withstand quantum attacks.[62] In 2021, the National Standardization Development plan emphasized the importance of standards in the governance of emerging technologies, including quantum.[63] This is part of a broader effort to achieve technological self-reliance and allow China to reduce its dependence on foreign technologies and to bolster its national security.

---

57 ETSI (n.d.(b)).

58 European Commission (2022a).

59 NIST (2024a).

60 Davis et al. (2025a).

61 China National Institute of Standardization (n.d.).

62 Swayne (2025b).

63 People's Republic of China (2021).

Nevertheless, it does engage in international collaboration, but the aim is to enhance China's influence over global standards.

In the UK, the British Standards Institute plays a pivotal role in driving standards related to quantum technologies and the Department for Science, Innovation and Technology oversees the implementation of the UK National Quantum Strategy, which was published in 2023.

In April 2025, Standards Australia released a draft standard, AS 5405 *Quantum technology—Reference guide to quantum computing*, for public comment. The draft standard "specifies a hierarchical description of concepts in the field of quantum computing and provides guidance on preparing guidelines for due diligence related activities".[64] An accompanying report explains that "[e]xtensive, high-quality quantum standards development will be required for quantum technologies to realize their maximum potential and deliver the greatest benefits for people and society."[65] These documents must be seen in light of the Australian government's National Quantum Strategy, which identifies "Standards and frameworks that support national interests"[66] as one of five themes through which Australia aims to establish itself as a key global player in QTs.

It is critical to remark that these examples of national bodies do not operate in silos. For example, CEN and CENELEC have agreements with their respective international counterparts (ISO and IEC) that attempt to develop common standards in parallel, to reduce duplication. Furthermore, as discussed above, many national bodies form a key part of operations within international organizations to help ensure that standards achieve key objectives including interoperability and collaboration.

2.4.4 Objectives and Rationales for Standards

As described above, standards are a common means of governing emerging technologies, including nanotechnologies, AI, and QTs, due to their perceived advantages in facilitating innovation without allowing undue risks to proliferate. Standards are particularly apt for governing QTs as the current state-of-the-art demands an agile governance system that can adapt quickly to changing circumstances and societal needs. Standards, as a "softer" governance approach thus appear to be more adaptable and capable of responding to new information[67] than traditional legislation.

One way that standards facilitate innovation is that their creation process provides a means for knowledge sharing between actors with differing backgrounds, knowledge and interests.[68] Provided that standards are developed in a way that ensures meaningful and inclusive participation, which is not a given, the resulting outputs

---

64 Standards Australia (2025).

65 Langford and Devitt (2025).

66 Department of Industry, Science and Resources (2025, 36).

67 Johnson (2019).

68 Van Deventer et al. (2022).

can represent the distilled wisdom of those with various relevant sources of expertise.[69] This expertise can arise from technical knowledge, the needs of the stakeholders, and the knowledge of how emerging technologies may impact the wider landscape. This pooling of knowledge acts as a foundation for finding a consensus that helps to attain compatibility and the technical, legal and semantical interoperability between products and services. Example includes standards that provide a set of technical vocabulary and terminology that can be used by all stakeholders, such as ISO/IEC 4879:2024 that facilitates the exchange of research and concepts, and those that aim to provide a common set of benchmarking techniques to enable a harmonized assessment of the performance of implemented quantum technologies, such as IEEE P7131. The resulting standards enhance the dissemination of knowledge between researchers and facilitate the cost-effective transition of technologies to market. In that regard, standards can also promote the establishment of so-called regulatory sandboxes and testbeds for quantum technologies, which are right now at the forefront of national and global policy initiatives.[70] These environments will allow quantum technologies to be tested in controlled settings, enabling regulators to gather insights and refine their governance strategies before quantum innovations are widely adopted.[71] By embedding regulatory components into testbeds from the start, policy-makers aim to ensure that quantum innovations can transition smoothly from the research stages to market implementation, with appropriate safeguards in place.[72] A robust and interoperable body of standardized quantum technologies would thus support the functioning of such sandboxes. If well-proven and accepted, standards might even minimize the need for such regulatory sandboxes that can be complex, costly, and demand a high regulatory capacity.

The consensus from a wide range of stakeholders produces another benefit as this can encourage the uptake of a technology, triggering additional investment that encourages further innovation. The combination of private and public sector expertise acknowledges the limits to a government's ability to regulate, and that power premised upon democratic justifications are nevertheless limited in their appropriateness. Instead, it is highly desirable to have some contribution from the private sector, such as their role in developing standards, as it best ensures these stakeholders can work together to shape markets that align with commercial incentives and public values. The balance of guidance and scope for development means that standards are less likely to impose onerous costs of commercial stakeholders nor stray too far from public values.[73]

[69] IEC (2021).

[70] H.R. 2739 Quantum Sandbox for Near-Term Applications Act of 2023 (proposed) (2023). UK Department for Science, Innovation & Technology (2024).

[71] Choucair (2024).

[72] Choucair (2024).

[73] Cantero Gamito (2021).

2.5 The Challenges and Limitations of Governance through Standards

This section discusses some of the challenges surrounding the use of standards to govern QTs. Some of the difficulties relate to QTs themselves and the difficulties they specifically present. Others relate to the concept of standards more generally and the difficulties of regulating at an international level, especially during particularly turbulent geopolitical times.

2.5.1 *Perceptions of Standardization Bodies*

The acceptance of standards as a legitimate means of governance depends, in part, on perceptions of the bodies that develop them. If these bodies are seen as transparent, inclusive, and technically competent, their outputs are more likely to be accepted and implemented. However, if they are perceived as dominated by particular national or corporate interests, or as lacking accountability, their output may be viewed with skepticism or even rejected. This is particularly relevant in the context of QTs where the stakes are high and the development ecosystem is international. The international bodies, such as ISO, and national standards bodies that are involved in the creation and dissemination of standards are well-respected and often praised for prioritizing expertise over commercial interests.

However, concerns about the influence of commercial interests over bodies involved in the creation of standards is not solely hypothetical. In the EU Commission's 2022 New Standardization Strategy, it had expressed concerns about the growing influence of foreign companies on European standardization.[74] In particular, it highlighted the influence of Huawei, a Chinese company, upon ETSI's Industry Specification Group on Securing AI and the ability of foreign companies to do more than participate as ETSI members, but also vote on important decisions and be part of the management.[75] Subsequently, the EU downgraded ETSI's role when it published its draft standardization request for the AI Act. The request was addressed only to CEN and CENELEC, despite ETSI's relevant expertise and the EU's history of addressing such requests to all three entities.[76] Instead, CEN and CENELEC were directly to merely consult with ETSI, based upon its acknowledged expertise and previous work in this area.[77]

Nevertheless, the many international standards organizations are respected as impartial experts, and it is important to distinguish the more formal standards development organizations from their informal counterparts. The latter usually only

[74] European Commission (2022a).

[75] Kanevskaia et al. (2024).

[76] European Commission (2022b).

[77] European Commission (2022b, 11).

consists of industry stakeholders whose objective is to align the development of a technology with their commercial interests.[78]

2.5.2 *Difficulties in Segmenting QTs for Standardization Purposes*

QTs span an array of technologies that have different uses and are currently at different stages of maturity. Some have posited that one of the difficulties associated with efforts to standardize QTs is thus how to delineate between different technologies and purposes in a way that would be manageable and cohesive. For example, the European Quantum Flagship roadmap features four domains that delineate the technologies into those related to quantum computing, quantum communication, and quantum metrology and sensing. This may make sense when the focus is on the different potential uses of QTs, but this segmentation could obfuscate commonalities between these domains, such as their underlying hardware, which is highly relevant to standardization.[79]

Relatedly, it is not always possible to fully distinguish between quantum technologies and others, as evidenced by the efforts of ISO/IEC JTC 1/SC 27 as discussed in Sect. 2.4. One can see lines being blurred between classical and quantum computing, given the use and development of hybrid schemes, quantum simulation on classical machines, and cloud-based quantum computing. Similarly, other QTs intersect with fields like condensed matter physics, nanotechnology, and photonics, making it difficult to draw clear boundaries between what constitutes a 'quantum technology' and what falls under adjacent scientific domains. This ambiguity can complicate efforts to develop coherent standards in different ways. First, it means it is not always clear which technologies should be included in the scope of quantum-specific governance frameworks. Second, these links and overlaps increase the risk of duplicative efforts that may lead to outcomes that are inconsistent with each other.

2.5.3 *The Timing of Standards*

There is much literature on the Collingridge dilemma as a phenomenon that applies to law, but the same concerns may also relate to softer forms of governance, such as standards. Whilst classical computing has now converged upon dominant architectures, quantum computing currently lacks a universally accepted hardware or software model, although certain main techniques are in the process of being established, due to its nascent and rapidly evolving state.[80]

---

[78] Werle and Iversen (2006).

[79] Van Deventer et al. (2022).

[80] Preskill (2018).

Instead, there are a plethora of approaches that are all competing for dominance. For example, superconducting circuits (used by IBM and Google), trapped ions (used by IonQ and Honeywell), neutral atoms (used by QuEra), and photonic systems (used by Xanadu and PsiQuantum) all compete in the hardware space. These systems differ significantly in their control protocols, error rates, and scalability approaches.[81] Similarly, on the software side, the volatility of algorithmic and compiler-level innovation complicates efforts to define stable programming standards or interfaces. Quantum error correction—a foundational requirement for fault-tolerant systems—has multiple competing codes (e.g., surface code, Bacon-Shor, color code), each with different implications for architecture and implementation.[82]

Benchmarking presents another challenge as there is a risk that metrics such as quantum volume, circuit layer operations per second (CLOPS), and logical fidelity are used inconsistently across companies and research institutions. This will make objective comparisons difficult and potentially lead to technological fragmentation.

This range of approaches and systems is common when a technology is immature, and standards provide a key means of preventing this from becoming fragmented and inhibiting efforts at collaboration and interoperability. This suggests that it is an appropriate time to introduce standards to promote before this existing array of approaches and systems become so entrenched that it proves impossible to gain the necessary consensus to pass a standard.

2.5.4 Standards' Adaptability and Responsiveness

Where standards are referenced by law or are used by companies to demonstrate legal compliance, it is important to consider how far they can adapt and respond to technological developments. This is a point often used to criticize the legal regulation of emerging technologies and, as standards and law entwine, it is pertinent to consider its applicability to this context. One aspect of this critique is the risk that regulation, whether legally enforceable or de facto deemed to be a requisite to demonstrate regulatory compliance, may lock-in technologies down a regulatory path that was determined by now outdated information and approaches. This may have wider consequences where the technologies enable complementary technologies and create network effects. The setting of standards may not just shape the development of what the standard applies to, but also related technologies, products, and services. That said, ISO standards are periodically updated on a five year to adapt and respond to technological changes. This enables, for instance, the ISO 27001 for information security to reflect the state-of-the-art in technical and organizational measures for cybersecurity which companies implement to demonstrate compliance with Art. 32 GDPR security of processing without having to revise the GDPR. Similarly, ISO 13485, defining the requirements for medical device quality

[81] Devitt (2016).

[82] Gambetta et al. (2021).

management systems (QMS), goes through periodic updates to ensure quality and safety of medical devices without requiring legislative or regulatory changes for the EU Medical Device Regulation or the FDA quality system regulation.[83]

Another consideration is that the various bodies producing standards can create a complex landscape in these are not well coordinated. There are some synergies between bodies. For example, some regional and international bodies draw membership from national standard development bodies, which can facilitate some cohesion. However, it does not guarantee a complete consensus. Furthermore, there is also the issue of competition between regional and international standards development bodies, as there is no mechanism in place to ensure harmonization or to prevent the duplication of effort. Efforts have been made to reduce the scope for duplication, through the Vienna Agreement between CEN and ISO and the Frankfurt Agreement between CENELEC and IEC. This does not prevent the standards development bodies associated with the EU pushing forward with its own agenda nor from derogating from international standards. These agreements seek to facilitate the optimal use of resources and expertise to prevent duplication of effort and allow for information exchange to take place to increase the transparency of standardization efforts.[84] The development of QTs is thus somewhat shaped by broader geopolitical concerns, a point explored further below, and given the current tumultuous geopolitical climate it is unclear how far national states will try to exert pressure on the development of standards to align with domestic preferences.

2.5.5 The Potential of State Influence

This chapter has focused upon standards setting organizations but, particularly in the context of QTs because they are deeply entangled with geopolitical considerations. QTs have the potential to revolutionize fields such as cryptography, defense, and high-performance computing, making them strategically vital. As a result, states view leadership in quantum computing as a matter of national security and economic competitiveness and have begun to recognize that the ability to shape standards may be a source of bolstering their own power and maintaining their technological sovereignty.[85] Therefore, in contrast to the relatively open and cooperative environment of medical device standardization, the governance of QTs, including the creation of standards, is increasingly an arena of competition between states over emerging technologies, including QTs.[86] Where this encourages competition rather than collaboration, such actions may become a technical barrier to trade between states where they are used to protect domestic markets.[87]

---

[83] Aboy et al. (2025).

[84] CEN and CENELEC (2025).

[85] Blind (2025).

[86] Rühlig (2022).

[87] CEN-CENELEC (2023).

Some have accused the US's previous administration of being too directly involved in the setting of standards relating to QTs and "sidelining experts" to potentially undermine the collaborative process that traditionally underpins the development of standards.[88] The US administration by-passed the American National Standards Institute (ANSI), the official national standards body of the United States, and instead directly engaged with other States.[89] Furthermore, the US has increasingly moved away from ANSI, selecting the National Institute of Standards and Technology (NIST) to administer the U.S. National Committee (USNC) Technical Advisory Group (TAG) to ISO-IEC/JTC3 on Quantum Technologies that could be construed as efforts to increase US political influence of the setting of standards.[90] There is still legitimacy in a State's interest in QTs but there is a risk that such premature or overbearing action may stifle innovation. This threat to the proper development of standards is neutralized if they continue to be created in a voluntary, open, participatory, and rules-based process.

It therefore seems unlikely, although not entirely impossible, for a State to capture the process of making standards. However, the geopolitical tensions associated with certain QTs may inhibit consensus being reached within standards organizations or lead to "satisficing" wherein common ground can only be achieved within areas that are not contested by divergent interests. The difficulties in reaching consensus with standards setting organizations may also lead to States leading their own efforts to standardize QTs, such as NIST's efforts to lead the formalization of PQC algorithms being met by China, through its Institute of Commercial Cryptography Standards (ICCS), which operates under the Chinese Cryptography Standardization Technical Committee, soliciting proposals for PQC algorithms.[91]

2.5.6 Exploring the Legitimacy of Standards as a Form of Governance

The increasing reliance upon standards as instruments of governance has prompted growing scrutiny of their legitimacy. Standards are usually developed through processes that significantly differ from traditional legislative processes, whilst potentially exerting similar effects, especially when they are referenced within regulatory frameworks. This raises important questions about the democratic legitimacy of standards and the actors involved in their creation.

One potential critique is that standards may be disproportionately shaped by private actors that could steer the development of technologies, including QTs, down a regulatory path that may not align with broader societal views. This concern is particularly acute when standards are used to demonstrate legal compliance across

[88] Swayne (2024).

[89] Swayne (2024).

[90] Cory (2024).

[91] Swayne (2025b).

different jurisdictions, effectively functioning as a form of de facto law. While these concerns are valid, the critique risks oversimplifying the institutional architecture of international standardization. International standards bodies such as the International Organization for Standardization (ISO) and the International Electrotechnical Commission (IEC) are composed of national standards bodies from member states, including BSI (UK), DIN (Germany), and ANSI (USA), albeit the US has begun to rely upon NIST in the context of QTs. These bodies are generally public or quasi-public institutions and often directly linked to state regulatory frameworks. This structure introduces a layer of public oversight and national accountability that potentially enhances the legitimacy of standards where they are incorporated into regulatory frameworks. Nonetheless, the presence of national bodies does not eliminate concerns about legitimacy. Participation in standardization processes, even at the national level, often remains limited to technical experts and industry representatives. Civil society organizations, SMEs, and the general public are frequently underrepresented, particularly in domains where standards intersect with ethical, social, or human rights considerations. Moreover, the influence of powerful industry actors can be channeled through national bodies, blurring the line between public oversight and private interest.

Questions of legitimacy are difficult because the concept of legitimacy itself is complex. Legitimacy in the context of standards development can take different forms. This includes the concepts of "input legitimacy" concerning who can participate in the production of standards, "throughput legitimacy" which relates to the design of the decision-making process and the quality of interactions that are facilitated, and "output legitimacy" that incorporates what interests are represented in the developed standard.[92]

2.5.6.1 Input Legitimacy

Taking each in turn, the development of standards has been criticized for lacking input legitimacy through the exclusion of non-expert stakeholders and the public and underrepresentation of small and medium enterprises (SMEs) and civil society organizations.[93] This may be more acceptable where standards deal only with highly technical questions, but those developing standards are increasingly asked to grapple with questions at the intersection of technology and ethics. For example, the European Commission has directed the European standardization organizations to consider ways in which standards can ensure the fundamental rights of individuals.[94] However, standards are a problematic means of performing such a task because they are best suited to defining and measuring concepts, rather than determining which competing

[92] Werle and Iversen (2006).

[93] Kallestrup (2017).

[94] Soler Garrido et al. (2024).

interests should be given priority, or what residual level of risk or unfairness is acceptable in each situation.[95]

Even where standards deal with purely technical matters, such as definitions, the influence of industry representatives over the process has seen criticism. As previously discussed above, the EU Commission has already downgraded ETSI's role in relation to harmonized standards under the AI Act due to its concerns about the level of influence held by foreign commercial entities within ETSI. One issue relates to the concept "evasive entrepreneurship" that describes efforts to minimize losses associated with the formal legal structure by using standards, including those related to purely technical matters,[96] to create a path dependency best suited to the needs of the most powerful industry actors involved in standards development. The Commission's decision to minimize the role of ETSI has proven controversial, with some arguing that foreign influence is not so undesirable as the benefits of standardization as a regulatory tool is rooted in the influence of private industry.[97] Their role helps, in principle, to ensure the outputs retain a non-political character and respond to the realities of developing emerging technologies. However, such critiques should not be overstated as the international standards setting organizations are composed of national standards bodies that do have some public accountability, either through being a public institution or by operating within or through domestic laws. Nevertheless, the presence of national bodies does not fully mitigate concerns about inclusivity and representativeness. Participation in these national bodies often remains limited to large industry players and technical experts, with minimal involvement from civil society or smaller enterprises. Furthermore, as demonstrated by the EU's decision to award ESTI a mere advisory role, the influence of private actors is not eliminated by the public status of national bodies; rather, it is often channeled through them.

The role of industry and transnational nature of standards development mean that they foster a more decentralized approach to the governance of emerging technologies. This could foster improved international cooperation, but this outcome is less certain in the context of QTs. Their potential implication for national security and scope for weaponization mean that States are very interested in ensuring their development aligns with their national priorities.[98] Moreover, the industries for certain QTs may develop into "winner-takes-all" economies, wherein their benefits are disproportionately captured by one or a selection of companies, or a specific country or region. Other frontier technologies, such as semiconductors,[99] have quickly seen concentrated dominance and significant economic moats,[100] which are vociferously protected by corporate interests—and, often, the governments within which those corporate interests reside.

---

95 Gornet and Maxwell (2024).

96 Hagemann et al. (2018).

97 Rühlig (2022).

98 Johnson (2019).

99 Grimes and Du (2022).

100 Watts et al. (2024).

2.5.6.2 Throughput Legitimacy

The shift towards standards responding to less technical issues also raise concerns about throughput legitimacy, relating to the decision-making process and the interactions that are facilitated through this process. The development of standards was not designed to accommodate difficult normative concepts relating to risks including fundamental rights and other ethical principles. To the extent that QTs may raise such questions, the legitimacy of standards as a regulatory tool is increasingly threatened but it is important to remember that current standards developments are more within the domain in which standards are a highly appropriate and useful form of governance e.g. harmonizing vocabulary. Nevertheless, the potential of QTs to be used to break public key encryption raises issues for individuals' rights to privacy and their freedom of expression, yet the forums in which these standards are developed may lack the procedural safeguards typically associated with democratic deliberation.[101]

Concerns relating to fundamental rights in particular raise very tricky questions as to the appropriateness of standards as a means of governance. Some argue that the technology is not yet at a stage to pose such a threat, which means regulation in the form of legislation is not needed *now*[102] but this is not a universally held belief.[103] Nevertheless, the seemingly inevitable development of QTs and uncertainty as how the technology will develop, particularly with regards to who will drive the development and use QTs suggests some form of regulation is desirable. In some ways, standards could be a beneficial tool here. They could provide a set of early guardrails that steers the development of technologies down a path that aligns with fundamental rights and freedoms. Furthermore, the international nature of many of the key standards development organizations could ensure that potential human rights issues are responded to at a global level and prevent countries from lowering their fundamental rights protections to gain an economic advantage. One major issue is the lack of transparency relating to the development history of standards, and the respective contributions of different members. The gaps in the data make it hard to evaluate the legitimacy of the decision-making process. Nevertheless, an element of privacy is desirable because there is a need to prevent the disclosure of confidential information that may be shared by private actors to ensure standards respond to the real-word wants and needs of industry.[104] Furthermore, to the extent that States are able to influence the decisions made by these bodies, standards may be pushed down a path that attempts to enhance QT development in such States.

[101] Van Daalen (2025).

[102] Van Daalen (2025).

[103] Van Daalen (2025), Davis et al. (2025a).

[104] Barrett (2024).

2.5.6.3 Output Legitimacy

In terms of output legitimacy, while the references to fundamental rights within standards may push the development of QTs in a more socially responsible direction, there is a risk that this will be done through an economic lens that could introduce an undesirable path dependency that favors certain commercial interests.[105] While the involvement of national standards bodies in ISO/IEC processes introduces a degree of public accountability, it does not necessarily ensure that the outputs of standardization reflect the public interest. A reliance upon industry experts is not inherently problematic, as standards are designed to facilitate interoperability and collaboration, but it could risk the underrepresentation of societal values. This means that, in the long run, when legislation does become an appropriate option given the maturity of QTs, this economically driven approach could already somewhat baked into any laws.[106] Laws are heavily influenced by any existing forms of regulation and governance, either directly or indirectly as the current regulatory landscape will influence discourse. The ways in which QTs are, and will be, discussed builds a shared understanding of what they are, including their respective opportunities and their risks. These shape what are deemed to be acceptable solutions, and structure the roles of those involved in the regulatory process.[107] Once embedded in legal frameworks, standards can entrench particular technological trajectories and regulatory assumptions. For example, if early QT standards are shaped primarily by the interests of dominant industry actors, they may encode assumptions about acceptable levels of risk or privacy that reflect those actors' priorities rather than a broader societal consensus. Even when standards reference fundamental rights, they often do so in abstract or procedural terms, without engaging with the substantive trade-offs such rights entail. This is particularly problematic in areas like encryption, where the stakes involve not just technical performance but the protection of core democratic freedoms.

An unquestioning reliance upon standards to inform future legislative risks the promotion and an understanding of societal values and the public interest that have been shaped by standard development organizations without considering if their content aligns with how they are conceived by States and public institutions. Moreover, questions concerning risks to fundamental rights will nearly always raise difficult normative questions that are not within the remit of the current technical expertise of standards development organizations. In this context, the hybrid nature of the standardization system, often public or quasi-public in structure, but often private in operation, raises difficult questions about how to ensure that the outputs of standardization serve wider societal interests. The challenge is not simply to increase participation or transparency, but to develop mechanisms that can meaningfully integrate diverse perspectives into the substantive content of standards. Where there is a need to make trade-offs that include contested societal values, standards are not apposite as they

[105] Johnson (2019).

[106] Bacchi (2007).

[107] Black (2002).

stray further from the justification for relying upon such organizations. Harking back to the Collingridge dilemma, it may be too soon to legislate, but that doesn't stop the establishment of norms that will nevertheless constrain certain behaviors and promote others.

2.5.6.4 Legitimacy and the Rule of Law

Certain types of standards raise distinct concerns within the EU. The EU relies, in part, on harmonized standards to flesh out certain aspects of EU legislation, which are requested by the EU Commission but developed by European Standards Organizations (ESOs). The procedure for this is set out in EU Regulation 1025/2012 and the ECJ has held that such standards have legal effects[108] This does not mean they become legislation, rather that they complement the EU legislation that they implement, because they provide a means of demonstrating conformity with the law.[109] This means that individuals retain the freedom and ability to demonstrate compliance with the law by some other means.

ESOs are classed as private entities under EU Regulation 1025/2012[110] that are not subject to the same oversight as the law-making institutions within the EU. This means that harmonized standards should benefit from copyright protection and thus ESO should be able to require payment for access. Therefore, the creation and dissemination of harmonized standards creates a tension between the ability of private entities that develop standards being able to protect their work through copyright, and thus require payment for access to the documents, and the rule of law, that requires laws to be transparent and accessible. The extent to which copyright protections should apply to standards considering the public interest in their accessibility is unclear. In 2024, the Grand Chamber of the EU Court of Justice discussed this tension in a case concerning how far commercial interests should be protected where harmonized standards are explicitly incorporated into legislation.[111] Here, the ECJ found that the public interest *did* outweigh commercial considerations because, in that instance, compliance with the standards was "manifestly mandatory"[112] as the requirements set out in the standards were used within the legislation to determine compliance. Furthermore, the Court also stressed specific Articles within the founding EU Treaties that emphasized the importance of the rule of law, which

[108] Case C-613/14, James Elliott Construction Limited v Irish Asphalt Limited of 27 October 2016.

[109] Tzoulia (2025).

[110] Regulation(EU) No 1025/2012 of the European Parliament and of the Council of 25 October 2012 on European standardisation, amending Council Directives 89/686/EEC and 93/15/EEC and Directives 94/9/EC, 94/25/EC, 95/16/EC, 97/23/EC, 98/34/EC, 2004/22/EC, 2007/23/EC, 2009/23/EC and 2009/105/EC of the European Parliament and of the Council and repealing Council Decision 87/95/EEC and Decision No 1673/2006/EC of the European Parliament and of the Council.

[111] Case C-588/21, Public.Resource.Org, Inc. and Right to Know CLG v European Commission Judgment of the Court (Grand Chamber) of 5 March 2024.

[112] Case C-588/21, Public.Resource.Org, Inc. and Right to Know CLG v European Commission Judgment of the Court (Grand Chamber) of 5 March 2024 para. 79.

requires access to EU laws and for individuals to ascertain their rights and obligations,[113] and the principles of transparency and openness, including the right of access to documents enshrined in the EU Charter.[114] However, the Court did not articulate this finding to be a blanket rule, and it thus remains unclear as to when the public interest will outweigh commercial copyright protections because the decision provided no guidance or criteria for how to weigh these competing interests. The need to clearly articulate how to balance these competing interests will only become more acute as standards continue to drift from purely technical questions to ones that concern fundamental rights and ethics.

2.5.7 The Enforcement of Standards

As the previous section made clear, harmonized standards within the EU have legal effects and certain standards have been deemed to be "manifestly mandatory" due to difficulties in demonstrating conformity with the law by alternative means to those set out in the relevant standards. Beyond EU harmonized standards, the enforceability of standards is not uniform. Standards can gain some form of legal enforceability where they are incorporated into contracts, insurance, and other forms of liability.[115] Standards can have a *de jure* legal effect where they become relevant to decisions made by the World Trade Organization (WTO) regarding the Technical Barriers to Trade Agreement (TBT Agreement). The aim of this agreement is to prevent Member States from using standards as a means of unjustifiably treating imported goods less favorably or imposing other forms of unnecessary barriers to international trade. This does not preclude a Member State from creating their own standards where none exist or deviating from existing international standards. However, if a deviation occurs then a Member State is required to provide a reasonable explanation for any divergences. It is unclear how QTs will be treated under this agreement, due to their potential national security implications. This is an area that the TBT Agreement recognizes as one where no Member State should be prevented from taking measures necessary for its essential security interest.

Beyond the references to standards in law or by institutions capable of enforcing agreements, it should not be forgotten that another reason for companies to abide by standards is they can operate as a de facto pre-requisite to certain forms of regulatory approval and market access. Standards can thus streamline regulatory compliance across several jurisdictions to provide an incentive for their use, irrespective of their lack of legal enforceability. They continue to operate with substantial normative and practical force, even in the absence of formal legal codification.

---

[113] Case C-588/21, Public.Resource.Org, Inc. and Right to Know CLG v European Commission Judgment of the Court (Grand Chamber) of 5 March 2024, para. 81.

[114] Case C-588/21, Public.Resource.Org, Inc. and Right to Know CLG v European Commission Judgment of the Court (Grand Chamber) of 5 March 2024, para. 84.

[115] Johnson (2019).

There is no single answer as to whether this enforceability is an advantage or disadvantage of standards as a key means of governing QTs. However, even the existence of these differences potentially introduces a level of uncertainty that undermines the certainty that standards are supposed to promote.

2.6 State Influence Over Standards

Though standards are not a creature of a State's legislative process, this does not mean standards exist beyond the reach of a State's influence and, in many cases, cannot be considered as a purely private form of governance. This point is particularly applicable to the development of standards within the EU to the extent that the EU can be considered a quasi-State.[116] As the previous section discussed, the EU can trigger the creation of standards and incorporate them into legislation to bestow legal effects upon them, which may be conceived as a form of regulated self-regulation. This process also provides the means for the EU to reject existing standards and replace them with their own. For example, when the EU updated the Medical Devices Regulation[117] it altered the scope of the rules as they applied to devices that had both a medical and non-medical purpose. Under Article 1(3) of the Medical Devices Regulation, such devices must "fulfil cumulatively the requirements applicable to devices with an intended medical purpose and those applicable to devices without an intended medical purpose" that runs contrary to established standards, such as ISO 13485:2016, which introduced a division between those purposes.[118] But how can this phenomenon and the intricate interplay be conceptualized and described in more detail? And, what about state influences in other regions of the world?

2.6.1 Standards as a Hybridized Form of Governance

The EU is not alone in attempting to exert influence over what may appear to be a purely private form of self-governance. Technology has never been truly apolitical, but QTs may be considered a rather extreme example of a technology that States are attempting to exert influence over its development at a time that is usually characterized by private self-regulation. As this is not a new phenomenon, discussions concerning standards have already explored their increasingly hybridized nature,

[116] Pelinka (2011).

[117] Regulation (EU) 2017/745 of the European Parliament and of the Council of 5 April 2017 on medical devices, amending Directive 2001/83/EC, Regulation (EC) No 178/2002 and Regulation (EC) No 1223/2009 and repealing Council Directives 90/385/EEC and 93/42/EEC (Text with EEA relevance).

[118] Fosch Villaronga and Golia (2019).

which emphasizes the role of private and public actors in their development. Therefore, acknowledging standards as a hybridized form of governance is not novel, but the focus has still tended to remain on the industry actors, as the actors with the expertise and, usually, in charge of any enforcement.[119] This section will thus focus more upon the role of States and the means in which they have already begin to exercise power to influence the development of QTs. This is done through indirect means that may nevertheless guide the development of standards that will act as a precursor to hard law. These alternatives provide scope for standards to align with the wishes of States that are more successful in influencing forms of governance that apply to developing technologies.

The following focuses on these alternate mechanisms to explore how the US, EU, and China are seeking to influence the development of QTs, as the three entities that claim to be leading the way in developing QTs. The reasons for States' efforts to steer the development of technologies are similar those that underpin the motivations of industry actors, albeit on a larger scale. States seek to develop technologies in a way that aligns with their needs and priorities to reduce their technological and economic dependence on other States. Their national strategies often prioritize self-reliance and security over interoperability. There is reluctance to align with standards that could cede influence to geopolitical rivals. Such techno-nationalist and techno-regionalist approaches, which have grown in importance during the last 5 years, threaten to fragment global standards and hinder cross-border compatibility.[120]

2.6.2 US Efforts to Influence Standards—Enhancing US Leadership Through Technical Standards

While the US has a regulatory culture that prefers to industry-led responses to issues faced by emerging technologies, such as coordination problems, the State is not entirely absent. One means of influencing QT development is funding and, compared to some jurisdictions, the US allows the private sector significant scope to complement publicly funded efforts and those funded via miliary agencies. Funding has the potential to direct technologies down certain paths as it allows private actors to reduce the risks arising from technologies not developing as intended. It may also incentivize private actors to prioritize certain strands of research and development, where it appears they have better prospects for achieving external funding. The US National Institute for Science and Technology (NIST) recently published an Implementation Roadmap that demonstrates its efforts to support standards development organizations in the implementation of emerging technologies to sustain national technical leadership.[121]

[119] Werle and Iversen (2006).

[120] Kop et al. (2024a).

[121] NIST (2024b).

Beyond examples of soft power, the US has also introduced legislation that attempts to gauge a better understanding of the actors involved in the development of standards. The United States Innovation and Competition Act[122] specifically stated that its policy in QTs included the need to enhance US leadership in "technical standards-setting bodies and avenues for developing norms regarding the use of emerging critical technologies."[123] This policy sought to achieve several objectives, including remaining in a global leadership role and, in particular, ensuring China did not dominate the Indo-Pacific region, subvert democratic societies, distort global market, manipulate international trade, coerce other nations, or see its technological advantages to undermine individual freedoms or nations' security interests. This legislation was ultimately incorporated into the CHIPS and Science Act.[124] With this development, all references to China were removed from the legislative text but the desire for US involvement in the development of QTs at an early stage was made clearer. Section 10661 of the CHIPS and Science Act concerns Quantum Networking and Communications and discusses NIST's role as one to facilitate the development and standardization of a range of QTs, including quantum cryptography, quantum networking, communications, and sensing technologies and applications. Though no longer explicit, the United States Innovation and Competition Act, as a precursor to the current legislation, indicates the driver for this regulatory approach to quantum technologies and what the US seeks to achieve through its involvement in developing standards. The tech decoupling of the US and China is further demonstrated by the US Department of Commerce's decision to place several Chinese quantum firms (e.g., QuantumCTek and the Hefei National Laboratory) on its Entity List, restricting their access to U.S. technology.[125] The current tensions between US and Chinese approaches to developing technologies is not limited to QTs, and has arisen in relation to other technologies, most notably 5G technologies.[126]

This demonstrates that there are limits to the ability of standards to foster collaboration and interoperability where the efforts of States, such as the US, limit the potential for international collaboration, impedes access to components needed for prototype development, and discourages firms from aligning with international standards if they fear potential trade penalties. Nevertheless, this point should not be pushed too far as there are examples of international cooperation taking place between the national standards bodies of countries including the US, as exemplified by ISO/IEC JTC3 on Quantum Technologies. This Joint Technical Committee was launched in January 2024[127] and has 28 participating countries, including China and the US, alongside 10 observer countries.[128] It has already published ISO/IEC 4879:2024,[129]

122 S.1260—United States Innovation and Competition Act of 2021 (2021).

123 S.1260—United States Innovation and Competition Act of 2021, (2001), Section 3004.

124 H.R.4346—CHIPS and Science Act (2022).

125 Sanders (2021).

126 Kim et al. (2020).

127 ISO and IEC (2024b).

128 IEC (2025).

129 IEC/ISO JTC 3.

on vocabulary relating to quantum computing that applies to all types of organizations that look to exchange quantum computing concepts, and has drafted ISO/IEC AWI TR 18157 that relates to an introduction to quantum computing.[130] This cooperation perhaps highlights the differences between State approaches to quantum computing and the approaches of the national standards bodies who form the membership of the ISO and the divergences and convergences between the approaches of states and national standards bodies will be a point of interest regarding the future development of quantum governance.[131]

2.6.3 EU Efforts to Influence Standardization—Rights and Resistance Against Corporate Influences

In contrast to China and the US, the EU is not a nation state but its coordination of Member State laws and activities within the EU make it global leader in the development of emerging technologies, including QTs. The Chapter has already discussed the ways in which standards and legislation may interact with one another in the EU, and that harmonized standards may provide a direct source of obligations within a wider piece of legislation. The creation of standards through a request by the EU Commission to the European SDOs does not mean the resulting harmonized standards will be different to existing international standards but alignment is not guaranteed. For example, there are differences in the understanding of risk within the EU AI Act, that will shape European standards produced under the auspices of this legislation, and existing standards, such as ISO/IEC 23894, that governs risk management.[132] As the EU continues to focus on the establishment and functioning of its internal market and the protection of fundamental rights and freedoms as protected by EU law, the greater this risk of divergence from international standards.

An EU-centric approach to developing standards does not preclude the input of non-EU stakeholders. Chinese firms played a significant role in the development of standards relating to other emerging technologies, such as AI and 5G, but this did raise concerns. The EU has sought to push for a greater role for National Standards Bodies within the development of standards and the downgrading of ETSI, the SDO that is most greatly influenced by industry interests, to an advisory role in the creation of standards related to the AI Act. Nevertheless, the changes have not reduced the scope of foreign participation in the technical work, as distinct from voting and decision-making. Furthermore, where standards do align with pre-existing international standards, it supports criticisms that EU SDOs lack legitimacy as the stakeholders within them have little scope to develop standards due to the pre-existence of international standards.

---

[130] IEC/ISO JTC 3.

[131] ISO (n.d.(b)).

[132] Tartaro (2023).

The EU's coordination function is evident in its 2018 launch of the Quantum Technology Flagship, a long-term research and innovation initiative that seeks to solidify the EU's position as a leader in QT development. This is part of a plethora of actions taken by the EU to foster a collaborative approach to "unlock the transformative power of quantum" and "develop a fully-fledged European quantum ecosystem."[133] The EU has not yet pushed forward with a significant legislative agenda as it has done with AI and the digital sector.

2.6.4 Chinese Approaches in Standardization—The dawn of a "Beijing Effect"?

China has also sought to influence QTs at this early stage in their development, in ways that directly and indirectly relate to the development of standards. One rather direct means of influence is its increased participation and leadership in the largest global SDOs, making it now one of the key figures in developing standards. For example, between 2012 and 2023, China tripled its number of leadership positions within the ISO, surpassing Japan, France, and the UK.[134] China has also dramatically increased the number of committees in which it participates, becoming the nation with the highest number of participating memberships.[135] This does not necessarily translate to an increased influence over the outputs, especially as there is still significant participation by western states, but is a demonstration of intent to play a much larger and more active role in shaping the development of emerging technologies. Standards are developed upon the participation and consensus of members, so an increase in the number of Chinese representatives is likely to lead to a greater influence over any outputs. Just as the EU benefitted from a "Brussels Effect" in the wake of the General Data Protection Regulation, which influences data governance beyond EU borders, the increased participation of China here may be rooted in a desire to propagate a "Beijing Effect" in the governance of emerging technologies at an earlier stage of their governance.

Many have expressed concerns that China's desire to infuse its values into the development of standards has "compromised" SDOs, especially as, in contrast to other jurisdictions, the national body that represents China at two key SDOs is a public entity.[136] This has led to concerns that Chinese influence over standards has shifted from an acceptable level of influence to one that distorts the relevant bodies to unjustifiably integrate its preferred values into global standards. However, the evidence to support such contentions is not publicly available as voting patterns and submission rates within SDOs are not made publicly available and some state that

[133] European Commission (n.d.).

[134] Barrett (2024).

[135] Barrett (2024).

[136] Barrett (2024).

China's increased influence is merely a corollary of its growth as an economy.[137] QTs will benefit from this economic growth as China has already built a National Laboratory for Quantum Information Science and has invested billions as part of a broader industrial strategy to increase self-sufficiency, industrial competitiveness, and create favorable path dependencies.[138] This is particularly pertinent to QT development in China as the National Laboratory for Quantum Information is already subject to export controls from the US.[139] This means it would need to obtain a license to acquire technologies that originate from the US, which is highly unlikely in the current geopolitical climate.

2.7 The Path Forward: Promising Areas, Practical Challenges, and Strategic Considerations

Certain domains in quantum technology are well-suited for early standardization, as demonstrated by areas where many standardization activities[140] are taking place including the field of Post-Quantum Cryptography (PQC). NIST currently leads the effort to standardize quantum-resistant cryptographic algorithms alongside international experts and through transparent processes. Final selections were announced in 2022, with migration guidance now underway.[141] Benchmarking Frameworks are another area which is also well-suited for standardization. Metrics such as IBM's quantum volume,[142] which is an example of a system-level performance benchmark, or the QED-C suite of application-oriented benchmarks[143] could help create shared performance baselines, even if full hardware interoperability remains out of reach These early efforts could help avoid long-term fragmentation.

However, there are also a variety of challenges associated with standardization activities in the quantum technology sector. Standardization efforts in quantum are further complicated by a diverse stakeholder landscape. Governments, large tech firms, startups, universities, international standard bodies, and defense organizations all approach quantum with different incentives. Furthermore, the timing of standards remains a difficult question, and relies upon a plethora of factors that may be outside the control of stakeholders involved in the creation and dissemination of standards. The following section draws from the insights gained in the previous section and provides a structured overview and analysis of selected key practical challenges to standardization efforts in quantum technologies.

137 Barrett (2024).

138 Lee et al. (2022).

139 Bureau of Industry and Security, Department of Commerce (2024).

140 Aboy et al. (2025).

141 NIST (2022).

142 Cross et al. (2019).

143 Lubinski et al. (2024).

2.7.1 Export Controls and Trade Restrictions

As elaborated by Davis et al.,[144] QTs are increasingly subject to export controls and technology transfer restrictions. Under the Wassenaar Arrangement, several components related to QTs—including types of PQC and advanced sensors—are regulated.[145] Due to increasing difficulties in achieving consensus within key multilateral regimes like the Wassenaar Arrangement, States are increasingly resorting to national measures to restrict the export of frontier technologies.[146] These restrictions apply to both quantum computers, and the materials, infrastructure and software necessary to develop and use them.[147]

This could lead to significant fragmentation of approach to QTs internationally as countries, and companies, adapt to the QTs that are available to them, or make the most economic sense in light of trade restrictions. Most obviously, the countries against whom export controls and trade restrictions are aimed (i.e., threats to national security and geopolitical rivals) may be excluded from certain types of, or approaches to, QTs. However, this fragmentation also extends to countries traditionally seen as allies, with a "patchwork"[148] of rules beginning to emerge even within EU Member States that are typically aligned on these measures. The increased volume and divergence of measures aimed at QTs mean that achieving a level of consensus required to standardize is significantly more challenging.

2.7.2 Open Innovation Versus Strategic Secrecy

Open standards such as TCP/IP and USB demonstrate that openness has historically accelerated technological development. Yet, quantum technology's security implications, particularly in cryptography, have prompted more cautious behavior from governments and defense agencies, sometimes resulting in non-disclosure of technologies by public or private actors due to demands for the protection of state secrets.[149]

Private firms are also protective of their IP, including copyrights, patents and trade secrets.[150] Cloud-accessible platforms like IBM Q and Amazon Braket offer Application Program Interfaces (APIs) that are not fully standardized, limiting portability and supplier interoperability. This behavior, while commercially rational, may inhibit the emergence of broadly adopted interface standards and demonstrates the risks of

---

[144] Davis et al. (2025b).

[145] Wassenaar Arrangement (2019, 2025).

[146] Davis et al. (2025b).

[147] Davis et al. (2025b).

[148] European Commission (2024, 8).

[149] Davis et al. (2025a).

[150] Kop et al. (2022), Rantala and Giardini (2024).

entrusting private industry with an overly significant role in the early governance of emerging technologies.

These tensions between open scientific collaboration and concerns related to national and regional security, trade secrets and IPRs are not novel, but there is a risk that these become particularly acute in the QT and standardization context[151] This inhibits the level of international cooperation and collaboration that is required to ensure the creation of a standard with the prerequisite consensus of relevant actors.

It is therefore critical that the standards and regulations that develop around QTs are steeped in the global best-practice forums as offered by SSOs. It is in the interest of States to participate, but QTs raise particular national security concerns that are currently undermining these efforts. In the United States, current rules from the Bureau of Industry and Security prevent some technologies from being shared in standards development arenas like SSOs. This has meant that when entity-listed Chinese organizations are involved, US representatives have been forced to withdraw from the development of that specific standard.[152]

2.7.3 Standard Essential Patents and FRAND Licensing

The legal framework governing intellectual property, particularly Standard Essential Patents (SEPs), will also play a defining role in shaping interoperable standards, as well as the direction and accessibility of innovation. Given the increasing reliance on interoperability and common protocols in areas such as quantum communications, quantum computing architectures, and post-quantum cryptography, the integration of SEPs into standardization regimes has become both legally salient and economically consequential.

SEPs are patents that claim technology is deemed necessary for compliance with a formalized standard. As such, implementers cannot build compliant products without infringing the SEP unless they obtain a license. In exchange for the market power conferred by standard essentiality, SEP holders are generally required to license their patents on Fair, Reasonable, and Non-Discriminatory (FRAND) terms. The FRAND obligation is designed to prevent hold-up, facilitate access to essential technologies, and encourage efficient participation in global innovation markets.[153] While the FRAND framework is well developed in telecommunications and information technology sectors, it nevertheless has given rise to different judicial interpretations. Besides that, recent legal and policy developments highlight growing concerns that the current SEP ecosystem lacks the requisite transparency, consistency, and dispute resolution mechanisms needed to support emerging technology markets.[154] Accordingly, it is likely that quantum technologies could further challenge the current SEP

[151] Kop et al. (2022).

[152] NIST (2021).

[153] See the recitals of the recently withdrawn proposal by the European Commission (2023).

[154] Intellectual Property Office (2025).

system, but a deeper exploration of potential challenges and responses fall outside this chapter's scope.

2.8 Lessons to Be Learned from Other Technologies

As described above, quantum standardization faces interlocking challenges: technical immaturity, global power struggles, regulatory restrictions, and competing stakeholder interests. The additional complexities of SEPs and FRAND licensing underscore the need for proactive frameworks that promote innovation while preventing monopolistic control. However, it would be an exaggeration to argue such complexities render QTs a completely novel challenge to existing governance mechanisms. Discussions concerning emerging, yet still more mature, technologies such as AI may provide some fruitful insights for those involved in the governance of QTs. Nevertheless, certain differences remain, and it is important to remain cognizant of the unique characteristics of QTs and their place in wider geopolitical climates and sociotechnical landscapes.

Justifications for standards as a legitimate form of governance are rooted in the expertise of those involved in their creation are only persuasive where that expertise aligns with the standard's purpose and content. Similarly, if standards serve as a means of promoting collaboration and interoperability by providing a common set of terminologies or measurements, then there should be little scope for disagreement over their application. Where standards are used to govern more normative questions, such as the appropriateness or reasonableness of a technology's use, or to expand upon the fundamental right's dimensions of technologies, they erode their justifications for use. These issues risk standards losing their ability to effectively coordinate and provide a robust foundation for technologies to flourish.

The issue is thus not one of just legitimacy, but also the usability of standards. Therefore, we advocate for standards to focus more upon the tasks that they were originally designed for and to allow more normative matters to be resolved via a more suitable mechanism with the appropriate expertise to determine such matters over how and when technologies should be used. This chapter has focused on some of the larger, formal standardization setting organizations, but this does not mean they are the only relevant actors. Just as informal industry bodies coalesce around certain technologies, the governance of QTs may benefit from similar efforts from civil society organizations and similar bodies, whilst leaving standards to do the job that they were initially conceived to perform.

The EU, as a matter of urgency, must elaborate the criteria implied in *Public.Resource.Org*[155] that would determine when a standard, irrespective of their copyright protections, should be made public due to the implied transparency requirements inherent to the rule of law. The need for clarity is evident, but this will not

[155] Case C-588/21, Public.Resource.Org, Inc. and Right to Know CLG v European Commission Judgment of the Court (Grand Chamber) of 5 March 2024 (2024).

be an easy task, and no outcome will be universally acclaimed. The importance of the public knowing their duties, obligations, and rights is unquestioned, but it is not clear how often such information is contained within standards. It is important that any criteria recognizes that efforts to reduce copyright protection may disincentivize participation by private actors. This may lead to a reduction in the quality of standards and mean that any outputs may not be viewed as an authoritative consensus. Finally, this chapter highlights the complexity of the standards setting landscape and, given the concerns over technological fragmentation, it is critical that there are cooperation and collaboration between the different bodies. Those involved in the development of standards must have recourse to the Vienna and Frankfurt agreements that try to facilitate alignment between standards issued by international bodies. The Vienna Agreement sets out cooperation arrangements between ISO and CEN and the Frankfurt Agreement does the same between IEC and CENELEC. This could be a useful tool where national security concerns may impinge upon international collaborative efforts.

2.9 Conclusion

Standards offer a flexible, globally harmonized path to govern early-stage quantum technologies while preserving innovation, security, and international cooperation.[156] Early standardization in post-quantum cryptography, benchmarking, and interoperability protocols shows promise and should be pursued. In fact, the various QT standard initiatives address many of the quantum ELSI concerns raised by scholars. Nevertheless, changes in regulatory understandings of what emerging technologies can achieve, going beyond product safety to include fundamental rights protections in some instances, and current geopolitical climate requires a careful examination of when and where they are used. Standards remain a key means of supporting innovation through creating shared understandings of key terminology, enhanced interoperability, and facilitating collaboration between a range of relevant stakeholders across multiple sectors and borders. As QTs mature, the strategic use of international consensus standards can offer a common foundation upon which research, commercialization, and oversight can develop in an effective manner that mitigates fragmentation to promote globally coherent innovation trajectories.

Whilst standards are "voluntary" in a technical sense, their deeper integration into legislative frameworks and how they can provide a clear means of demonstrating regulatory compliance means that, in reality, they operate more as mandatory requirements. This blurring between soft law and hard law shows how standards have an influence beyond their formal status. As QTs begin to develop across a range of important sectors, including communications, security, and computing, this quality is likely to become a pervasive attribute of standards. This suggests that standards will become a core component of emerging compliance and governance frameworks.

[156] Aboy et al. (2025).

At the same time, the chapter underscores that reliance on standards is not without challenges. Questions of legitimacy, inclusiveness, and geopolitical influence remain salient, particularly as standards become more closely tied to normative concerns and strategic state interests. Furthermore, in light of some of the applications of QTs and their relationship with national security, how far standards can become globalized to provide a truly streamlined regulatory experience. International consensus regarding QT standards will require long-term trust-building, institutional leadership, and a commitment to balancing sovereignty with interoperability. Only through such coordinated action can the promise of quantum technology be realized as a shared global infrastructure, rather than a fragmented arena of strategic competition. Realizing the full potential of international standards to guide the trajectory of QT development entails a more nuanced understanding of standards as part of a complex and layered regulatory framework. They remain a key tool for providing the requisite adaptability and authority to encourage responsible technological development that can support commercial interests and long-term goals in the broader public interest.

Acknowledgements This work was made possible through the generous support of the Novo Nordisk Foundation (NNF) via a grant for the scientifically independent Collaborative Research Program in Bioscience Innovation Law (Inter-CeBIL Program—Grant No. NNF23SA0087056). Any use of AI in this manuscript adheres to ethical guidelines for use and acknowledgement of AI in academic research. Each author has made a substantial contribution to the work, which has been thoroughly vetted for accuracy, and assumes responsibility for the integrity of their contributions in accordance with the ethical guidance on AI use and disclosure set out by Porsdam Mann et al.

References

Aboy, M., Gasser, U., Cohen, I.G., Kop, M. (2025) Quantum technology governance: A standards-first approach. *Science* 389(6760):575–578.

Aboy, M., Price, W.N., Raker, S. (2023) Mapping the patent landscape of medical machine learning. *Nature Biotechnology* 41(4):461–468.

Ajagekar, A., You, F. (2022) Quantum computing and quantum artificial intelligence for renewable and sustainable energy: An emerging prospect towards climate neutrality. *Renewable and Sustainable Energy Reviews* 165:112493.

Bacchi, C. (2007) The Ethics of Problem Representation: Widening the Scope of Ethical Debate. *Policy and Society* 26(3):5–20.

Barrett, T. (2024) Standards Development Organisations in an era of strategic competition. Available at: https://www.ussc.edu.au/standards-development-organisations-in-an-era-of-strategic-competition. Accessed 12 May 2025.

Black, J. (2002) Regulatory Conversations. *Journal of Law and Society* 29(1):163–196.

Blind, K. (2025) Standardization and Standards: Safeguards of Technological Sovereignty? *Technological Forecasting and Social Change* 210(C):123873.

British Standards Institution (2025) BSI Royal Charter. Available at: https://www.bsigroup.com/en-GB/about-bsi/bsi-royal-charter/. Accessed 7 Jul 2025.

Bureau of Industry and Security, Department of Commerce (2024) Commerce Control List Additions and Revisions; Implementation of Controls on Advanced Technologies Consistent With Controls Implemented by International Partners. Available at: https://www.federalregister.gov/documents/2024/09/06/2024-19633/commerce-control-list-additions-and-revisions-implementation-of-controls-on-advanced-technologies. Accessed 13 May 2025.

Cantero Gamito, M. (2021) From Private Regulation to Power Politics: The Rise of China in AI Private Governance Through Standardisation. Available at: https://papers.ssrn.com/abstract=3794761. Accessed 14 Apr 2025.

CEN, CENELEC (2025) ISO and IEC. Available at: https://www.cencenelec.eu/european-standardization/international-policy/iso-and-iec/. Accessed 5 May 2025.

CEN-CENELEC (2023) Standardization Roadmap on Quantum Technologies. Available at: https://www.cencenelec.eu/media/CEN-CENELEC/AreasOfWork/CEN-CENELEC_Topics/Quantum%20technologies/Documentation%20and%20Materials/fgqt_q04_standardizationroadmapquantumtechnologies_release1.pdf. Accessed 2 Apr 2025.

Chen, L., Lange, T., Moriai, S. (2023) Post-Quantum Cryptography: Part I - General. ISO/IEC JTC1 SC27 WG2, SC 27 Committee Document 208 Available at: https://committee.iso.org/sites/jtc1sc27/home/wg2.html. Accessed 15 Sep 2025.

China National Institute of Standardization (n.d.) Welcome to CNIS. Available at: https://en.cnis.ac.cn/bzygk_329/kyly/. Accessed 11 Aug 2025.

Choucair, C. (2024) UK Government Releases Strategic Quantum Regulation Plan to Encourage Innovation and Support Global Leadership UK Government Releases Strategic Quantum Regulation Plan to Encourage Innovation and Support Global Leadership. Available at: https://thequantuminsider.com/2024/10/08/uk-government-releases-strategic-quantum-regulation-plan-to-encourage-innovation-and-support-global-leadership/. Accessed 29 May 2025.

Cihon, P. (2019) Standards for AI Governance: International Standards to Enable Global Coordination in AI Research & Development. Available at: https://www.governance.ai/research-paper/standards-for-ai-governance-international-standards-to-enable-global-coordination-in-ai-research-development. Accessed 06 Oct 2025.

Contreras, J. (2019) Technical Standards, Standards-Setting Organizations and Intellectual Property: A Survey of the Literature (with an Emphasis on Empirical Approaches). In: Menell, P.S., and Schwartz, D. (eds.) *Research Handbook on the Economics of Intellectual Property Law, Volume II* (Edward Elgar Publishing, Cheltenham).

Cory, N. (2024) The Biden Administration Overreacts Responding to China's Role in Setting Standards for Quantum Technologies. Available at: https://itif.org/publications/2024/07/29/the-biden-administration-overreacts-in-responding-to-china-s-role-in-setting-standards-for-quantum-technologies/. Accessed 9 Jul 2025.

Cross, A.W., Bishop, L.S., Sheldon, S., et al. (2019) Validating quantum computers using randomized model circuits. *Physical Review A*. 100:032328.

Danish Business Authority, Danish Quantum Community (2024) 16 Danish Quantum Use Cases: Practical Insights into Applications of Quantum Technologies Across Industries. Available at: https://dqc.dk/wp-content/uploads/2024/12/16-Danish-Quantum-Use-Cases-December-2024.pdf. Accessed 06 Oct 2025.

Dansk Standard (2025) About Danish Standards - Danish Standards. Available at: https://www.ds.dk/en/about-danish-standards. Accessed 7 Jul 2025.

Davis, P.,A.,E., Aboy, M., Bygrave, L.A., et al. (2025a) EU Cybersecurity Regulation in the Quantum Age. Available at: https://papers.ssrn.com/sol3/papers.cfm?abstract_id=5383838. Accessed 06 Oct 2025.

Davis, P.,A.,E., Aboy, M., Minssen, T. (2025b) Regulatory Challenges and Opportunities of Export Controls on Quantum Computing. Available at: https://papers.ssrn.com/sol3/papers.cfm?abstract_id=5404548. Accessed 06 Oct 2025.

Department of Industry, Science and Resources (2025) National Quantum Strategy. Available at: https://www.industry.gov.au/publications/national-quantum-strategy. Accessed 06 Oct 2025.

Devitt, S.J. (2016) Performing quantum computing experiments in the cloud. *Physical Review A* 94(3):032329.

ETSI (n.d.(a)) Membership of ETSI. Available at: https://www.etsi.org/membership. Accessed 7 Jul 2025.

ETSI (n.d.(b)) ETSI - About Us. Available at: https://www.etsi.org/about. Accessed 18 Apr 2025.

European Commission (n.d.) Quantum | Shaping Europe's digital future. Available at: https://digital-strategy.ec.europa.eu/en/policies/quantum. Accessed 13 May 2025.

European Commission (2022a) An EU Strategy on Standardisation - Setting global standards in support of a resilient, green and digital EU single market. Available at: https://ec.europa.eu/docsroom/documents/48598. Accessed on 06 Oct 2025.

European Commission (2022b) A Notification under Article 12 of Regulation (EU) No 1025/2012 - Draft standardisation request to the European Standardisation Organisations in support of safe and trustworthy artificial intelligence. Available at: https://ec.europa.eu/docsroom/documents/52376. Accessed 06 Oct 2025.

European Commission (2024) White Paper on Export Controls. Available at: https://eur-lex.europa.eu/legal-content/EN/TXT/?uri=celex:52024DC0025. Accessed 06 Oct 2025.

European Commission (2023b) Proposal for a Regulation of the European Parliament and of the Council on Standard Essential Patents and Amending Regulation (EU)2017/1001. Available at: https://single-market-economy.ec.europa.eu/publications/com2023232-proposal-regulation-standard-essential-patents_en. Accessed on 06 Oct 2025.

European Committee for Standardization (n.d.) CEN Community - List of members. Available at: https://standards.cencenelec.eu/dyn/www/f?p=CEN:5. Accessed 7 Jul 2025.

Fosch Villaronga, E., Golia, A.J., (2019) Robots, standards and the law: Rivalries between private standards and public policymaking for robot governance. *Computer Law & Security Review* 35(2):129–144.

Gambetta, J., Javadi-Abhari, A., Johnson, B., et al. (2021) Driving quantum performance. Available at: https://www.ibm.com/quantum/blog/circuit-layer-operations-per-second. Accessed 15 September 2025.

Gornet, M., Maxwell, W. (2024) The European approach to regulating AI through technical standards. *Internet Policy Review* 13(3):1–27.

Grimes, S., Du, D. (2022) China's emerging role in the global semiconductor value chain. *Telecommunications Policy* 46(2):101959.

Hagemann, R., Huddleston Skees, J., Thierer, A. (2018) Soft Law for Hard Problems: The Governance of Emerging Technologies in an Uncertain Future. *Colorado Technology Law Journal* 17(1):37–130.

IEC (2021) Quantum Information Technology - White Paper. Available at: https://www.iec.ch/basecamp/quantum-information-technology. Accessed on 06 Oct 2025.

IEC (2025) IEC - IEC/ISO JTC 3 Structure. Available at: https://www.iec.ch/dyn/www/f?p=103:29:388850622726::::FSP_ORG_ID,FSP_LANG_ID:49854,25. Accessed 1 Jul 2025.

IEC/ISO JTC 3 (2024) ISO/IEC 4879:2024. Available at: https://www.iso.org/standard/80432.html. Accessed 17 Apr 2025.

IEC/ISO (2025) JTC 3 ISO/IEC AWI TR 18157. Available at: https://www.iso.org/standard/85203.html. Accessed 1 Jul 2025.

IEEE (2022) P1943: Standard for Post-Quantum Network Security. Available at: https://development.standards.ieee.org/myproject-web/public/view.html#pardetail/9872. Accessed 17 Apr 2025.

Intellectual Property Office (2025) Consultation on Standard Essential Patents. Available at: https://www.gov.uk/government/consultations/consultation-on-standard-essential-patents-seps/consultation-on-standard-essential-patents. Accessed 15 Sep 2025.

ISO (n.d.(a)) Eesti Standardikeskus (EVS). Available at: https://www.iso.org/member/1721.html. Accessed 15 Sept 2025.

ISO (n.d.(b)) ISO - Members. Available at: ISO. https://www.iso.org/about/members. Accessed 17 Apr 2025.

ISO (2015) ISO Membership Manual. Available at: https://www.iso.org/publication/PUB100399.html. Accessed 06 Oct 2025.

ISO (n.d.(c)) ISO/IEC JTC 1/SC 27 - Information security, cybersecurity and privacy protection. Available at: https://www.iso.org/committee/45306.html. Accessed 17 Apr 2025.

ISO, IEC (2024a) ISO/IEC Guide 2:2004. Available at: https://www.iso.org/standard/39976.html. Accessed 06 Oct 2025.

ISO, IEC (2024b) IEC and ISO launch new joint technical committee on quantum technologies. Available at: https://www.iso.org/news/new-joint-committee-quantum-technologies. Accessed 1 Jul 2025.

ISO/IEC JTC 1/SC 27 (2023a) ISO/IEC 23837–1:2023. Available at: https://www.iso.org/standard/77097.html. Accessed 17 Apr 2025.

ISO/IEC JTC 1/SC 27 (2023b) ISO/IEC 23837–2:2023. Available at https://www.iso.org/standard/77309.html. Accessed 17 Apr 2025.

ISO/IEC JTC 1/SC 27 (2025) ISO/IEC WD TR 25544. Available at: https://www.iso.org/standard/90711.html. Accessed 17 Apr 2025.

ITU Telecommunication Standardization Sector (2020) Y.3800. Available at: https://www.itu.int/rec/T-REC-Y.3800-202004-I!Cor1/en. Accessed 17 Apr 2025.

ITU-T (2025) Global information infrastructure, Internet protocol aspects, next-generation networks, Internet of Things and smart cities. Available at: https://www.itu.int/rec/T-REC-Y/en. Accessed 17 Apr 2025.

Johnson, W.G., (2019) Governance Tools for the Second Quantum Revolution. *Jurimetrics* 59(4): 487–522.

Kallestrup, M. (2017) Stakeholder Participation in European Standardization: A Mapping and an Assessment of Three Categories of Regulation. *Legal Issues of Economic Integration* 44(4): 381–393.

Kamara, I. (2024) European cybersecurity standardisation: a tale of two solitudes in view of Europe's cyber resilience. *The European Journal of Social Science Research* 37(5):1441–1460.

Kanevskaia, O., Panagiotis, D., Bijlmakers, S. (2024) The European Telecommunication Standards Institute (ETSI): in search for legitimacy and resilience of European standardisation. *The European Journal of Social Science Research* 37(5):1269–1288.

Karlsson-Vinkhuyzen, S.I., Vihma, A. (2009) Comparing the legitimacy and effectiveness of global hard and soft law: An analytical framework. *Regulation & Governance* 3(4):400–420.

Keil, T. (2002) De-facto standardization through alliances—lessons from Bluetooth. *Telecommunications Policy* 26(3-4):205–213.

Kim, M., Lee, H., Kwak, J. (2020) The changing patterns of China's international standardization in ICT under techno-nationalism: A reflection through 5G standardization. *International Journal of Information Management* 54:102145.

Kop, M., Aboy, M., De Jong, E., et al. (2024a) Towards Responsible Quantum Technology: Safeguarding, Engaging and Advancing Quantum R&D. *UC Law Science and Technology Journal* 15(1):63–94.

Kop, M., Aboy, M., De Jong, E., et al. (2024b) Ten principles for responsible quantum innovation. *Quantum Science and Technology* 9(3):035013.

Kop, M., Aboy, M., Minssen, T. (2022) Intellectual property in quantum computing and market power: a theoretical discussion and empirical analysis. *Journal of Intellectual Property Law & Practice* 17(8):613–628.

Langford, N.K., Devitt, S.J. (2025) Quantum Technologies and Standardisation Globally and in Australia. Available at: https://www.standards.org.au/documents/quantum-technologies-and-standardisation-globally-and-in-australia. Accessed 06 Oct 2025.

Lee, J., Zhang, E., Creemers, R. (2022) China's Standardisation System – trends, implications and case studies in emerging technologies. Available at: https://leidenasiacentre.nl/wp-content/uploads/2022/04/Chinas-standardisation-system.pdf. Accessed 06 Oct 2025.

Lubinski, T., Goings, J.J., Mayer, K., et al. (2024) Quantum Algorithm Exploration using Application-Oriented Performance Benchmarks. Available at: https://arxiv.org/pdf/2402.08985. Accessed on 06 Oct 2025.

NIST (2021) Comment on FR Doc # 211026–0219. Available at: https://www.regulations.gov/comment/NIST-2021-0006-0033. Accessed 12 May 2025.

NIST (2024a) Quantum information science. Available at: https://www.nist.gov/quantum-information-science. Accessed 11 Aug 2025.

NIST (2024b) U.S. Government National Standards Strategy for Critical and Emerging Technologies (USG NSSCET): Implementation Roadmap. Available at: https://www.nist.gov/system/files/documents/2024/06/26/USG%20NSSCET_REPORT_v6_26.pdf. Accessed 06 Oct 2025.

Pelinka, A. (2011) The European Union as an Alternative to the Nation-State. *International Journal of Politics, Culture, and Society* 24(1–2):21–30.

People's Republic of China (2021) National standardization development outline. Available at: https://perma.cc/CB6V-VQDV. Accessed 06 Oct 2025.

Perrier, E. (2022) The Quantum Governance Stack: Models of Governance for Quantum Information Technologies. *Digital Society* 1(3):22.

Preskill, J. (2018) Quantum Computing in the NISQ era and beyond. *Quantum* 2:79–99.

Rantala, J., Giardini, M. (2024) IP Guidelines for Quantum Technologies. Quantum Flagship Coordination and Support Action QUCATS Available at: qt.eu/media/pdf/IP_Guidelines_for_Quantum_Technologists_2024.pdf. Accessed 06 Oct 2025.

Rühlig, T.N. (2022) Technical Standardization and Innovation in a Change Geopolitical Landscape. In: Deiaco, E., Wernberg, J. (eds) *Rethinking boundaries and revisiting borders: conditions for innovation, entrepreneurship and economic integration in an interconnected world*. (Swedish Entrepreneurship Forum, Stockholm).

Sanders, C. (2021) China criticizes U.S. for putting Chinese firms on trade blacklist. Available at: https://www.reuters.com/business/us-restricts-exports-dozen-more-chinese-companies-2021-11-24/. Accessed 06 Oct 2025.

Soler Garrido, J., De Nigris, S., Bassani, E., et al. (2024) Harmonised Standards for the European AI Act. Available at: https://publications.jrc.ec.europa.eu/repository/handle/JRC139430. Accessed 06 Oct 2025.

Standards Australia (2025) AS 5405:2025. Available at: https://store.standards.org.au/product/as-5405-2025. Accessed 06 Oct 2025.

Swayne, M. (2025a) KETS Quantum Security Futureproofs Critical Infrastructure for Government Contract. Available at: https://thequantuminsider.com/2025/04/25/kets-quantum-security-futureproofs-critical-infrastructure-for-government-contract/. Accessed 19 Jun 2025.

Swayne, M. (2025b) China Launches Its Own Quantum-Resistant Encryption Standards, Bypassing US Efforts. Available at: https://thequantuminsider.com/2025/02/18/china-launches-its-own-quantum-resistant-encryption-standard-bypassing-us-efforts/. Accessed 9 Jul 2025.

Swayne, M. (2024) U.S. Overreach on Quantum Standards Risks Undermining Private Sector Leadership, Policy Expert Warns. Available at: https://thequantuminsider.com/2024/08/10/u-s-overreach-on-quantum-standards-risks-undermining-private-sector-leadership-policy-expert-warns/. Accessed 9 Jul 2025.

Tartaro, A. (2023) Towards European Standards Supporting the AI Act: Alignment Challenges on the Path to Trustworthy AI. Available at: https://papers.ssrn.com/sol3/papers.cfm?abstract_id=4470766. Accessed 06 Oct 2025.

Teubner, L.K., Henkel, J., Bekkers, R. (2021) Industry consortia in mobile telecommunications standards setting: Purpose, organization and diversity. *Telecommunications Policy* 45(3):102059.

The UK Government, British Standards Institution (2024) Memorandum of Understanding between the United Kingdom Government and the British Standards Institution in Respect of its Activities as the United Kingdom's National Standards Body. Available at: https://www.bsigroup.com/en-GB/about-bsi/governance/standards-governance/. Accessed 06 Oct 2025.

Tzoulia, E. (2025) Harmonized Standards in the Public Domain? Better Not .... *IIC - International Review of Intellectual Property and Competition Law*. 56:692–712.

UK Department for Science, Innovation & Technology (2024) Regulating quantum technology applications: government response to the RHC. Available at: https://www.gov.uk/government/publications/regulating-quantum-technology-applications-government-response-to-recommendations-made-by-the-regulatory-horizons-council/regulating-quantum-technology-applications-government-response-to-the-rhc. Accessed 29 May 2025.

van Daalen, O. (2025) Human Rights-Compatible Quantum Computing Governance. In: van Daalen, O. (ed.) *From Encryption to Quantum Computing: The Governance of Information Security and Human Rights*. (T.M.C. Asser Press, The Hague).

van Deventer, O., Spethmann, N., Loeffler, M., et al. (2022) Towards European standards for quantum technologies. *EPJ Quantum Technology* 9:1–41.

Wassenaar Arrangement (2019) List of Dual-Use Goods and Technologies & Munitions List (Dec. 2019). Available at: https://www.wassenaar.org/list-of-dual-use-goods-and-technologies-munitions-list-dec-2019/. Accessed 15 Sep 2025.

Wassenaar Arrangement (2025) What is the Wassenaar Arrangement? Available at: https://www.wassenaar.org/the-wassenaar-arrangement/. Accessed 15 Sep2025.

Watts, R., Valantasis, G., Ruelas, C. (2024) A Systematic Approach for Identifying Companies with Economic Moats. Available at: https://www.spglobal.com/spdji/en/research/article/a-systematic-approach-for-identifying-companies-with-economic-moats/. Accessed 06 Oct 2025.

Werle, R., Iversen, E.J. (2006) Promoting Legitimacy in Technical Standardization. *Science, Technology & Innovation Studies* 2:19–39.

Wu, Y., Weil, T. (2022) Recent Developments of Nanodiamond Quantum Sensors for Biological Applications. *Advanced Science* 9(19):2200059.

Chapter 3
A Governance Stack Framework for Quantum Technology Applications in Life Sciences: Examining Ontological and Integration Challenges

Elija Perrier and Mateo Aboy

3.1 Introduction

3.1.1 Motivation

Life sciences represent a promising area for the application of quantum information technology (QIT).[1] By leveraging the properties of quantum computing (QC), quantum sensing (QS) and quantum communication (QCM), QIT offers prospects for improved pharmaceutical synthesis, diagnostic tools, medical device design, biological system modelling, and bioinformatics processing and encryption. Quantum cryptography and communication offer potentially heightened security over sensitive personal data. Combined with the revolution in artificial intelligence,[2] QIT is anticipated to herald a new phase in life sciences innovation.[3]

---

[1] McKinsey & Company (2024).

[2] Fu et al. (2025), Thierer (2021).

[3] Flöther (2023), Pyrkov et al. (2024).

E. Perrier (✉)
Centre for Quantum Software and Information, University of Technology, Sydney, Australia

Centre for Law, Medicine and Life Sciences (LML), University of Cambridge, Cambridge, UK

M. Aboy
Centre for Law, Medicine and Life Sciences (LML) and Centre for Intellectual Property and Information Law (CIPIL), University of Cambridge, Cambridge, UK

M. Aboy et al. (eds.), *Quantum Technology Governance II*, Perspectives in Law, Business and Innovation, https://doi.org/10.1007/978-981-92-3768-5_3

For these reasons, QIT applications in the life sciences are a major focus of research and innovation globally.[4] Yet the developmental trajectory of QIT remains uncertain.[5] The technology is nascent. Its reliability and risks arising from its use are unclear.[6] This mismatch—an early-stage, high-risk QIT entering a mature life sciences sector—creates a central governance dilemma of how to integrate QIT governance within existing regulatory regimes.[7] Striking the right governance balance is central to realizing the gains and mitigating the risks from QIT life sciences applications.[8] In addition to the integration challenge, there is a second governance dilemma arising from the use of QIT in the life sciences—one which is ontological in nature. Neither life sciences nor prospective QIT governance regimes significantly address how the unique features of quantum ontology upon which QIT is based—entanglement, no-cloning, superposition, and inherently stochastic measurement—affect governance (which is based on classical assumptions of physical processes and information).

3.1.2 *Two Types of Governance Dilemmas*

The application of quantum information technologies in the life sciences introduces two distinct governance dilemmas that shape the regulatory landscape.

3.1.2.1 Technical Dilemmas

The first, a technical dilemma, emerges from the fundamental differences between the quantum ontology underpinning QIT and the classical ontology that forms the basis of existing life sciences regulation. Quantum properties such as superposition and entanglement, the no-cloning, and inherent stochasticity in measurement contrast sharply with the classical assumptions of deterministic measurement and reproducible data, creating challenges for regulatory frameworks that rely on stable, verifiable information.

---

[4] Baiardi et al. (2023), Chakraborty et al. (2023), Flöther (2025), Ghamsari and Baniasadi (2024), Liu et al. (2022), Pal et al. (2024a, b), Shimada et al. (2025), Yukawa et al. (2025), Azevedo et al. (2022), Abbott (2021), Batra et al. (2021), Blunt et al. (2022), Casares et al. (2022), Emani et al. (2021), Heidari et al. (2024), Kiani et al. (2020), Kirsopp et al. (2022), Krunic et al. (2022), Landman et al. (2022), Li et al. (2021a, b), Maheshwari et al. (2023), Malone et al. (2022), Marchetti et al. (2022), Mensa et al. (2023), Moradi et al. (2022), Outeiral et al. (2021), Sagingalieva et al. (2023), Sarkar et al. (2021), Zinner et al. (2022a, b).

[5] Preskill (2018), Preskill (2021).

[6] Perrier (2022).

[7] Compare with analysis of AI integration within governance regimes (see Aboy et al. 2024).

[8] Marchant (2020).

3.1.2.2 Integration Dilemmas

The second, an integration dilemma, concerns the harmonization of nascent QIT governance, which is still developing and often focused on areas like cybersecurity and dual-use controls, with the mature regulatory structures of the life sciences, such as those governing pharmaceuticals and medical devices. These dilemmas highlight the tension between fostering QIT-driven innovation and maintaining the rigorous oversight required to ensure safety and efficacy in life sciences applications, necessitating careful consideration of how governance can adapt to accommodate QIT's unique characteristics while leveraging existing frameworks. Broadly, the integration dilemma stems from aligning the different governance characteristics of life sciences (sometimes referred to as harmonization challenges[9]) and QIT,[10] which are based on fundamentally different ontologies.

3.1.3 Governance Responses

These dilemmas in turn shape two primary governance responses which QIT life sciences regulation must address: (1) How life sciences governance of QIT may need to adapt to accommodate the unique (*sui generis*[11]) effects of non-classical quantum ontology; and (2) How to consistently integrate existing QIT governance (regarding dual use, export controls and so on) within life sciences governance. Addressing these dilemmas—including assessing the fit of existing governance regimes and identifying required changes to handle unique QIT impacts—is central to this chapter, which aims to inform QIT-based advancements in the life sciences.[12]

3.1.4 Contributions

To this end, we make four principal contributions to the literature on QIT within the life sciences.

3.1.4.1 Effects of QIT Ontology

We specify how QIT's non-classical ontological foundations—superposition, entanglement, and no-cloning—differ from classical information processing and identify

---

[9] Marchant et al. (2009), Marchant and Abbott (2012).

[10] Marchant and Wallach (2015).

[11] Moses (2011).

[12] Marchant et al. (2011).

a number of life sciences use cases that could be impacted by these quantum-specific features.

3.1.4.2 Quantum Technology in the Life Sciences State of the Art Review

We review the state of the art in quantum technology applications within the life sciences, summarizing prospective uses of quantum computing for complex simulations such as protein folding and genomic analysis, quantum sensing for high-resolution imaging and biomarker detection, and quantum communication for secure data transmission in healthcare and genomics, drawing on recent literature to highlight emerging trends, technical limitations, and innovation opportunities.

3.1.4.3 Regulatory Gaps

We examine potential regulatory gaps resulting from QIT's nascency versus the life sciences' mature governance frameworks (primarily in the United States). We highlight where QIT use may give rise to novel regulatory dilemmas arising from regulatory assumptions that information is processed classically.

3.1.4.4 QIT Life Sciences Case Study

We present a hypothetical case study involving the use of QC in the context of pharmaceutical innovation to illustrate how quantum ontological considerations may require adapting classical governance approaches.

3.1.5 Structure

This chapter is structured as follows. Section 3.2 presents an overview of the life sciences technology stack and sectors into which QIT are likely to be integrated. Section 3.3 summarizes QIT applications in the life sciences, focusing on QC, QS and QCM. Section 3.4 sets out key analysis of how QIT differs from classical technology, adopting the paradigm of information to identify QIT's sui generis effects. Section 3.5 explores the governance dilemmas arising from the technical differences between quantum and classical information systems in the life sciences. Sections 3.6 to 3.7 explore governance dilemmas from integration with existing regulation. Section 3.8 ties the analysis together using a hypothetical case study examining the governance implications of using quantum simulation for pharmaceutical drug innovation. Sections 3.8 onwards conclude with discussion of future directions in QIT life sciences governance research.

3.1.6 Related Work

Current approaches within the literature considering the intersection of QIT and the law tend to focus upon the effects of QIT, such as potential decryption,[13] or how QIT may allow more powerful computation.[14] However, much governance analysis of QIT (including in the life sciences[15]) tends not to focus specifically on the impact of the fundamental ontological differences between classical and quantum systems. And rarely is discussion of QIT firmly situated in the context of information processing.[16] While the consequences of these differences may be minimal from a regulatory perspective, comprehensive analysis remains limited. Although the FDA has begun to issue guidance on emerging technologies such as AI in health and medicine,[17] these frameworks do not yet address the unique, quantum-specific issues that underpin the governance dilemmas explored here. Consequently, existing FDA guidelines provide a starting point for broader oversight of advanced computational tools but leave the intricacies of quantum systems largely uncharted.

This chapter aims to address this gap with respect to QIT governance in a life sciences context. It advances current debate further by articulating how these integral features of quantum ontology have practical consequences for how the intersection of QIT and the life sciences is regulated. Together with other work in this volume, it aims to contribute to research into QIT governance by squarely identifying what is *sui generis* about the use of QIT in the life sciences.

To do so, we adopt a *governance stack* model[18] for analyzing QIT life sciences regulation. The core idea behind this approach is twofold: (1) that QIT apply at specific locations in the life sciences technical stack, such as being a resource for computational simulation or data processing, where QIT effects allow for novel or differentiated outcomes compared with classical computations; and (2) that governance instruments can be framed as intervening at some level in this technical stack by imposing obligations or rights on stakeholders with respect to elements in the stack, be it as proscriptions or prescriptions on how, for example, computation unfolds (proscriptions on simulating), or how activities, such as clinical trials, are undertaken, how products are disseminated or on the use of outputs of technologies.

---

[13] Watrous (2018).

[14] Marchant et al. (2024), Kop (2021a, b), Kop et al. (2023), Kop et al. (2024a), Coenen et al. (2022), Coenen and Grunwald (2017), de Wolf (2017), DiVincenzo (2017), Grinbaum (2017), Johnson (2018), Perrier (2022), Vermaas (2017).

[15] Kop et al. (2024b, c).

[16] Watrous (2018).

[17] U.S. Food and Drug Administration (2025f).

[18] Perrier (2022).

3.2 The Life Sciences Stack Model

To understand any governance implications of QIT for the life sciences, it helps to first identify the key areas within the life sciences technical stack into which QIT technology would be integrated. To do this, we focus our analysis upon the hierarchical systems upon which life sciences are built. Specifically, we use a *life sciences (technology) stack* as a means of identifying at what level in the life sciences natural hierarchy life science technology and practices, including research, operate.

3.2.1 What Are the Life Sciences?

Life sciences are anchored in biological sciences dealing with living organisms and life processes.[19] The scope of phenomena covered by the life sciences is extensive. It includes homeostasis, order and structure, metabolic processes and growth, adaptation, response to stimuli, reproduction, mortality and population dynamics such as heredity, evolutionary development and even autonomy.[20] Life sciences subject matter includes not just items classified as living, but also includes their inorganic components, such as biochemical molecules, including DNA. The breadth and scope of life makes life sciences an expansive and multi-faceted set of disciplines within which QIT may be utilized.

For the purposes of understanding the key likely applications of QIT in life sciences sectors and, moreover, any governance implications arising from such applications, it is useful to frame life sciences subject matter in terms of a hierarchical stack from the atomic scale through the level of organisms, to animals, humans and society more broadly. Life sciences technologies can then be seen as utilizing elements in the stack or acting upon elements in the stack – and, for our purposes, encoding or utilizing information that level in the stack. It also assists in understanding at what level in the stack life sciences activity is taking place, such as design, control and effect. We set out one example of the stack below.

3.2.1.1 Atomic

The smallest units of matter, including atoms (C, H, O, N, P, S) and their subatomic particles (protons, neutrons, electrons).

[19] Carroll (2009), Koshland (2002), Luisi (1998), Macklem and Seely (2010), Tirard et al. (2010).

[20] Koshland (2002), Macklem and Seely (2010), Tirard et al. (2010), Luisi (1998), Carroll (2009), Ruiz-Mirazo et al. (2004).

3.2.1.2 Molecular

Comprises basic molecules (e.g., water, CO_2) and large macromolecules like proteins, DNA/RNA, lipids, and carbohydrates.

3.2.1.3 Cellular

Involves organelles (nucleus, mitochondria, etc.) and cells themselves (prokaryotes vs. eukaryotes) as the fundamental units of life.

3.2.1.4 Tissue

Consists of groups of similar cells (epithelial, connective, muscle, nervous) working together for a specific function.

3.2.1.5 Organ

Formed by multiple tissue types (e.g., heart, lungs) that perform specialized tasks within an organism.

3.2.1.6 Organ System

Coordinated networks of organs (circulatory, respiratory, digestive) that collectively carry out complex bodily processes.

3.2.1.7 Organism

An independent living entity, which may be single-celled (bacteria, yeast) or multicellular (plants, animals, fungi).

3.2.1.8 Population

A group of organisms of the same species in a particular area that can interbreed and produce fertile offspring.

3.2.2 Inputs, Processes and Outputs

To assess how QIT is or can be used in the life sciences (and any governance consequences) at each level in the stack, it is useful to borrow a computational analogy of input/output processes. Life sciences subject matter may serve as inputs into a process, such as regulations covering the use of biological substances like genetic material or organisms in a laboratory. Alternatively, the process itself may be the subject of life sciences regulation, as in the use of biological processes to synthesize chemicals or medicines, which are subject to assurance requirements. Outputs of a process may fall under life sciences classification, for example, the manufacture of biological organisms or derived biologics. Finally, a technology or process may have a direct impact on life sciences subject matter without involving it as an input, process, or output. A similar framing can also be used for QIT. Quantum information may be an input into a process; or QIT may simply take classical inputs and evolve them using quantum processing; or the outputs of QIT may be quantum data; or the impact of an exogenous factor may be upon QIT itself.

We also leverage a distinction between embedded and non-embedded. Specific QIT applications may be embedded within life sciences subject matter (e.g. quantum dot sensors[21] within living organisms or substrates) or non-embedded (such as a quantum computer). Those technologies that directly interact with life sciences subject matter, such as medicines acting upon human or biological subjects, or which utilize biological subject matter, tend to attract a higher degree of regulation than non-embedded and non-interacting devices such as information processing devices. We only cover a small division of how life sciences and quantum information may be used as inputs, processes or outputs. This framing is useful for several reasons summarized below.

3.2.2.1 Quantum Effects Manifest at Smallest Scales

Quantum information processing occurs only at very small scales (at the atomic or molecular scale). While QIT require sophisticated engineering at multiple scales, quantum circuits that actually perform quantum information processing are engineered via the manipulation of sub-atomic (e.g. electron) or molecular-level features.

3.2.2.2 The Effects of QIT Are Informational

The primary effects of QIT are informational. The way in which QIT affects life sciences is thus mediated (for the most part) through its effects on information which

[21] Ali et al. (2023), Belal et al. (2024), Bukowski and Simmons (2002), Clift and Stone (2012), Tiwari et al. (2021).

is converted to classical form (e.g. measurement statistics) and then forms the basis of interventions in the life sciences stack.

3.2.2.3 Most QIT is Non-embedded

QIT in the life sciences is primarily concerned with non-embedded information processing. The exception to this is quantum sensor technology which may be in certain cases embedded within life-sciences subject matter (e.g. organisms) or used in production processes.

3.2.2.4 Quantum Information is Not Directly Accessible

While quantum systems are ontologically distinct from classical, the input and output of information is classical in form. Surrounding all QIT is necessarily classical architecture that allows conversion of information from quantum to classical.

3.2.2.5 QIT is Embedded Within Classical Information Processing Technology

Quantum processes involved in QIT may only be a subset of the information processing that is occurring. Thus a quantum algorithm used for life sciences simulation will comprise classical and non-classical gates, for example. Discerning the specifically *quantum* effect (e.g. quantum advantage obtainable) may be difficult.

The consequences are that—embedded quantum sensors aside—the primary use cases for QIT are as non-embedded measurement, communication and computational devices whose outputs then can influence other apparatuses or decisions which in turn affect life sciences subject matter (QC does not act directly on an organism or biological substrate for example).

3.2.3 Technical Stacks and Governance

A familiarity with the life sciences stack helps identify exactly what it is that is being governed and the site where governance, such as the law, seeks to impose constraints or obligations upon use. For example, sometimes governance is expressed in terms of obligations upon specific legally-recognized entities.

Alternatively, governance may be directed to how an object or thing is used regardless of who is doing so. For example, QC simulations of chemical reactivity or interactivity typically address the atomic and molecular levels of the stack; a quantum dot sensor might target the cellular, organ, or tissue level; or a QCM device for encrypting and transmitting health data could be framed as operating at the organism level or below.

The level of the life sciences stack within which QIT operates in turn affects how that use of QIT is governed. To this end, the law can be framed as imposing obligations upon stakeholders with respect to subject matter at one or more specific levels in the life sciences technical stack. This may include obligations or standards relating to how information regarding atomic interactions is obtained or simulated; the types of chemicals or compositions which may be permissible; the types of organisms which may be cultivated or the appropriate methods for diagnosing a disease; or overall population health, such as relating to epidemiology.

Such a taxonomic hierarchy is important in enabling a mapping of QIT applications to life sciences. It promotes a level of analytical precision that is crucial when seeking to distinguish exactly how the use of QIT may affect, if at all, governance regimes. In the next section, we set out an overview of prospective use cases of QIT in the life sciences.

3.2.4 Life Sciences Sectors Relevant to QIT and Illustrative Potential Applications

The intricacy of life sciences is reflected in it being subject to among the most complex regulatory ecosystems of all the sciences. This complexity makes analyzing the full gamut of regulatory changes that may be necessary or desirable from the use of QIT challenging. A useful starting point to approach this complexity is via the division of life sciences into different sectors. Such divisions are multidisciplinary. They are united broadly by the scientific study of and development of applications using or applicable to biological systems. We set out the sectorial division in Table 3.1 together with a few motivating examples of QIT relevant to each sector (which we examine in more detail in the next section).

The framing above is useful to partition the different applications of QIT and governance regimes into workable segmentations. The divisions above represent the major life sciences sectors where QIT is likely to have a practical impact. In this chapter, we primarily focus upon the pharmaceutical sector and potential specific applications of QIT that are likely or expected to materialize (e.g. with respect to drug discovery and information processing).

Table 3.1 Life sciences sectors and potential applications of QIT

Sector	Description	QIT Potential Applications
Pharmaceuticals and biotechnology	Development of medical products such as drugs, vaccines and biologics utilizing a range of techniques such as genetic engineering and chemical synthesis	• Quantum simulation for drug discovery • QS for targeting drug delivery • QCM for collaboration
Medical devices	Design and manufacture of devices for use in life sciences contexts, such as instrumentation, automated machine technology, implants and prostheses and diagnostic tools	• Quantum simulation for medical device materials and scenario modelling • QS for diagnostics
Healthcare and clinical research	Public and private research institutions, hospitals, foundations, clinics and pharmaceutical companies, focused on the advancement of health and medical science, healthcare delivery and clinical trial procedures	• QC for large-scale patient data analysis (e.g., personalized medicine, population health) • QS for ultra-precise diagnostic imaging (e.g., improved MRI, PET) • QCM for secure telemedicine and cross-institutional data sharing
Genomics and bioinformatics	Information processing of genetic data for medicine discovery, personalized treatment and simulation of biological systems	• QC for rapid genome sequence alignment and variant detection • Quantum simulation of protein–DNA/RNA interactions for gene regulation insights • QCM for secure storage and sharing of sensitive genomic data
Regenerative medicine and tissue engineering	Developing synthetic or alternative biological substitutes, such as via stem cell research or bioprinting, for repairing or replacing damaged biological components such as tissue and organs	• Quantum simulation to model complex cell and tissue growth processes (e.g., scaffold design) • QS for high-resolution monitoring of tissue engineering and stem-cell differentiation • Quantum optimization algorithms for multi-parameter tuning (e.g., nutrient delivery, environmental conditions) in regenerative research and clinical applications

3.3 Quantum Technology Applications in the Life Sciences

Quantum applications in the life sciences—be it directly via simulations or indirectly via prospective quantum chemistry—have garnered significant attention due to the prospective innovations in drug discovery,[22] device manufacture and therapeutic treatment they may facilitate.[23] For this reason, applications of QIT for biomedical computational and data sciences represent a major research focus with respect to advanced information technologies.[24] As we set out below, research into QIT in the life sciences tends to focus upon its application in the health and pharmaceutical life sciences sectors.[25] Prospective applications of QIT include improved chemistry and physics simulations,[26] solving problems in computational biology and biochemical research,[27] design and synthesis and diagnostics.[28]

QIT has further application across biomedical research, biological and molecular synthesis and medical imaging. Quantum algorithms such as quantum Fourier transforms, quantum phase estimation and hybrid quantum–classical algorithms have application across medical imaging.[29] QIT has application in biological sequence data analysis, including gene identification, mutation detection, and phylogenetic analysis, improving the scale and speed of multiomics data analysis.[30] These are just a few examples of the potentially expansive remit of QIT in the life sciences.

3.3.1 QIT Life Sciences Taxonomies

How to taxonomise QIT in the life sciences is contextual and taxonomies vary: (1) *QIT-wise*: based on the class of QIT utilized; (2) *Sector-wise*: focuses on the use of QIT by sectors listed above, particularly in pharmaceutical, bioinformatics and medical device contexts, (3) *Life sciences stack-wise*: based on where and how QIT impacts the existing life sciences stack; and (4) *Governance-wise*: where QIT use is organized according to governance taxonomies, such as QIT subject to FDA oversight, pharmaceutical regulations, or medical device regulations and so on. Our focus below adopts a QIT-wise approach in order to identify key *sui generis* effects. In Sect. 3.8 we concentrate sector-wise, examining realistic workflows as part of a hypothetical example of pharmaceutical innovation and drug discovery. To this end,

---

[22] Zinner et al. (2022a, b).

[23] Aslam et al. (2023).

[24] McWeeney et al. (2023), Emani et al. (2021).

[25] Flöther (2023), Liu et al. (2022), Flöther (2025), Baiardi et al. (2023), Sharples et al. (2021), McWeeney et al. (2023), Aslam et al. (2023).

[26] Daley et al. (2022).

[27] Emani et al. (2021).

[28] Flöther et al. (2022).

[29] Landman et al. (2022).

[30] Chakraborty et al. (2023).

we set out a brief summary of leading prospective use cases of QC, QS and QCM below.

3.3.2 Quantum Computing

Quantum computing utilizes quantum mechanical properties such as superposition and entanglement[31] in ways that may potentially render tractable computationally intensive tasks in the life sciences. Examples of prospective applications include protein-folding simulations,[32] virtual drug screening,[33] and clinical data classification.[34] QC also shows promise for accelerating genomic sequence alignment,[35] improving drug candidate prioritization,[36] and enabling finer-grained disease-risk modelling. In Table 3.2, we set out a few specific prospective QC applications in the life sciences identified in the literature.

3.3.3 Quantum Sensing

Quantum sensing in the life sciences involves information acquisition from living and non-living matter.[37] Quantum sensors facilitate hyper-sensitive measurement and detection at higher resolutions and smaller scales than many classical measurement devices.[38] Moreover, QS can in certain cases allow non-invasive measurement of fine-grained structures in ways that is difficult with classical technologies, including improving magnetoencephalography, MRI and PET scanning and microscopic imaging.[39] Their ability to measure and thus construct more detailed schema of life sciences structures and processes also means they have potential application with nanotechnology in improved targeting of treatments in therapeutic contexts.[40] Quantum sensors—such as quantum dot-based sensing technologies[41]—are the most advanced type of QIT, already being utilized in experimental research within the life sciences. A few potential uses cases are set out below in Table 3.3.

---

[31] Nielsen and Chuang (2011).

[32] Casares et al. (2022).

[33] Batra et al. (2021).

[34] Maheshwari et al. (2023).

[35] Sarkar et al. (2021).

[36] Blunt et al. (2022).

[37] Ghamsari and Baniasadi (2024).

[38] Aslam et al. (2023).

[39] Yukawa et al. (2025).

[40] Shimada et al. (2025).

[41] Ali et al. (2023).

Table 3.2 Prospective applications of quantum computing in the life sciences

Sector	Detail
Genomics and clinical research	• *Gene Sequence Alignment/Assembly*: Quantum algorithms may speed up DNA sequencing and analysis, which can be computationally difficult using classical methods[42] • *Protein Structure/Interactions*: Quantum-enhanced algorithms may improve prediction of protein folding, structure identification, and interactions, especially in the case of complex or synthesized compounds.[43] Simulation of protein–ligand interactions, crucial for drug development, is also a prospect[44] • *Drug Discovery and Screening*: QC simulation of molecular dynamics may speed up virtual screening of drug candidates via improved assessment of efficacy and toxicity[45]
Diagnostics	• *Medical Imaging Analysis*: Quantum machine learning offers in principle improvements in medical imaging (e.g. mammograms and X-rays) in terms of accuracy and efficiency[46] • *Disease Risk Prediction*: Quantum techniques can facilitate improved analysis of data to predict and classify disease characteristics, including Alzheimer's, cardiovascular disease and cancer survival rates[47]
Treatments and interventions	• *Therapy Persistence and Clinical Outcomes*: Quantum algorithms have been successfully benchmarked against classical methods for predicting treatment persistence[48] • *Public Health Applications*: Quantum algorithms have been explored for outbreak prediction applications, such as COVID-19, based on disease data analysis[49] • *Precision Oncology*: QC offers prospects for use in adaptive radiotherapy to enable more personalized treatment for cancer[50]

42 Prousalis and Konofaos (2019), Sarkar et al. (2021).

43 Robert et al. (2021).

44 Malone et al. (2022), Kirsopp et al. (2022).

45 Li et al. (2024), Kiss et al. (2022), Mensa et al. (2023), Albrecht et al. (2023).

46 Landman et al. (2022), Azevedo et al. (2022).

47 Kathuria et al. (2020), Moradi et al. (2022), Kavitha and Kaulgud (2022).

48 Krunic et al. (2022), Heidari et al. (2024).

49 Kairon and Bhattacharyya (2021).

50 Niraula et al. (2021).

Table 3.3 Prospective applications of quantum sensing in the life sciences

Sector	Detail
Biomedical imaging and diagnostics	Quantum sensors offer enhanced capabilities for visualizing biological structures and detecting disease markers with improved sensitivity and resolution: • Magnetoencephalography (MEG) and Magnetocardiography (MCG) for non-invasive brain imaging and heart diagnostics[51] • *MRI and PET*: Quantum correlations may be harnessed to improve signal-to-noise ratios in MRI and PET[52] • Microscopic imaging and biomarker detection: detection of biomarkers for improved targeting
Cellular analysis	Quantum sensors enable precise measurements of physical and chemical parameters within biological microenvironments, offering insights into fundamental life processes at the cellular and molecular level: • *Intracellular Thermometry*: NV centers in nanodiamonds can act as nanoscale thermometers for local probing of temperature-dependent biological processes[53] • *Parameter sensing*: detection of magnetic and electric fields, temperature, pressure, and molecular diffusion with high sensitivity, allowing measurements in organelles like mitochondria • *Single molecule spectroscopy and cellular activity monitoring*: positioning NV centers nanometers away from target spins, techniques like single-protein NMR and single-molecule ESR become possible and measurements of action potentials of single neurons[54]
Treatments and interventions	QS contributes to therapeutic interventions and enhances drug delivery and monitoring: • *Targeted Drug Delivery*: Quantum dots are being investigated to enhance the targeting and delivery of drugs to tumors • *Theranostics*: Quantum sensors may be employed for theranostic applications, combining diagnostics and therapy, allowing for the identification and targeting of disease[55] • *Thermotherapies*: Nanodiamonds containing NV centers can be used for in vivo temperature calibration during thermotherapeutic treatments[56]

3.3.4 Quantum Communication

Quantum communication uses protocols like quantum key distribution (QKD) and using protocols such as QKD and entanglement-assisted protocols to support quantum-secured communication and to offer heightened protection to sensitive data.

---

[51] Aslam et al. (2023).

[52] Yukawa et al. (2025).

[53] Correa et al. (2015).

[54] Ghamsari and Baniasadi (2024).

[55] Wang et al. (2018).

[56] Soumya et al. (2023).

Table 3.4 Prospective applications of quantum communication in the life sciences

Category	Detail
Healthcare and clinical research	• Utilize quantum key distribution (QKD) for secure telemedicine, ensuring patient consultations and imaging files remain confidential • Reduce risks of unauthorized interception of sensitive patient data using quantum-secured communication protocols.
Pharmaceuticals and biotechnology	• Employ secure quantum data storage to protect proprietary compound libraries, drug formulations, and clinical trial findings from hacking • Enable encrypted collaboration among R&D teams using QKD-protected communication channels for exchanging sensitive research data
Genomics and bioinformatics	• Implement post-quantum encryption to safeguard large genomic datasets and multi-decade longitudinal studies from future quantum decryption • Ensure secure sharing of patient genomic information across research institutions while complying with data privacy regulations

Prospective examples include its use in telehealth communications security, securing clinical trial records or large-scale genomic archives. QCM potentially offers robust safeguards against classical eavesdropping and future quantum decryption attacks,[57] allowing biotech and healthcare institutions to share high-sensitivity information with stronger guarantees of confidentiality and data integrity. A few prospective uses of QCM applications in the life sciences are set out in Table 3.4.

Taken together, QC, QS and QCM applications illustrate how QIT may augment innovation, analytics, and collaboration in the life sciences. Yet these properties stem from fundamentally non-classical nature of quantum systems —entanglement, measurement-induced collapse, no-cloning— which, as we discuss below, in part are distinct from long-standing assumptions embedded in governance regimes regarding reproducibility, data verification, and security. In the following section, we examine how such intrinsic quantum effects render QIT qualitatively distinct from classical information systems upon which modern life science is founded.

[57] Alagic et al. (2022), Bernstein and Lange (2017).

3.4 Why QIT is Different: The Role of Information

3.4.1 Information as a Core Analytical Lens

QIT are fundamentally information technologies. The response to the question regarding how to shed light on the *sui generis* effects of QIT naturally lands, therefore, upon the concept of information. Below, we draw upon the concept of information as a means of organizing and ordering life sciences and QIT activities, their synthesis and governance. The use of information as an organizing principle according to which technical and regulatory analysis may be conducted is well-motivated for the following reasons.

3.4.1.1 Information is Central to Modern Life Sciences

Information is a foundational element of the life sciences[58] and QIT's impact is primarily upon information.

3.4.1.2 Information is Central to Life Sciences Governance

Much governance of life sciences concerns ensuring scientific procedures for data acquisition, privacy, patentability, diagnosis, drug design and development and medical product devices are trustworthy, accurate and reliable—all characteristics which ultimately can be framed in informational terms.

3.4.1.3 Information is Central to Innovation

Innovation in the life sciences is driven foundationally by information—the pipeline from ideation, preliminary research, through to clinical trials and rigorous verification is contingent upon information as its lifeblood.[59]

3.4.1.4 QIT Are Fundamentally Information Technologies

QIT is fundamentally about information processing.[60]

---

[58] Gatenby and Frieden (2007).
[59] Akcigit and Liu (2016).
[60] Watrous (2018).

3.4.1.5 Information Allows Us to Benchmark Classical Versus Quantum Effects

QIT can be compared against classical information processing upon which the life sciences are built (e.g. comparing quantum and classical simulation efficacy).

3.4.1.6 Informational Differences Inform Where Regulatory Responses Are Required

Information theory is also a useful way of understanding regulatory theory.[61] Examples include understanding governance dynamics in terms of information asymmetries within economics.[62]

For this reason, information is chosen as our core analytical lens in this work as a means of connecting the diverse frameworks applying to the life sciences.[63] We explore a number of these differences below in more detail given their pivotal role in the differences between life sciences and QIT.

3.4.2 *Information in the Life Sciences*

Information theory is typically framed in a stateful manner. Information states represent an encoding of data about the system (e.g. in a register). The process of encoding into states occurs via the information system physically interacting with the environment, such as a measurement apparatus or device. Doing so allows a representation of the phenomena to be constructed via the measurement process.

3.4.2.1 Life Sciences Depend upon Accurate measurement

The reliability of measurement and measurement apparatuses, data encoding and information processing protocols is crucial to the trustworthiness of life sciences.

---

[61] Hildebrandt (2016), Hildebrandt (2018).

[62] Cai et al. (2015).

[63] By information theoretic we mean in a paradigmatic governance and jurisprudential sense. Nevertheless, more technically focused analysis could very well examine how formal information theory concepts (where systems are described in terms of registers, channels and measured in various ways) in principle could also be applied for finer-grained analysis of how life sciences information differs from and is similar to that in quantum formalism (see Watrous (2018) for detail).

3.4.2.2 Life Sciences Require Verification

Highly rigorous requirements for pre-trial research, clinical trials and post-approval monitoring of technologies or products, such as pharmaceuticals or medical devices, rely upon verification of information.

3.4.2.3 Life Sciences Assume Data Behave Classically

Data privacy, data security, reproducibility requirements are based on classical information assumptions as distinct from quantum ones. We explore these informational characteristics in more detail below.

3.4.3 Life Sciences Are Built upon Classical Information Assumptions

The first primary difference in how life sciences and quantum science treats information is ontological.

3.4.3.1 Life Sciences Assume Classical Information Processing

Existing life sciences regulations typically assume that all relevant properties (e.g., of a drug molecule, a medical device, or patient data) arise from classically behaving systems. By contrast, QIT is subject to quantum information processing.

3.4.3.2 Life Sciences Data Uncertainty is Distinct from Quantum Uncertainty

Uncertainty about such systems may be *epistemic*, the result of incomplete knowledge or measurement error, or *aleatory*, the result of the inherent stochasticity of the system itself.[64] Under standard interpretations of quantum mechanics, quantum uncertainty is often treated as fundamentally ontological:[65]certain observables (like an electron's spin) do not have definite values until measured, and measurement itself changes the system's state.[66] We explore this fundamental distinction in more detail below.

---

[64] Jiang et al. (2018).

[65] Luo (2005).

[66] Wiseman and Milburn (2010).

3.4.4 QIT Process Life Science Data Differently

QIT differ in fundamental ways from classical digital computing and data processing.[67] These differences are not merely of degree or scale (faster processors or more memory etc.). They are also difference of kind. They arise from the unique properties of quantum mechanics (superposition, entanglement, no-cloning, and measurement-induced collapse) which QIT are specifically designed to leverage. In the life sciences, safety, efficacy, and reproducibility of information is central to managing risk. However, both the nature of such information and how it is processed (including acquired, transformed and communicated) are fundamentally *classical*. This stands in contrast to the quantum case.

3.4.4.1 QS Acquires Information Differently

QS is about acquiring information that is more fine-grained, higher-resolution or simply infeasible to obtain using classical means.

3.4.4.2 QC Processes Information Differently

QC is about processing quantum information—that information stored in quantum states—in ways that satisfy the postulates of quantum mechanics. Information is processed in ways that are fundamentally distinct from classical computation, prospectively enabling faster computation and the solving of problems in complexity classes too difficult for classical computation. QIT has both a scalar effect but also a *sui generis* effect by enabling previously intractable computations to become tractable.

3.4.4.3 QCM Transmits Information Differently

QCM uses quantum correlations and quantum key distribution protocols to support secure communication alongside classical channels.

Examples which we examine in more detail below include simulations for pharmaceuticals e.g. quantum simulations of protein interactions[68] may yield probabilistic predictions rather than a single deterministic outcome. Quantum-based sensors (e.g., embedded quantum dots) might return results that are inherently stochastic with additional randomized measurement uncertainty not present in classical equivalents.

---

[67] Nielsen and Chuang (2011).

[68] Malone et al. (2022).

3.4.5 *Unique Quantum Properties Differ from Classical Counterparts*

The unique quantum mechanical properties identified above are precisely what underpin the novel power and capabilities of QIT and motivate their use in the first place. These properties are non-classical characteristics.[69] We set these out below (see other chapters in this series for in-depth discussion of each). We reiterate the key properties below the effects of which for governance we examine further on.

3.4.5.1 Superposition

Quantum states can exist in superposition of states rather than a definitive single state.

3.4.5.2 Entanglement and Non-locality

Quantum systems can be entangled, exhibiting non-local correlations among their measurement statistics.

3.4.5.3 Quantum Measurement

Observing a quantum state irreversibly influences it, unlike classical systems where the same data register can be read multiple times.

3.4.5.4 No-Cloning

Identical copies of an unknown quantum state cannot be made, complicating data duplication and auditing procedures.[70]

3.4.5.5 Stochasticity and Error

Under standard interpretations of quantum mechanics, outcomes in quantum systems are treated as intrinsically probabilistic, rather than just a matter of incomplete knowledge. Quantum systems are highly sensitive to physical and logical errors, requiring error correction to function.[71]

---

[69] Nielsen and Chuang (2011).

[70] Wootters and Zurek (1982).

[71] Gottesman (2010).

Together each of these effects or characteristics of quantum mechanics give rise to fundamental differences by comparison with classical physics. The consequences of these differences are significant from both a technical perspective (in terms of QIT capabilities) but also, as we focus on below, from a governance perspective.[72]

3.5 Governance Dilemmas: Technical Differences of QIT

The technical differences between classical and quantum ontology shape governance outcomes in a number of ways. To assess this, we now turn to examine the two classes of governance dilemma—technical and integrative—that arise from the use of QIT in life sciences contexts.

3.5.1 Life Sciences Regulation Assumes Classical Ontology

These distinctive features of QIT have implications for information processing and thus technological innovation in the life sciences. They also have implications for life sciences governance. Most life sciences regulatory frameworks are based upon classical assumptions about information. Legal systems have long managed uncertainty via probability and burden-of-proof doctrines, quantum systems embed phenomena whose unique ontology may, in specific situations, require adjustment to how the law reckons with irreducible uncertainty.[73] Additionally, ownership, copying, evidence, and even causation may require new or adapted interpretations when the underlying technology is governed by quantum mechanics rather than classical physics such as in the case of information stored using shared entangled resources. Finally, what counts as admissible in silico evidence[74] may require modification to accommodate quantum uncertainty.

These properties provide considerable opportunity for advanced medical computational innovations, being the basis for the power of QC, the fine-grained sensitivity of QS and protocols of QCM. But they also give rise to novel governance challenges.[75] Below we list out categorically how quantum ontology, such as the distinctive, non-classical nature of quantum systems, may in particular circumstances have important consequences for legal, regulatory, and ethical frameworks.[76]

[72] Coenen et al. (2022).

[73] Moses (2017).

[74] Terstappen and Reggiani (2001).

[75] Johnson (2018).

[76] Kop et al. (2024a).

3.5.2 Categories of QIT Impact on Life Sciences Governance

The impacts of QIT on life sciences governance can be classified as set out in Table 3.5.

We utilize these categories in our case study below to assess the impact of QIT and prospective governance responses as a result. We now briefly explore a few of these categorical governance consequences in more detail arising from the superposition, entanglement, quantum measurement, no cloning and stochasticity below.

3.5.3 Superposition States

Quantum superposition allows a qubit to occupy a coherent combination of multiple basis states simultaneously, rather than a single definite state as in classical systems. Superposition specifically challenges the assumption that experimental inputs and intermediate computational steps can be pinned to a single, well-defined state at any given time:

- In life sciences governance, this means regulatory protocols may need to accommodate the fact that quantum computations or quantum sensors operate on entangled states.
- Verifying how a superposed system evolves or produces outcomes will rely on statistical sampling from repeated experiments, since a single measurement collapses the superposition and certain underlying quantum coherences.

3.5.4 Non-locality and Entanglement

Quantum entanglement allows two or more qubits to share non-local correlations. Measuring one qubit can affect the correlated state description of the other. This may have consequences for legal and regulatory contexts where the physical location of data or materials is often crucial (e.g., for export controls, data residency requirements, or cross-border clinical trials):

- If qubits are entangled across different laboratories or even different countries, classical definitions of location or possession may become problematised.
- If quantum-encrypted medical data is partially entangled across international sites (such as via a quantum internet), questions may arise regarding jurisdiction over distributed quantum-secured data systems.

Table 3.5 Prospective impacts of QIT in the life sciences

Category	QIT issues
Data input and measurement	• Regulation usually assumes measurements or input data to be repeatedly observable and thus classically reproducible • Quantum measurements collapse quantum states. Obtaining data requires repeated experiments to derive measurement statistics, potentially complicating how regulators view stable input data or repeated measures
Verification and reproduction	• Regulators often rely on classically reproducible datasets, assuming identical conditions yield identical results, which can be copied, validated, or retested • QIT results are probabilistic. No-cloning rules mean the same quantum state cannot be simply replicated for direct re-testing • Validation requires multiple experiments, error-correction, and statistical convergence, potentially requiring new protocols for proving reproducibility
Privacy and security	• Classical information governance (e.g. under the Health Insurance Portability and Accountability Act of 1996 (HIPAA) and GDPR) assumes encryption over classical channels with typical key management and recognized attack vectors • Compliance uses established frameworks (e.g., TLS/SSL) for data in transit and at rest. These may be rendered vulnerable by QC's prospective decryption capabilities.[77] QKD and entanglement-based encryption offer ultra-secure channels but also novel complexities (no straightforward intercept or key escrow) • Post-quantum cryptography standards may vary and affect accessibility of data
Auditing and control	• Auditing protocols may presume data can be cloned identically multiple times to verify origin, integrity, and authenticity • Electronic data may be required to be continuously accessible for inspection which is difficult in the quantum case • Quantum data cannot be cloned; entangled state information might be co-owned across geographic borders • Auditors may need to rely on statistical footprints or repeated state preparations, and classical location-based verification models may fail if partial qubits reside in different jurisdictions • Control of quantum systems may be more difficult than classical counterparts
Ownership, IP and disclosure	• Quantum properties may give rise to questions of ownership e.g. in the case of entangled information • Patent and disclosure rules generally assume that a disclosed invention can be sufficiently reproduced or enabled by a skilled person; enablement demands that a skilled person can replicate the invention or data generation under normal lab conditions • No-cloning and specialized quantum hardware limit straightforward replication. Quantum simulations of molecular designs may require distinct quantum hardware with noise-correction • Patent offices might need adapted guidance related to the written description, enablement and best mode requirements for QIT inventions

[77] Alagic et al. (2024).

3.5.5 *Quantum Measurement is Different*

Quantum measurement[78] is fundamentally different from classical measurement. In quantum mechanics, measurement irreversibly collapses a superposed state into one observed outcome. Unlike classical data, which can be inspected repeatedly, a single quantum state cannot be measured twice in the same way without altering it. This is a fundamental ontological feature of quantum systems. This stands in stark contrast to classical data, which in principle can be reproduced by repeatedly querying (interacting with) the system without affecting the informational state of the data register. Some of the consequences of these differences may impact pharma and medical devices.

For a pharmaceutical company using a quantum computer to generate data supporting an Investigational New Drug (IND) (see Sect. 3.8.5), verification regulations (which assume classical reproducibility of data) may need adjustment. The governance outcome may require *identical measurement statistics* within certain error thresholds of a simulation.

Similarly, medical device regulations and standards which require re-testing or revalidation of device performance may be complicated where the device leverages quantum information obtained via quantum measurement, such as via embedded quantum dots, or measurement statistics of quantum computational algorithms.

3.5.6 *No Cloning*

The quantum no-cloning theorem[79] forbids creating an identical copy of an arbitrary unknown quantum state. This means that in effect we must measure not just one quantum system multiple times, but rather multiple quantum systems—or the same quantum system that is re-prepared into an identical initial state—many times over. Quantum states cannot simply be copied or reproduced as classical states can be. For life sciences regulation, this is distinct from classical assumptions about data sharing and reproducibility, where copying or distributing data for independent verification is standard. Because of the no-cloning prohibition, regulators cannot simply request a duplicate quantum state for parallel testing purposes. Instead, they must rely on statistical consistency across multiple re-prepared states, in contrast to the typical classical replication model central to current verification and auditing frameworks.

---

78 Wiseman and Milburn (2010), Nielsen and Chuang (2011).

79 Wootters and Zurek (1982).

3.5.7 *Stochasticity and Error*

Quantum systems are inherently stochastic. Moreover, the quantum mechanical properties of such systems render them subject to noise and decoherence in ways that are distinct from classical information technologies used in the life sciences.[80] This susceptibility necessitates robust error-correction schemes—such as logical qubits and stabilizer codes—that could complicate standard validation procedures.

Stochastic processes not only introduce probabilistic output (making direct replication less straightforward) but also demand specialized protocols for demonstrating that fault-tolerant states were adequately maintained throughout an experiment or simulation, or where quantum state or process tomography is relied upon.

Thus, life sciences governance may need to factor in error correction protocols and thresholds (or set specific fidelity thresholds) e.g. where validation through repeated runs is required to achieve confidence in results, and classical notions of re-testing or duplicating data for independent analysis must be replaced by new frameworks that account for quantum-specific uncertainty, random sampling, and multi-run statistical convergence.

3.6 Governance Dilemmas: Integration into Existing Governance Regimes

3.6.1 *Life Sciences Governance is Mature, Quantum Governance is Nascent*

As noted above, realizing these potential benefits while managing material risks arising from the integration of QIT within life sciences requires a detailed and close study of governance. Life sciences governance is mature and highly sophisticated. Quantum governance is nascent. Innovation occurs within well-established and proven governance regimes with fine-grained and highly specific requirements that enable higher risk activities to be undertaken.[81]

Life sciences is also highly complex, prescriptive and routinised with implicit and explicit approaches to risk encoded within its structure. It also involves some of the most highly regulated areas of scientific, technological and economic activity, from the extensive requirements surrounding prototyping, testing and commercialization of medical devices and medicines, to the complex regulatory networks governing healthcare and clinical trials. How to solve the pacing problem of innovation,[82]in order to ensure QIT innovation can advance rapidly while maintaining appropriate guardrails required by the life sciences, remains an open challenge.

---

80 Joos et al. (2013).

81 Marchant et al. (2009).

82 Moses (2011), Marchant et al. (2011).

3.6.2 Innovation Dilemmas

How to square the circle so to speak such that experimental and untested technologies—and the higher degree of risk this entails—may be applied usefully to the life sciences with its fine-grained management of risk is important to both fields. From an innovation perspective, the different stages of maturity and speeds at which innovation in QIT and life sciences move presents a dilemma to innovation. QIT remains highly experimental. Innovation in QIT requires such early-stage sector flexibility, including the flexibility to fail. And its governance is by contrast undeveloped, with the primary emerging areas of governance being those focused upon cybersecurity,[83] intellectual property[84] and dual-use considerations.[85]

A hypothetical example of this dilemma may arise if a quantum-computing startup seeks to use NISQ-era machines to model novel gene therapies. In principle, rapid prototyping could reveal optimized vectors or delivery mechanisms for CRISPR-based edits within weeks. However, existing FDA and NIH rules may mean each simulation-derived compound or procedure might trigger a new round of IND submissions or complex institutional review board requirements. This level of oversight, while necessary to protect human subjects, can slow the pace of quantum-driven innovation if regulators are unclear as to how to handle QIT data. As a result, some QIT applications could remain locked in protracted preclinical or exploratory stages, delaying both commercial viability and broader scientific validation of frontier techniques. Addressing these innovation dilemmas will be important in the context of implementing the purpose of innovation initiatives such as the National Quantum Initiative Act.[86]

3.6.3 Dual Use and Export Control Regimes

In the United States, both life sciences and QIT are governed by dual-use frameworks designed to mitigate malicious exploitation while fostering beneficial research and commercial innovation. However, these dual use and export controls differ fundamentally due to contrasting national security imperatives inherent to each field.

Life sciences regulations focus to a considerable extent on preventing biological agents from being weaponized.[87] This emphasis involves extensive monitoring of pathogens, toxins, and genetically engineered organisms, grounded in tangible threats to public health and biosecurity.

[83] Quantum Computing Cybersecurity Preparedness Act of 2022.

[84] Alter (2025).

[85] Export Control Reform Act (ECRA) of 2018.

[86] Raymer and Monroe (2019), National Quantum Initiative Act of 2018.

[87] For example the Public Health Security and Bioterrorism Preparedness and Response Act of 2002 and the Select Agent Program (42 CFR Part 73, 7 CFR Part 331, and 9 CFR Part 121).

By contrast, QIT is subject to specific *Export Administration Regulations* (EAR)[88] coverage primarily due to its implications for cybersecurity and national defense. For example, QC and encryption technologies can potentially decrypt sensitive communications and bypass traditional cybersecurity defenses, posing acute risks to critical national security infrastructure. As a result, quantum regulation may target the specific dimensions of QIT, such as algorithmic intellectual property, software-defined quantum systems, and entanglement-based communications.

Differing imperatives for dual use of related technologies are not uncommon.[89] These distinct priorities reflect an essential divergence: life sciences governance emphasizes physical containment and biosafety controls for concrete biological threats, whereas dual use regimes for QIT encompass regulation of intangible, software-driven quantum capabilities along with hardware.[90] Consequently, enforcing dual-use controls on QIT may involve addressing challenges such as abstract algorithm management, secure cloud-based quantum computing access, and complex international research collaborations,[91] necessitating specialized oversight mechanisms distinct from those used in the life sciences.[92]

3.7 Lessons from AI Regulation

3.7.1 AI and Life Sciences Regulation

Over the last decade, regulators including the FDA have been gradually developing policy positions regarding the governance of AI in the life sciences.[93] The FDA addresses artificial intelligence and machine-learning functionality within its *software as a medical device* (SaMD) guidance.[94] The FDA has referenced definitions of artificial intelligence consistent with 15 USC 9401(3) being a machine-based system that can, for a given set of human-defined objectives, make predictions, recommendations, or decisions influencing real or virtual environments. AI includes such systems which use machine- and human-based inputs to perceive real and virtual environments, and which can abstract such perceptions into models through analysis in an automated manner; and use model inference to formulate options for information or action (covering, for example, reasoning models). Machine-learning refers to the statistical techniques by which those engines improve as new data accumulate.

---

[88] Export Administration Regulations 15 CFR chapter VII, subchapter C.

[89] Anstis et al. (2023).

[90] Anstis et al. (2023).

[91] Marchant and Wallach (2015).

[92] Marchant et al. (2024).

[93] Joshi et al. (2024).

[94] U.S. Food and Drug Administration (2025a).

The FDA's approach to AI regulation[95] has primarily been via an iterative soft-governance approach that seeks to utilize guidance regarding how AI technologies would fit within existing regulatory pathways. Early guidance included the *Predetermined Change Control Plan* (PCCP)[96] process in 2019 which set out guidance for terms upon which manufacturers ought to pre-specify the scope and verification methods for future algorithm updates. Following this, the 2021 AI/ML SaMD Action Plan[97] outlined the FDA's roadmap on AI and medical devices, while setting out discussion regarding methodological recommendations and real-world monitoring. In particular, the guidance takes a risk-based approach. It concentrates upon categories of software modification that may require premarket submission including changes that (a) introduce new risks or modify existing risks that could result in significant harm; (b) affect risk controls mitigating harm; and (c) significantly affect clinical functionality or performance specifications of devices.

3.7.1.1 Technical Guidance

Since then, the FDA has updated its guidance in more detail: (1) *Good Machine Learning Practice* (GMLP) Guiding Principles[98] sets out ten guiding principles covering data quality, algorithm transparency and human-AI interaction; (2) a Transparency for ML-Enabled Devices Principles[99] document urges plain-language labelling and post-market disclosure of algorithm drift; and (3) PCCP Guidance setting out recommendations relating to submission of PCCPs for AI-enabled devices.[100]

3.7.1.2 Marketing Guidance

The FDA guidance on life-cycle and marketing-submission expectations for AI-enabled device software functions has thus sought to harmonise existing approaches and provide more specific advice on data provenance, update frequency and performance monitoring.

3.7.1.3 Incremental Approach

The FDA has thus adopted an incremental approach which is in keeping with much AI governance in the US at the federal level. Such an approach makes sense as it

95 Stephens (2025), Warraich et al. (2025).

96 U.S. Food and Drug Administration (2024a).

97 U.S. Food and Drug Administration (2021).

98 U.S. Food and Drug Administration (2025b).

99 U.S. Food and Drug Administration (2024b).

100 U.S. Food and Drug Administration (2024c).

aims to build on existing governance. Specific items of relevance to QIT include the requirement of a prospective change-management plan for adaptive algorithms; codification of good machine-learning practice in non-binding principles; a prioritization of transparency for both clinicians and regulators and maintenance of cross-center alignment so that drugs, biologics and devices face coherent evidentiary standards. The result is an example regulatory framework for AI that is sufficiently flexible to adapt to technology as it evolves. It complements FDA discussion papers and guidance on AI in drug manufacturing and other life science sectors.[101]

3.7.2 *Implications of QIT Integration*

The FDA's approach to AI regulation therefore provides both an illustrative guide and an existing framework into which QIT regulation can integrate.[102] Firstly, in many cases QIT systems will be likely complemented by AI systems, thus forming one larger computational system which would arguably fall within the definition of an 'AI system' itself (even if the specific learning protocols themselves remain classical rather than quantum in nature). Drawing a clear demarcation between where classical technology (and AI) ends and QIT begins may nevertheless be challenging due to the fact that QIT is necessarily embedded within classical systems. Secondly, from a governance stack perspective, it is likely as we suggest below that existing methods of, for example, handling uncertainties, can be adapted to handle QIT-specific differences. Thirdly, depending on the regulatory regime, *QIT as a medical device-* or *QIT in a medical device*-style guidance would arguably complement existing AI governance and so would reasonably be expected to form part of the FDA's future approach to quantum technology integration. This is especially the case when it comes to integration: in the AI context the FDA has worked with a range of other agencies[103] to seek to align the responsible use and governance of AI for medical products and healthcare—a coordinated approach that would suit QIT in life sciences.

3.7.2.1 Regulation Already Handles Uncertainties

As noted above, the inherent ontological indeterminacy of QIT systems[104]—from measurement stochasticity to no-cloning results—stands in contrast to classical information systems. However, the early experience of AI guidance suggests that the extent to which regulation needs to adapt to cater for such differences may be less significant. For example, the FDA already accepts stochastic outputs in clinical statistics, in

[101] U.S. Food and Drug Administration (2025c).

[102] Branco and Sousa (2025).

[103] U.S. Food and Drug Administration (2025e).

[104] Luo (2005).

silico simulations, and AI-enabled diagnostic classifiers.[105] The guidance (updated in early 2025) explicitly contemplates process models that update in real time as new data arrive and means of handling uncertainty (or the 'credibility' of a component) and verification protocols—for judging uncertain information and evidence. These approaches ought to also apply to QIT, but with modifications required to deal with differences identified above and quantum-specific features, such as error correction or noise metrics (e.g. logical error rates, sampling variance).

3.7.2.2 Classical Auditing and Risk Assessment Can Provide a Guide

FDA guidance above also sets out recommendations relating to model provenance, training-data quality, and version control—key features of auditing which also would apply to the use of QIT. For example, the FDA's PCCP framework set out detailed specifications relating to disclosure of modifications by the use of AI in order to enable its monitoring and auditing. In the QIT case, similar technological artefacts such as computational and process logs, hardware-noise details, and evidence that identical initial states, when re-prepared, converge to the same distribution within defined confidence bounds would arguably fulfil similar audit functions. Where no-cloning prevents literal duplication, statistical reproducibility based on repeated state preparation might become an acceptable substitute analogous to multiple-batch strategies accepted by the FDA in other contexts (e.g. ANDA and NDA processes).

Overall, the FDA's developing methods for adapting to AI technological innovation are likely to directly apply to many QIT life sciences use cases. They will also provide a useful starting point for assessing adaptations to FDA regulation that are desirable in order to accommodation QIT technology without the need for significant regulatory reform. The same graduated approach—innovation-accommodating soft governance in the short term supported by data-driven performance benchmarks and, once full fault-tolerant systems arrive, specific regulation and integration into the life-sciences governance stack—is therefore a likely course of action.

3.8 Case Study: QC for Pharmaceutical Innovation

3.8.1 Case Study

In this section, we examine the regulatory dilemmas described above in the context of a hypothetical case study of a pharmaceutical producer (denoted a 'sponsor' in line with typical regulatory nomenclature) using QC simulations for pharmaceutical innovation. QC offers a method to simulate molecular and protein-level interactions

[105] U.S. Food and Drug Administration (2025d).

in ways that may be more accurate and more computationally feasible than classical computing.[106] This is especially the case for complex multi-body systems and large biomolecules. Quantum simulations can potentially accelerate pharmaceutical innovation by reducing time and cost involved in screening candidate compounds, predicting toxicity, and optimizing protein–ligand binding in ways classically infeasible or prohibitively resource-intensive.[107] We consider how the use of such QC simulations would fit within the FDA's established framework for demonstrating safety, efficacy, and reproducibility of drug products. We map out a generic pharmaceutical innovation lifecycle below, for each stage identifying technical uses of QIT and relevant governance issues arising.

3.8.2 Pharmaceutical Innovation Lifecycles

The typical lifecycle pathway of pharmaceutical innovation for drug discovery involves the following steps[108] under Title 21 (*Food and Drugs*) of the CFR. We set them out in Table 3.6.

We discuss each stage in more detail below.

3.8.3 Drug Discovery

3.8.3.1 Technical

Drug discovery focuses on identifying compounds or biologics that can modulate a disease target, typically leveraging computational tools alongside lab-based experiments. This is the first primary stage for the use of quantum simulations. In our case study, we assume a sponsor uses a fault-tolerant quantum computer to run high-precision molecular simulations (e.g., variational quantum eigensolvers or quantum phase estimation) to predict interaction energies, protein–ligand binding affinities, or structural conformations. The benefit of the quantum simulation is in efficiency, scale and tractability. Classical simulations rely heavily on simplifying approximations to render computations of interactions feasible. By contrast, QIT may be able to capture electron correlations more accurately (currently the ability to do so is limited in scale).

106 Kirsopp et al. (2022).

107 Mensa et al. (2023).

108 Mantus and Pisano (2014).

Table 3.6 Prospective applications of QIT in the lifecycle pathway of pharmaceutical innovation for drug discovery

Stage	Detail	Prospective QIT applications
Drug discovery	Preliminary identification of disease targets, compound screening/optimization, basic in silico modelling, and laboratory assays	Quantum simulations (e.g., variational quantum eigensolvers, phase estimation) for high-precision modelling of molecular interactions More accurate protein–ligand binding predictions and conformational analysis
Preclinical testing	Laboratory (in vitro) and animal (in vivo) studies to assess toxicology, pharmacokinetics, and pharmacodynamics	Quantum-based toxicity/PK/PD simulations to assess off-target binding, absorption, and metabolic pathways Parallel use of quantum and classical methods for comprehensive early screening
Investigational New Drug (IND) application	Formal application to the FDA, compiling preclinical data and proposed clinical trial protocols for initial human studies	Quantum-augmented safety rationale for minimal off-target binding or unique mechanism-of-action insights Targeted trial design (e.g., identifying specific subpopulations) via quantum-derived data
Clinical trials	Multi-phase testing in human volunteers and patients to evaluate safety, dosage, and effectiveness	Dose-ranging and biomarker identification using quantum simulations of drug metabolism at finer electronic scales Potential adaptive trial designs based on real-time or interim quantum analyses
New Drug Application (NDA) submission	Comprehensive dossier of all preclinical and clinical data submitted to request marketing approval	Quantum-driven efficacy and safety data supplementing classical results (e.g., detailed receptor binding models) Highlighting how quantum computations capture complex reaction coordinates more accurately

(continued)

Table 3.6 (continued)

Stage	Detail	Prospective QIT applications
FDA review and approval	FDA evaluation of safety, efficacy, and manufacturing quality, potentially involving advisory committees and labelling negotiations	Demonstrations of quantum reproducibility (statistical convergence from multiple experiments) for binding selectivity or mechanistic synergy
Post-marketing surveillance (Phase IV)	Ongoing monitoring of real-world safety, efficacy, and rare adverse events after product launch	Quantum re-simulation of real-world data (adverse events, patient subgroups) to identify new risk signals or refine dosing
Manufacturing and quality control	Implementation of Good Manufacturing Practices (GMP)[109] to ensure consistent product safety, purity, and potency	Quantum simulations to optimize reaction conditions (e.g., temperature, crystallization) Potential for real-time quantum feedback loops in process analytics
Advertising and promotion	Regulation of promotional materials and campaigns to ensure truthful, non-misleading communication of drug benefits and risks	Quantum references in promotional materials (e.g., "Developed with quantum simulations") to differentiate R&D approach
Generic Drug Approval (ANDA)	Abbreviated application demonstrating bioequivalence to an already-approved reference product without repeating full clinical trials	Quantum modelling for fine-tuning generic formulations or predicting dissolution Enhanced equivalence analysis (e.g., minor formulation adjustments)
Post-approval changes and supplements	Regulatory pathways for modifying formulation, manufacturing processes, or labelling post-approval	Quantum re-simulation to evaluate impact of altered excipients, manufacturing steps, or labelling update
Withdrawal and recalls	Voluntary or mandatory removal of a drug from the market if new evidence deems it unsafe, ineffective, or misbranded	Quantum re-check of emergent toxicity mechanisms or off-target effects leading to voluntary or mandated withdrawal

[109] Current Good Manufacturing Process—for drug manufacturers is set out in 21 CFR Parts 210, 211, 212 and 312.

Table 3.7 Prospective governance issues and responses arising from the use of QIT in drug discovery

Category	Governance issue	Governance response
Data input and measurement	Quantum simulations require multiple measurements giving rise to distinct stochastically-based measurement statistics	Document repeated quantum experiments under GLP guidelines, maintaining fully compliant records of sampling and error rates
Verification and reproduction	FDA assumes reproducibility under stable conditions; quantum outputs are inherently probabilistic	Use statistical convergence and error mitigation approaches to demonstrate reproducibility within current GLP frameworks
Privacy and security	Early-stage R&D data may primarily be proprietary rather than personal data, though GDPR obligations can apply where personal data are processed	Maintain standard industrial data security protocols (e.g., encryption, access control) to protect proprietary quantum-derived research data
Auditing	Quantum measurement may be different from that expected as auditing typically expects cloneable data	Store classical logs for each quantum run, ensuring traceability under GLP audit trails rather than relying on replicating the quantum state
Ownership, IP and disclosure	Quantum-derived insights may be unpatentable if deemed natural phenomena	Pursue method or process patents (e.g., for novel quantum algorithms or computational techniques)

3.8.3.2 Governance

Drug discovery activity itself is not directly regulated by the FDA beyond broad ethical guidelines (e.g., NIH Guidelines, Public Health Service Act[110]). However, data from quantum simulations—if later used in IND or NDA submissions—must comply with *Good Laboratory Practice* (GLP) standards[111] for non-clinical laboratory studies data integrity. A possible QIT-related issue is ensuring that probabilistic outcomes and error rates do not undermine the reproducibility principle. If quantum-generated insights inform future regulatory filings, sponsors should document how many runs and error-mitigation steps were taken and keep robust electronic records[112] from the outset, even during early research. We summarize the issues and responses in Table 3.7.

[110] Public Health Service Act of 1944.

[111] 21 CFR §§ 58.1–58.219 (2024). Good Laboratory Practice for Nonclinical Laboratory Studies.

[112] 21 CFR §§ 11.1–11.300 (2024). Electronic Records; Electronic Signatures.

3.8.4 Pre-clinical Testing

3.8.4.1 Technical

Preclinical testing involves in vitro (cellular) and in vivo (animal) studies to assess safety (toxicity, tolerability), pharmacokinetics (PK), and pharmacodynamics (PD). QC may supplement or partially replace certain classical modelling steps—such as evaluating off-target binding or predicting absorption profiles—by more precisely simulating molecular-electron interactions. Quantum-based toxicity or PK/PD simulations usually run in parallel with lab experiments and thus represent another way for QIT to input into the innovation process.

3.8.4.2 Governance

Regulatory oversight in this stage focuses on GLP guidelines regarding reliable data practices. If quantum-simulation outputs (e.g., predicted toxicities) help justify moving a prospective drug forward, the FDA will expect GLP compliance in how those simulations were designed and archived. An important part of the technical documentation would involve explaining how repeated QIT simulations converge statistically and, moreover, explaining results in terms of measurement statistics. In addition, detailing error correction metrics (and success metrics) for simulations—such as average fidelities—would be important. Sponsors would also be recommended to maintain thorough logs of hardware parameters, sampling experiments, and final outcomes so that the FDA can evaluate the validity of quantum-derived safety assessments. We summarize these governance issues and potential responses in Table 3.8.

3.8.5 Investigational New Drug Application

3.8.5.1 Technical

An IND submission presents all preclinical findings, proposed trial protocols, manufacturing information, and investigator qualifications to the FDA. Detail and information about QC simulations would form an essential part of any IND where QC results are used as the basis for the submission.

Table 3.8 Prospective governance issues and responses arising from the use of QIT in pre-clinical testing

Category	Governance issue	Governance response
Data input and measurement	Quantum toxicity/PK/PD simulations must be aggregated statistically	Document hardware configurations and repeated runs in compliance with GLP, showing how quantum data inform in vitro/in vivo safety tests
Verification and reproduction	Regulators expect classical replicability; quantum no-cloning and probabilistic outputs raise new validation questions	Provide evidence of convergent quantum runs plus classical or experimental correlation to confirm toxicological predictions
Privacy and security	Preclinical data may not be patient-specific but may be commercially sensitive	Protect quantum-simulation files under standard trade secret and cybersecurity policies
Auditing	FDA inspections[113] rely on stable data logs; ephemeral quantum states challenge direct re-checking	Maintain robust electronic records documenting each quantum simulation, including software versioning and error-mitigation logs
Ownership, IP and disclosure	Patentability of quantum-simulated insights (e.g., predicted toxicity) can be unclear if they echo natural phenomena	Emphasize novel computational methods in patent applications; rely on method claims consistent with enablement standards

3.8.5.2 Governance

Under 21 CFR Part 312,[114] sponsors must submit an IND package detailing preclinical data and study protocols. Quantum-based safety or mechanistic claims must be reproducible enough to meet the FDA's threshold for initiating human trials. Important QIT governance issues include demonstrating how probabilistic simulations yield consistent conclusions about safety and proper / accurate presentation of information to FDA standards. Part 312 does not explicitly address quantum technologies, but the FDA could in principle require supplementary data to show that quantum outputs are valid. Sponsors must also conform to informed consent[115] and IRB review[116] obligations, ensuring the trial design—potentially shaped by quantum predictions—does not pose unjustified risks. We summarize these issues and responses in Table 3.9.

[113] 21 CFR §§ 58.1–58.219 (2024). Good Laboratory Practice for Nonclinical Laboratory Studies.

[114] 21 CFR §§ 312.1–312.160 (2024). Investigational New Drug Application.

[115] 21 CFR §§ 50.1–50.56 (2024). Protection of Human Subjects.

[116] 21 CFR §§ 56.101–56.124 (2024). Institutional Review Boards.

Table 3.9 Prospective governance issues and responses arising from the use of QIT at the IND application stage

Category	Governance issue	Governance response
Data input and measurement	Quantum methods and descriptions of data would need to be included, but the nature of measurements is not explicitly addressed	Provide aggregated quantum simulation results and explain measurement procedures in the IND submission to meet FDA expectations
Verification and reproduction	FDA demands reproducible preclinical findings prior to human trials; quantum outputs are inherently probabilistic	Corroborate quantum-derived safety data with classical evidence to meet the reproducibility threshold
Privacy and security	IND documents would rarely hold protected patient information at this stage, but sponsor data must remain secure	Use routine data safeguards (e.g., encryption at rest/in transit) and control access to quantum simulation results in the IND filing
Auditing	FDA might request audits of IND data; quantum states do not allow direct duplication of data	Present classical logs/statistical analyses as part of the IND record for potential FDA inspections
Ownership, IP and disclosure	Early publication or disclosure of quantum-based safety insights can affect patent timelines	Time patent filings for quantum methods prior to public IND disclosures to preserve IP rights under U.S. first-to-file rules

3.8.6 Clinical Trials

3.8.6.1 Technical

Clinical trials proceed in a phased manner: Phase I (safety, dosing), Phase II (efficacy, side effects), and Phase III (large-scale confirmation) (21 CFR § 312.21). Information obtained from quantum simulations may be used at each stage e.g. to guide dose-ranging or identify the most relevant biomarkers by modelling drug metabolism at a sub-atomic electron level. QIT may also be used for interim analyses: information processed using QC could be used to adjust trials as they are underway.

3.8.6.2 Governance

Clinical trials are subject to requirements of 21 CFR Part 312. If quantum-based modelling leads to adaptive trial decisions—such as narrowing patient cohorts or adjusting dosage mid-study—the FDA and IRBs may require evidence that quantum outputs are robust (i.e., not purely exploratory). The sponsor must keep electronic

Table 3.10 Prospective governance issues and responses arising from the use of QIT during clinical trials

Category	Governance issue	Governance response
Data input and measurement	Adaptive trials might incorporate quantum-based dose predictions; 21 CFR Part 312 does not expressly cover the use of quantum data	Document quantum data inputs in real-time and ensure IRB-approved protocols reflect the probabilistic nature of these measurements[118]
Verification and reproduction	IRB/FDA (21 CFR § 50.25, 21 CFR § 56.111) expect clear explanations and robust replication of dosing rationales; quantum metrics are less transparent	Perform multiple quantum runs plus confirmatory classical modelling to justify trial modifications; maintain full records for each change
Privacy and security	Patient data remains under HIPAA; merging it with quantum computations in cloud-based HPC might introduce extra security layers	Implement HIPAA-compliant encryption for data movement into quantum platforms and, if used, consider QKD for especially sensitive information
Auditing	Mid-trial auditing typically checks stable endpoints; quantum-based adaptive decisions complicate sponsor monitoring	Provide thorough protocols for each quantum-driven decision point, enabling regulators to track how trial modifications arise from QIT outcomes
Ownership, IP and disclosure	Patent scope could be impacted if quantum-aided trial design reveals new uses or formulations unexpectedly	Draft broad method claims covering quantum-driven medical use expansions, ensuring compliance with FDA's stance on labelling for new indications

records in compliance with 21 CFR Part 11,[117] ensuring a full audit trail of any quantum-run parameters that inform trial modifications. Regulators may also seek clarity on how quantum predictions directly relate to patient safety or selection criteria. Table 3.10 below summarizes key prospective issues and responses.

3.8.7 New Drug Application (NDA)

3.8.7.1 Technical

An NDA compiles all preclinical and clinical data to prove safety, efficacy, manufacturing quality, and labelling accuracy. Quantum simulations could appear in the integrated summary of effectiveness—demonstrating, for instance, how a drug binds to multiple receptor isoforms or how different functional groups influence efficacy.

[117] 21 CFR §§ 11.1–11.300 (2024). Electronic Records; Electronic Signatures.

[118] 21 CFR §§ 56.101–56.124 (2024). Institutional Review Boards.

Sponsors might highlight quantum's ability to model complex reaction coordinates more precisely than classical high-performance computing (HPC).

3.8.7.2 Governance

Under 21 CFR Part 314,[119] the FDA reviews an NDA's content[120] and labelling compliance. If quantum modelling underpins significant efficacy or safety arguments, the FDA could request additional data showing how the sponsor validated quantum outputs. The sponsor must detail any probabilistic ensemble of runs and error-mitigation used to reach stable conclusions. Given the FDA's preference for standardizable data, bridging or replicate results may still be required. If quantum results or methods depart from typical classical methods, the FDA can ask for advisory committee input on reliability or novel method acceptance. It would be likely that the FDA would also seek data evidencing error-correction thresholds reached and quantum-specific performance metrics, such as fidelities. Table 3.11 sets out prospective issues and responses from use of QIT at the NDA stage.

3.8.8 FDA Approval

3.8.8.1 Technical

During the formal review, FDA staff and possibly external advisory committees scrutinize clinical trial data, labelling proposals, and any underlying computational analyses. QC–based evidence might explain mechanistic synergy or confirm binding selectivity. However, quantum hardware noise, limited qubit capacity, and the stochasticity of quantum measurements and error-correction problems can raise questions about reproducibility and reliability. Sponsors may be required to demonstrate measurement statistics converge to reproducible distributions based on multiple experiments.

3.8.8.2 Governance

Key statutory provisions include 21 CFR Part 314 (NDA review procedures) and the FDA's general authority under the *Federal Food, Drug, and Cosmetic Act* (FD&C Act). Panels may question how quantum simulations offer advantages over classical HPC simulations (given prospective trade-offs with error tolerances). The FDA may approve the application if overall benefits outweigh risks but may require labelling disclaimers referencing computational or theoretical data. No specific quantum

---

[119] 21 CFR §§ 314.1–314.650 (2024). Applications for FDA Approval to Market a New Drug.

[120] 21 CFR § 314.50 (2024). Content and Format of an Application.

Table 3.11 Prospective governance issues and responses arising from the use of QIT at the NDA stage

Category	Governance issue	Governance response
Data input and measurement	NDA requires comprehensive data. Quantum-based efficacy or safety data from measurement statistics are stochastic	Explain quantum measurement protocols in the NDA, showing how repeated sampling yields stable aggregated results for efficacy or safety claims
Verification and reproduction	FDA reviewers expect stable datasets; quantum noise must be shown not to undermine reliability	Provide error-mitigation logs and bridging in vitro/in vivo data to support quantum's probabilistic outcomes, satisfying NDA reproducibility norms
Privacy and security	NDA file confidentiality is protected by FDA regulations; quantum computations do not alter existing privacy rules	Maintain standard confidential NDA submissions, as quantum techniques do not inherently expand patient data usage at this stage
Auditing	FDA may conduct pre-approval inspections; ephemeral quantum states cannot be reloaded for direct re-checking	Keep detailed records of quantum parameters, noise thresholds, and run counts so FDA can trace data derivation steps in inspections
Ownership, IP and disclosure	Novel quantum-generated efficacy insights may require patent claims on dosing regimens or molecular scaffolds	File patent claims that differentiate quantum-assisted discoveries from mere laws of nature, focusing on unique computational processes or therapeutic uses

guidelines exist, so the FDA would apply standard review criteria (efficacy, safety, manufacturing) while scrutinizing the newness of quantum's error profiles and verifying compliance with other provisions such as 21 CFR Part 10 (administrative procedures) and application requirements.[121] Table 3.12 sets out a summary of the issues below.

3.8.9 *Post-marketing Surveillance*

3.8.9.1 Technical

Following FDA approval, sponsors are required to monitor a drug for rare or long-term adverse effects (Phase IV). Quantum simulations could in principle be utilized to do so via incorporating real-world adverse event data and re-running simulations to predict new risk signals or refine dosing in special populations. Compared to

[121] 21 CFR § 314.50 (2024). Content and Format of an Application.

Table 3.12 Prospective governance issues and responses arising from the use of QIT during the FDA approval process

Category	Governance issue	Governance response
Data input and measurement	Advisory committees and FDA staff may ask for clarifications on how quantum data were measured and aggregated	Present explicit protocols for quantum data collection, referencing relevant GLP/GMP compliance to reassure regulators of data integrity
Verification and reproduction	Quantum algorithms are still novel; FDA may doubt reproducibility if only minimal bridging data are provided	Strengthen bridging with classical HPC or lab data, and detail statistical confidence intervals from multiple quantum runs
Privacy and security	Generally, personal data security is not the main concern at approval, but sponsor trade secrets remain crucial	Protect quantum method specifics under FDA confidentiality rules
Auditing	FDA checks the reliability of all data sources; ephemeral quantum states complicate typical recheck approaches	Provide thorough quantum run logs (e.g., date/time, seed states, error-correction) ensuring an audit trail of how results were obtained
Ownership, IP and disclosure	Competitors might demand disclosure of quantum methods; sponsor must show they have adequate IP protection	Maintain trade-secret status for detailed quantum workflows if not patented, disclosing only as needed to FDA under confidentiality agreements

classical HPC analytics that rely on aggregate statistical methods, such simulations might capture subtle molecular pathways relevant to toxicity or off-label usage which cannot be modelled classically.

3.8.9.2 Governance

The FDA mandates adverse event reporting (21 CFR 314.80) and can impose Risk Evaluation and Mitigation Strategies (REMS) under FD&C Act § 505-1 in the event of actual or suspected adverse reporting. Any quantum-based findings that suggest label changes must be validated by additional data because post-market adjustments require robust evidence: if a QC simulation gave rise to an indication of imminent adverse outcomes, it remains an open question as to how this might be verified sufficiently to require such adjustments. Sponsors must maintain GLP standards if they do additional nonclinical experiments (e.g., quantum modelling of new safety concerns) to update the label. The FDA would consider quantum simulation data

Table 3.13 Prospective governance issues and responses arising from the use of QIT during post-marketing surveillance

Category	Governance issue	Governance response
Data input and measurement	Phase IV relies on real-world data; quantum re-simulation may need repeated runs to integrate post-approval adverse event data	Summarize quantum simulations with conventional epidemiological findings to detect new signals, complying with adverse event reporting requirements
Verification and reproduction	FDA would expect confirmatory data for label changes; quantum predictions alone may be insufficient	Provide bridging clinical or real-world evidence to validate quantum findings prior to label updates or modifications
Privacy and security	Patient-level data (HIPAA) might feed quantum re-simulations if analyzing real-world outcomes; secure handling is needed	Deploy standard HIPAA-compliant encryption/storage plus advanced QKD if extremely sensitive data is transmitted to quantum hardware
Auditing	FDA can audit post-marketing analyses quantum states preclude direct re-measurement	Retain thorough logs of each quantum run's conditions, aligning with monitoring guidelines for reanalysis if signals arise
Ownership, IP and disclosure	New post-market quantum findings might be deemed incremental discoveries with separate IP ramifications	Consider patent extensions or supplemental method claims for quantum-driven detection of new indications or subpopulations

but typically demands real-world or classical confirmatory data before altering official labelling. This speaks to the general requirement—and challenge—of how to verify quantum-based conclusions using classical procedures. A number of issues and possible responses are set out in Table 3.13.

3.8.10 Manufacturing and Quality Control

3.8.10.1 Technical

Manufacturing ensures consistent product quality via the aforementioned Good Manufacturing Practices. Quantum methods might optimize reaction conditions (e.g., temperature, pH) or crystallization by simulating molecular packing in a more precise manner. Real-time quantum feedback is theoretically possible for monitoring process variables albeit online (real-time) control differs for QC systems by contrast with their classical counterparts. However, current QIT hardware limitations make large-scale real-time control challenging due to the lack of scalable fault-tolerance.

3.8.10.2 Governance

21 CFR Parts 210 and 211 require validated manufacturing processes, batch records, and stable quality standards. If a sponsor uses a quantum-based software in control processes, that system must be validated for electronic records and signatures. Auditors would likely want to see how quantum-generated parameters or recipes are tested, documented, and repeated. Although no separate quantum GMP guidance exists, the FDA would expect the same reliability as classical software: sponsor must explain noise-handling and ensure final outputs meet reproducibility requirements for product safety and efficacy. Table 3.14 sets out prospective issues and responses.

Table 3.14 Prospective governance issues and responses arising from the use of QIT in relation to manufacturing and quality control requirements

Category	Governance issue	Governance response
Data input and measurement	Real-time quantum feedback loops for process analytics remain experimental; GMP does not specify quantum control requirements	Validate any quantum-based control software under GMP, showing reproducible final product specs despite probabilistic QIT outputs
Verification and reproduction	GMP relies on stable, repeatable processes; quantum noise might affect consistency of reaction conditions	Use error-corrected or statistically averaged quantum simulations to confirm each production batch meets specifications
Privacy and security	Manufacturing data is typically proprietary, with limited personal health info; quantum encryption is optional for corporate IP	Protect trade secrets with standard cybersecurity measures; adopt quantum-safe encryption if desired for internal or cross-plant data
Auditing	FDA inspections check manufacturing records; ephemeral quantum states cannot be re-created for direct re-inspection	Maintain classical logs and final product test results, referencing any quantum-driven optimizations as needed
Ownership, IP and disclosure	Novel quantum-optimized processes might be patentable as manufacturing methods	Patent method claims on quantum-driven process parameters; keep crucial quantum algorithms as trade secrets if not fully disclosed

3.8.11 *Advertising and Promotion*

3.8.11.1 Technical

Once a drug is approved, sponsors often promote its benefits and unique selling points. References to the use of QC might appear in marketing to underscore advanced R&D credentials. Technically, quantum claims might risk oversimplification or hype if not carefully couched. By contrast, classical HPC references are more established and recognized within the scientific community.

3.8.11.2 Governance

Under 21 CFR Part 202[122] and Office of Prescription Drug Promotion (OPDP) oversight, the FDA can take steps to ensure claims are not misleading. Quantum references must be substantiated by actual data linking the use of QIT to improved outcomes. The FDA may treat quantum claims much like AI claims requiring scientifically verifiable statements only. Failing to show a meaningful link between quantum modelling and clinical benefit could violate advertising regulations, even if the statements are technologically correct in a narrow sense. We summarize in more detail in Table 3.15.

3.8.12 *Generic Drug Approval*

3.8.12.1 Technical

Generic drugs must show bioequivalence to a reference listed drug. Quantum simulation might help optimize a generic formulation or predict dissolution properties with more precision than classical approaches. However, due to NISQ constraints on scaling and the absence of fully-fledged fault tolerant QC, actual implementation of large-scale and robust simulations remain prospective only. Thus sponsors would still typically be required to rely on in vitro bioequivalence tests.

3.8.12.2 Governance

The use of QC simulations in any attempt to establish bioequivalence is uncertain. In principle, a sponsor can incorporate quantum results in explaining minor formulation differences or improved manufacturing steps. Yet the FDA typically requires in vivo or in vitro bridging data to confirm equivalence. It is unclear whether quantum

---

[122] 21 CFR §§ 202.1–202.600 (2024). Prescription Drug Advertising.

Table 3.15 Prospective governance issues and responses arising from the use of QIT in connection with advertising and promotion

Category	Governance issue	Governance response
Data input and measurement	Promotional materials that cite quantum-based data must accurately reflect the nature of those measurements	Keep references to quantum findings truthful and explain the probabilistic aspect
Verification and reproduction	Claims about quantum-driven benefits need supporting reproducible data; black box quantum claims risk FDA scrutiny	Substantiate quantum claims with validated study results and disclaim any theoretical components not clinically corroborated
Privacy and security	Promotional data rarely contain PHI, so HIPAA rarely applies. Trade secret regarding QC processes ought to be safeguarded	Release only high-level summaries of quantum research publicly, retaining detailed computations for regulatory submissions or patent filings
Auditing	OPDP or FDA enforcement can review promotional materials	Provide OPDP with the classical summaries and evidence behind quantum claims, ensuring they meet non-misleading standards
Ownership, IP and disclosure	Over-promoting quantum discoveries without IP protection might invite competition or confusion	Time promotional announcements to align with patent filings; ensure no unapproved off-label quantum claims are made

simulation results would suffice. This raises ongoing questions regarding evidentiary standards for QC simulations. Table 3.16 sets out relevant issues and possible responses below.

3.8.13 Post-approval Changes/Supplements

3.8.13.1 Technical

Sponsors may in certain cases alter the formulation, labelling, or manufacturing of a drug after initial approval. As with the use of QC simulations at other steps, quantum simulation could in principle identify how changes to production parameters affect drug stability or efficacy. As above, justifying the conclusions and reliability of the QC simulations would depend upon how regulators handle quantum data.

Table 3.16 Prospective governance issues and responses arising from the use of QIT in relation to generic drug approval

Category	Governance issue	Governance response
Data input and measurement	Bioequivalence testing may incorporate quantum simulations, but the FDA largely expects classical in vitro/in vivo methods	Use quantum data as a supplementary approach to refine formulations but rely on traditional bioequivalence endpoints to satisfy applicable standards
Verification and reproduction	Standards demand proven equivalence; quantum's probabilistic results might not alone establish consistency	Support quantum findings with repeat classical or experimental comparisons to confirm bioequivalence
Privacy and security	Generic development data typically is not patient-specific; minimal new privacy concerns from quantum	Standard IP protections suffice; no specialized quantum security protocols required unless sponsor chooses to safeguard trade secrets further
Auditing	FDA can audit data submissions; ephemeral quantum states cannot be re-run for direct verification	Provide classical logs and replicate key simulations where possible, ensuring results are consistent
Ownership, IP and disclosure	Quantum improvements in generics may lead to method patents for establishing bioequivalence	Process patents may be filed if QC significantly improves the production of the drug

3.8.13.2 Governance

Significant changes require prior approval, while moderate changes may only need a supplemental application. The FDA would review how effectively the sponsor used QIT to justify the modification. Sponsors still must provide bridging data (batch tests, stability data, etc.) to confirm the quantum predictions. The FDA can reject or delay changes if the sponsor does not show a credible correlation between quantum outputs and real-world product consistency. Table 3.17 summarizes the issues below.

3.8.14 Withdrawals/Recalls

3.8.14.1 Technical

A drug may be voluntarily or mandatorily withdrawn if new evidence shows it is unsafe, ineffective, or misbranded. Quantum simulations might uncover a serious mechanistic toxicity route not obvious before. Classical reanalysis or real-world adverse events typically confirm these signals, but quantum re-checks can expedite the detection of potential emergent hazards. The use of QC in this case is interesting

Table 3.17 Prospective governance issues and responses arising from the use of QIT in relation to changes or supplements

Category	Governance issue	Governance response
Data input and measurement	Quantum re-simulation of altered formulations must be documented if used to justify a post-approval change	Provide an updated technical report with aggregated quantum data, explaining how the new conditions improve product quality or stability
Verification and reproduction	The FDA would expect data to confirm changes; quantum alone might be insufficient for revised labelling or manufacturing updates	Pair quantum-based predictions with classical or batch-level tests to show equivalence or superiority
Privacy and security	Post-approval changes typically concern product composition/ manufacturing; no major new patient data unless new indications are pursued	Continue standard protection of proprietary data; no additional HIPAA issues unless a new clinical population is tested
Auditing	FDA may audit supplements, requiring a stable record of quantum-based modifications	Include revised standard operating procedures detailing quantum simulations in the post-approval supplement submission
Ownership, IP and disclosure	Minor changes or supplements rarely yield major new IP; quantum-driven improvements might merit distinct process claims	If the quantum method itself is substantially innovative, consider filing an additional patent or maintaining it as a trade secret

in that it raises questions as to whether data from QC simulations used to identify adverse outcomes might be different from QC simulations used during a drug's approval process.

3.8.14.2 Governance

The FDA has authority to withdraw approval or request recalls. If the sponsor cites QC simulations, the FDA could still demand confirmatory data such as actual adverse event records. QIT might accelerate risk detection, but final regulatory decision still hinges on conventional risk analysis. Thus, it is unclear whether inferences drawn from QC simulations would be sufficient to justify recall of an approved product. Table 3.18 sets out issues and possible responses arising from QIT use at this stage.

Table 3.18 Prospective governance issues and responses arising from the use of QIT in the context of withdrawals and recalls

Category	Governance issue	Governance response
Data input and measurement	Quantum analyses might detect unforeseen toxicity or mislabeling, but these outcomes are probabilistic	Present classical follow-up data or real-world adverse event patterns to confirm quantum-detected signals under recall provisions
Verification and reproduction	FDA or sponsor requires classical proof of a serious safety problem; quantum-driven findings alone are unlikely to trigger withdrawals	Combine quantum signal detection with conventional re-checks or post-market evidence to justify product removal from market
Privacy and security	Recalls typically do not involve new patient data; no specific HIPAA/GDPR triggers	Maintain standard confidentiality for recall logistics, with no quantum-specific data security mandates
Auditing	FDA or sponsor audits recall decisions; ephemeral quantum states complicate re-running old analyses	Provide archived quantum logs and any classical re-validation to demonstrate how the withdrawal decision was reached
Ownership, IP and disclosure	Withdrawal or recall rarely generates new IP; sponsor may lose exclusivity if the product is permanently removed	Any quantum-based detection method remains sponsor IP, but the product's patent or exclusivity becomes moot if marketing authorization is pulled

3.9 Discussion and Outlook

This chapter has explored the integration of quantum information technologies into the life sciences, focusing on their potential to advance fields such as pharmaceutical drug discovery, bioinformatics, and medical device development.

We have identified two primary governance dilemmas: a technical dilemma, arising from the non-classical ontology of QIT that diverges from the classical assumptions embedded in life sciences regulation; and an integration dilemma, concerning the alignment of nascent QIT governance with the mature, risk-averse frameworks governing sectors like pharmaceuticals and biotechnology. By employing a life sciences stack model, spanning atomic-scale simulations to population-level analytics, we mapped QIT applications, including quantum computing for molecular modelling, quantum sensing for precision diagnostics, and quantum communication for secure data sharing. Our analysis introduced a *governance impact framework*, which helps to categorize QIT effects on data measurement, validation, privacy, auditing, and intellectual property, which we applied through a hypothetical case study on quantum simulation in pharmaceutical drug discovery to illustrate practical regulatory challenges and responses.

Despite the distinct features of QIT, existing life sciences governance frameworks, with their mature risk management practices and robust risk–benefit analysis, are likely flexible enough and well-equipped to accommodate QIT innovations. The established regulatory structures, such as the FDA's protocols for pharmaceuticals and medical devices, already manage uncertainties in clinical statistics and computational modelling, suggesting that QIT's probabilistic outputs can be addressed through extensions like statistical convergence thresholds and hybrid validation with classical experiments. Given the life sciences' extensive oversight mechanisms, designed to balance innovation with safety, this domain may represent one of the most feasible areas for integrating QIT, requiring primarily targeted quantum-specific guidance in specific areas.

Looking ahead, three research directions stand out. First, developing quantum-specific statistical standards can help regulators evaluate probabilistic QIT outputs, building on precedents from AI governance. Second, harmonizing QIT and life sciences regulations, particularly in dual-use and privacy domains, will ensure cohesive oversight. Third, interdisciplinary collaboration among regulators, scientists, and ethicists is essential to address QIT's unique challenges while leveraging stakeholder expertise. By adapting existing frameworks to QIT's distinct properties, governance can support responsible innovation, ensuring that QIT enhances life sciences advancements while maintaining rigorous standards for safety and efficacy.

3.10 Conclusion

This chapter explores the intersection of QIT and the life sciences, identifying opportunities and governance challenges. We outline two central dilemmas: 1) a *technical dilemma*, where QIT's non-classical features, including superposition, entanglement, no-cloning, and stochasticity, diverge from the classical informational assumptions of life sciences regulation; and 2) an *integration dilemma*, concerning the alignment of nascent QIT governance with the established, risk-averse frameworks of sectors such as pharmaceuticals and biotechnology. Using a life sciences stack model, we map QIT's potential applications, including quantum computing for drug discovery, quantum sensing for diagnostics, and quantum communication for secure data sharing.

Our contributions to the literature are as follows. First, we review the state-of-the-art QIT life science applications and specify how QIT's non-classical ontology may impact life sciences use cases, such as molecular simulations and biomarker detection, highlighting governance tensions in reproducibility, verification, and data integrity. Second, we propose a *governance stack framework* and use it to identify potential regulatory gaps in U.S. frameworks where classical expectations of deterministic data may not fully accommodate quantum outputs. Third, our hypothetical case study of quantum simulation in pharmaceutical drug discovery, from target identification to post-market surveillance, illustrates these potential challenges through a detailed workflow, showing how probabilistic quantum data may require adjusted evidentiary standards.

Despite these ontological differences, existing life sciences governance frameworks, built on classical assumptions, appear sufficiently adaptable to address QIT innovations. Current regulations, already equipped to handle uncertainties in clinical statistics and computational modelling, can likely extend to quantum stochasticity through methods like statistical convergence thresholds and hybrid validation with classical experiments. Quantum-specific guidance and standards may suffice to bridge most gaps. This suggests that integrating QIT into life sciences can leverage established regulatory structures without necessitating extensive reform.

Future research includes focusing on refining statistical standards for quantum outputs, harmonizing QIT and life sciences governance in areas like dual-use and privacy regulations, and fostering interdisciplinary dialogue among regulators, scientists, and ethicists. By adapting existing frameworks to QIT's unique features, governance can support innovation while maintaining the rigorous oversight required for safe and effective life sciences advancements.

In conclusion, the *governance stack framework* proposed here offers a structured analytical approach to help examine the ontological disparities and integration complexities that may arise when applying QIT to the life sciences. By layering QIT interventions across the hierarchical life sciences stack, this model helps *illuminate sui generis* quantum effects, such as superposition-driven probabilistic outcomes and entanglement-induced non-locality, which could challenge classical regulatory assumptions of determinism and reproducibility. Additionally, it helps address integration dilemmas by mapping nascent QIT oversight onto mature life sciences regimes, revealing potential regulatory gaps, with the goal of advancing the scholarly discourse on QIT governance and providing policymakers with actionable insights to support responsible deployment of quantum advancements in biomedicine.[123]

Acknowledgements This work was made possible through the generous support of the Novo Nordisk Foundation (NNF) via a grant for the scientifically independent Collaborative Research Program in Bioscience Innovation Law (Inter-CeBIL Program—Grant No. NNF23SA0087056). Any use of AI in this manuscript adheres to ethical guidelines for use and acknowledgement of AI in academic research. Each author has made a substantial contribution to the work, which has been thoroughly vetted for accuracy, and assumes responsibility for the integrity of their contributions in accordance with the ethical guidance on AI use and disclosure set out by Porsdam Mann et al.

References

Abbott A. (2021) Quantum computers to explore precision oncology. *Nature Biotechnology* 39(11): 1324–1325.

Aboy M., et al. (2024) Navigating the EU AI Act: implications for regulated digital medical products. *npj Digit. Med.* 7(1): 237.

[123] Porsdam Mann et al. (2024).

Akcigit U., Liu Q. (2016) The Role of Information in Innovation and competition. *Journal of the European Economic Association* 14(4): 828–870.

Alagic G., et al. (2022) *Status report on the third round of the NIST post-quantum cryptography standardization process.* National Institute of Standards and Technology.

Alagic G., et al. (2024) *Status Report on the First Round of the Additional Digital Signature Schemes for the NIST Post-Quantum Cryptography Standardization Process.* National Institute of Standards and Technology.

Albrecht B., et al. (2023) Quantum feature maps for graph machine learning on a neutral atom quantum processor. *Physical Review A* 107(4): 042615.

Ali MK., et al. (2023) Exploring the multifunctional roles of quantum dots for unlocking the future of biology and medicine. *Environmental Research* 232: 116290.

Alter KJ. (2025) U.S. export controls across time: Knowledge, technology, and China. *American Journal of International Law* 119(1), 180–195.

Anstis S., et al. (2023) Moving from Secrecy to Transparency in the Offensive Cyber Capabilities Sector: The Case of Dual-Use Technologies Exports. *Computer Law & Security Review* 48: 105787.

Aslam N., et al. (2023) Quantum sensors for biomedical applications. *Nature Reviews Physics* 5(3): 157–169.

Azevedo V., et al. (2022) Quantum transfer learning for breast cancer detection. *Quantum Machine Intelligence* 4(1): 5.

Baiardi A., et al. (2023) Quantum Computing for Molecular Biology. *ChemBioChem* 24(13):e202300120.

Batra K., et al. (2021) Quantum machine learning algorithms for drug discovery applications. *Journal of Chemical Information and Modeling* 61(6): 2641–2647.

Belal F., et al. (2024) Recent applications of quantum dots in pharmaceutical analysis. *Journal of Fluorescence* 34(1): 119–138.

Bernstein DJ., Lange T. (2017) Post-quantum cryptography. *Nature* 549: 188–194.

Blunt NS., et al. (2022) Perspective on the current state-of-the-art of quantum computing for drug discovery applications. *Journal of Chemical Theory and Computation* 18(12): 7001–7023.

Branco F., Sousa JJ. (2025) Chapter 2 - Artificial intelligence: A regulatory perspective. In: Pais A., Vitorino C., Nunes S., Cova T. (eds) *Artificial Intelligence for Drug Product Lifecycle Applications.* (Elsevier, United Kingdom).

Bukowski TJ., Simmons JH. (2002) Quantum dot research: current state and future prospects. *Critical Reviews in Solid State and Material Sciences* 27(3-4): 119–142.

Cai J., et al. (2015) Information asymmetry and corporate governance. *Quarterly Journal of Finance* 5(03): 1550014.

Carroll JD. (2009) A new definition of life. *Chirality* 21(3):354–358.

Casares PAM., et al. (2022) QFold: Quantum walks and deep learning to solve protein folding. *Quantum Science and Technology* 7(2): 025013.

Chakraborty C., et al. (2023) Quantum computing on nucleic acid research: Approaching towards next-generation computing. *Molecular Therapy Nucleic Acids* 33:53–56.

Clift MJD., Stone V. (2012) Quantum Dots: An Insight and Perspective of Their Biological Interaction and How This Relates to Their Relevance for Clinical Use. *Theranostics* 2(7): 668–680.

Coenen C., et al. (2022) Quantum Technologies and Society: *Towards a Different Spin. NanoEthics* 16(1): 1–6.

Coenen C., Grunwald A. (2017) Responsible research and innovation (RRI) in quantum technology. *Ethics and Information Technology* 19(4): 277–294.

Correa LA., et al. (2015) Individual quantum probes for optimal thermometry. *Physical Review Letters* 114(22): 220405.

Daley AJ., et al. (2022) Practical quantum advantage in quantum simulation. *Nature* 607(7920): 667–676.

de Wolf R. (2017) The potential impact of quantum computers on society. *Ethics and Information Technology* 19(4): 271–276.

DiVincenzo DP. (2017) Scientists and citizens: Getting to quantum technologies. *Ethics and Information Technology* 19(4): 247–251.

Emani PS., et al. (2021) Quantum computing at the frontiers of biological sciences. *Nature Methods* 18(7): 701–709.

Flöther F., et al. (2022) *Exploring quantum computing use cases for life sciences.* IBM Institute for Business Value.

Flöther F. (2023) The state of quantum computing applications in health and medicine. *Research Directions: Quantum Technologies* 1:e10.

Flöther F. (2025) Chapter 6 - Early quantum computing applications on the path towards precision medicine. In: Kelly L., Stanford WP. (eds) *Implementation of Personalized Precision Medicine.* (Elsevier, United States of America).

Fu L., et al. (2025) The applications and advances of artificial intelligence in drug regulation: A global perspective. *Acta Pharmaceutica Sinica B* 15(1): 1–14.

Gatenby RA., Frieden BR. (2007) Information Theory in Living Systems, Methods, Applications, and Challenges. *Bulletin of Mathematical Biology* 69(2): 635–657.

Ghamsari MS., Baniasadi F. (2024) Quantum for biology: Spectroscopy and sensing. *Innovation and Emerging Technologies* 11:2430005.

Gottesman D. (2010) An Introduction to Quantum Error Correction and Fault-Tolerant Quantum Computation. *Quantum information science and its contributions to mathematics, Proceedings of Symposia in Applied Mathematics* 63: 13–58.

Grinbaum A. (2017) Narratives of quantum theory in the age of quantum technologies. *Ethics and Information Technology* 19(4): 295–306.

Heidari N., et al. (2024) A quantum-enhanced precision medicine application to support data-driven clinical decisions for the personalized treatment of advanced knee osteoarthritis: development and preliminary validation of precisionKNEE_QNN. *Cureus* 16(1).

Hildebrandt M. (2016) Law as Information in the Era of Data-Driven Agency. *The Modern Law Review* 79(1): 1–30.

Hildebrandt M. (2018) Law as computation in the era of artificial legal intelligence: Speaking law to the power of statistics. *University of Toronto Law Journal* 68(Supplement 1):12–35.

Jiang C., et al. (2018) Probability-interval hybrid uncertainty analysis for structures with both aleatory and epistemic uncertainties: a review. *Structural and Multidisciplinary Optimization* 57(6):2485–2502.

Johnson WG. (2018) Governance Tools for the Second Quantum Revolution. *Jurimetrics* 59(4): 487.

Joos E., et al. (2013) *Decoherence and the Appearance of a Classical World in Quantum Theory* (Springer-Verlag Berlin Heidelberg, New York).

Joshi G., et al. (2024) FDA-Approved Artificial Intelligence and Machine Learning (AI/ML)-Enabled Medical Devices: An Updated Landscape. *Electronics* 13(3): 498.

Kairon P., Bhattacharyya S. (2021) COVID-19 outbreak prediction using quantum neural networks. In: Bhattacharyya, S., Paramartha, D., Kakali, D. (eds) *Intelligence Enabled Research.* (Springer, Singapore).

Kathuria K., et al. (2020) Implementation of a hamming distance-like genomic quantum classifier using inner products on ibmqx2 and ibmq_16_melbourne. *Quantum Machine Intelligence* 2(7):1–26.

Kavitha SS., Kaulgud N. (2023) Quantum K-means clustering method for detecting heart disease using quantum circuit approach. *Soft Computing* 27(18): 13255–13268.

Kiani BT., et al. (2020) Quantum medical imaging algorithms. arXiv:2004.02036.

Kirsopp JJ., et al. (2022) Quantum computational quantification of protein-ligand interactions. *International Journal of Quantum Chemistry* 122(22): 26975.

Kiss O., et al. (2022) Quantum neural networks force fields generation. *Machine Learning: Science and Technology* 3(3): 035004.

Kop M. (2021a) Establishing a legal-ethical framework for quantum technology. *Yale Law School, Yale Journal of Law & Technology (YJoLT), The Record.*

Kop M. (2021b) Ethics in the quantum age. *Physics World* 34(12): 31.

Kop M., et al. (2023) *Towards responsible quantum technology.* Harvard Berkman Klein Center for Internet & Society Research Publication Series.

Kop M., et al. (2024a) Ten principles for responsible quantum innovation. *Quantum Science and Technology* 9(3): 035013.

Kop M., et al. (2024b) A Brief Quantum Medicine Policy Guide. Harvard Law School, Petrie-Flom Center Bill of Health.

Kop M., et al. (2024c) *How Quantum Technologies May Be Integrated Into Healthcare, What Regulators Should Consider.* Stanford Law School.

Koshland DE. (2002) The Seven Pillars of Life. *Science* 295(5563): 2215–2216.

Krunic Z., et al. (2022) Quantum kernels for real-world predictions based on electronic health records. *IEEE Transactions on Quantum Engineering* 3: 1–11.

Landman J., et al. (2022) Quantum Methods for Neural Networks and Application to Medical Image Classification. *Quantum* 6:881.

Li J., et al. (2021a) Drug discovery approaches using quantum machine learning. In: *2021 58th ACM/ IEEE Design Automation Conference (DAC).* (IEEE).

Li J., et al. (2021b) Quantum Generative Models for Small Molecule Drug Discovery. *IEEE Transactions on Quantum Engineering* 2:1–8.

Li W., et al. (2024) A hybrid quantum computing pipeline for real world drug discovery. *Scientific Reports* 14(1):16942.

Liu H., et al. (2022) Prospects of quantum computing for molecular sciences. *Materials Theory* 6(1): 11.

Luisi PL. (1998) About various definitions of life. *Origins of Life and Evolution of the Biosphere* 28(4): 613–622.

Luo S. (2005) Quantum versus classical uncertainty. *Theoretical and Mathematical Physics* 143(2): 681–688.

Macklem PT., Seely A. (2010) Towards a Definition of Life. *Perspectives in Biology and Medicine* 53(3): 330–340.

Maheshwari D., et al. (2023) Quantum Machine Learning Applied to Electronic Healthcare Records for Ischemic Heart Disease Classification. *Human-centric Computing and Information Sciences* 13(06): 1–18.

Malone FD., et al. (2022) Towards the simulation of large scale protein-ligand interactions on NISQ-era quantum computers. *Chemical Science* 13(11): 3094–3108.

Mantus D., Pisano DJ. (eds) (2014) *FDA Regulatory Affairs.* (Taylor & Francis Group, Boca Raton).

Marchant GE., et al. (2011) *The Growing Gap between Emerging Technologies and Legal-Ethical Oversight: The Pacing Problem.* (Springer, Netherlands).

Marchant GE. (2020) Governance of Emerging Technologies as a Wicked Problem. *Vanderbilt Law Review* 73:1861–1877.

Marchant GE., Abbott KW. (2012) International Harmonization of Nanotechnology Governance Through "Soft Law" Approaches. *Nanotechnology Law & Business* 9: 393–399.

Marchant GE., et al. (2009) What Does the History of Technology Regulation Teach Us About Nano Oversight. *Journal of Law, Medicine & Ethics* 37(4): 724.

Marchant GE., et al. (2024) Learning from emerging technology governance for guiding quantum technology. *Rich JL & Tech* 31: 266.

Marchant GE., Wallach W. (2015) Coordinating Technology Governance. *Issues in Science & Technology* 31(4).

Marchetti L., et al. (2022) Quantum computing algorithms: Getting closer to critical problems in computational biology. *Briefings in Bioinformatics* 23(6): 437.

McKinsey & Company (2024) Quantum Computing: The Time to Act is Now. (Feb 2024). Available at: https://www.mckinsey.com/capabilities/mckinsey-digital/our-insights/tech-forward/quantum-computing-the-time-to-act-is-now. Accessed 5 Oct 2025.

McWeeney S., et al. (2023) Quantum Computing for Biomedical Computational and Data Sciences: A Joint DOE-NIH Roundtable. National Institutes of Health.
Mensa S., et al. (2023) Quantum machine learning framework for virtual screening in drug discovery: a prospective quantum advantage. *Machine Learning: Science and Technology* 4(1): 015023.
Moradi S., et al. (2022) Clinical data classification with noisy intermediate scale quantum computers. *Scientific Reports* 12(1):1–9.
Moses LB. (2011) Sui Generis Rules. In: Cutter, A., Gordijn, B., Marchant, GE., Pompidou, A. (eds) *The Growing Gap Between Emerging Technologies and Legal-Ethical Oversight: The Pacing Problem.* (Springer, New York).
Moses LB. (2017) Regulating in the Face of Sociotechnical Change. In: Brownsword R., Scotford E., Yeung K. (eds) *The Oxford Handbook of Law, Regulation and Technology.* (Oxford University Press, Oxford).
Nielsen MA., Chuang IL. (2011) *Quantum Computation and Quantum Information: 10th Anniversary Edition.* (Cambridge University Press, New York).
Niraula D., et al. (2021) Quantum deep reinforcement learning for clinical decision support in oncology: application to adaptive radiotherapy. *Scientific Reports* 11(1): 23545.
Outeiral C., et al. (2021) The prospects of quantum computing in computational molecular biology. *Wiley Interdisciplinary Reviews: Computational Molecular Science* 11(1): e1481.
Pal S., et al. (2024a) Future potential of quantum computing and simulations in biological science. *Molecular Biotechnology* 66(9): 2201–2218.
Pal S., et al. (2024b) Quantum computing in the next-generation computational biology landscape: From protein folding to molecular dynamics. *Molecular Biotechnology* 66(2):163–178.
Perrier E. (2022) The Quantum Governance Stack: Models of Governance for Quantum Information Technologies. *Digital Society* 1(3): 22.
Porsdam Mann S. et al. (2024) Guidelines for ethical use and acknowledgement of large language models in academic writing. *Nature Machine Intelligence* 6:1272–1274.
Preskill J. (2018) Quantum Computing in the NISQ era and beyond. *Quantum* 2: 79.
Preskill J. (2021) Quantum computing 40 years later. arXiv:2106.10522.
Prousalis K., Konofaos N. (2019) A quantum pattern recognition method for improving pairwise sequence alignment. *Scientific Reports* 9(1): 7226.
Pyrkov A., et al. (2024) Complexity of life sciences in quantum and AI era. *Wiley Interdisciplinary Reviews: Computational Molecular Science* 14(1): e1701.
Raymer MG., Monroe C. (2019) The US National Quantum Initiative. *Quantum Science and Technology* 4(2): 020504.
Robert A., et al. (2021) Resource-efficient quantum algorithm for protein folding. *npj Quantum Information* 7(1): 38.
Ruiz-Mirazo K., et al. (2004) A universal definition of life: autonomy and open-ended evolution. *Origins of Life and Evolution of the Biosphere* 34(3): 323–346.
Sagingalieva A., et al. (2023) Hybrid quantum neural network for drug response prediction. *Cancers* 15(10): 2705.
Sarkar A., et al. (2021) Estimating algorithmic information using quantum computing for genomics applications. *Applied Sciences* 11(6): 2696.
Sharples F., et al. (2021) Quantum Science Concepts in Enhancing Sensing and Imaging Technologies: Applications for Biology: Proceedings of a Workshop. National Academies of Sciences, Engineering, and Medicine.
Shimada T., et al. (2025) Nanobiodevices and quantum life science for future healthcare. *Analytical Sciences* 41: 601–607.
Soumya K., et al. (2023) A comprehensive review on carbon quantum dots as an effective photosensitizer and drug delivery system for cancer treatment. *Biomedical Technology* 4: 11–20.
Stephens K. (2025) FDA Proposes Framework for AI-Enabled Medical Devices. AXIS Imaging News. (8 January 2025).
Terstappen GC., Reggiani A. (2001) In silico research in drug discovery. *Trends in pharmacological sciences* 22(1): 23–26.

Thierer A. (2021) U.S. Artificial Intelligence Governance in the Obama-Trump Years. *IEEE Transactions on Technology and Society* 2(4):175–179.
Tirard S., et al. (2010) The definition of life: a brief history of an elusive scientific endeavor. *Astrobiology* 10(10): 1003–1009.
Tiwari PK., et al. (2021) Pivotal Role of Quantum Dots in the Advancement of Healthcare Research. *Computational Intelligence and Neuroscience* 2021(1): 2096208.
U.S. Food and Drug Administration. (2021) Artificial intelligence/machine learning (AI/ML)-Based Software as a Medical Device (SAMD).
U.S. Food and Drug Administration. (2024a) Predetermined Change Control Plans for Machine Learning-Enabled Medical Devices: Guiding Principles.
U.S. Food and Drug Administration. (2024b) Transparency for Machine Learning-Enabled Medical Devices: Guiding Principles.
U.S. Food and Drug Administration. (2024c) Marketing Submission Recommendations for a Predetermined Change Control Plan for Artificial Intelligence-Enabled Device Software Functions.
U.S. Food and Drug Administration. (2025a) Artificial Intelligence and Machine Learning in Software as a Medical Device.
U.S. Food and Drug Administration. (2025b) Good Machine Learning Practice for Medical Device Development: Guiding Principles.
U.S. Food and Drug Administration. (2025c) Artificial Intelligence for Drug Development.
U.S. Food and Drug Administration. (2025d) Using Artificial Intelligence & Machine Learning in the Development of Drug & Biological Products.
U.S. Food and Drug Administration. (2025e). Artificial Intelligence and Medical Products: How CBER, CDER, CDRH, and OCP are Working Together.
U.S. Food and Drug Administration. (2025f). Considerations for the Use of Artificial Intelligence To Support Regulatory Decision-Making for Drug and Biological Products.
Vermaas PE. (2017) The societal impact of the emerging quantum technologies: A renewed urgency to make quantum theory understandable. *Ethics and Information Technology* 19(4): 241–246.
Wang N., Liu GQ., Leong WH., et al. (2018) Magnetic criticality enhanced hybrid nanodiamond thermometer under ambient conditions. *Physical Review X* 8:011042.
Warraich HJ., et al. (2025) FDA perspective on the regulation of artificial intelligence in health care and biomedicine. *JAMA* 333(3): 241–247.
Watrous J. (2018) *The Theory of Quantum Information*. (Cambridge University Press, Cambridge).
Williamson ED. (2017) Life sciences today and tomorrow: emerging biotechnologies. *Critical Reviews in Biotechnology* 37(5): 553–565.
Wiseman HM., Milburn GJ. (2010) *Quantum Measurement and Control*. (Cambridge University Press, Cambridge).
Wootters WK., Zurek WH. (1982) A single quantum cannot be cloned. *Nature* 299(5886): 802–803.
Yukawa H., et al. (2025) Quantum life science: biological nano quantum sensors, quantum technology-based hyperpolarized MRI/NMR, quantum biology, and quantum biotechnology. *Chemical Society Reviews* 54: 3293–3322.
Zinner M., et al. (2022a) Quantum computing's potential for drug discovery: Early stage industry dynamics. *Drug Discovery Today* 26(7): 1680–1688.
Zinner M., et al. (2022b) Toward the institutionalization of quantum computing in pharmaceutical research. *Drug Discovery Today* 27(2): 378–383.

Chapter 4
Toward a Framework for Ethical Quantum Computing: Foundations and Research Directions

Elija Perrier

4.1 Introduction

Quantum information processing[1] (including quantum computing, quantum communication and quantum sensing) and machine learning represent two of the most significant fields of computational science to have emerged over the last half century. Over the last decade, large public investments, national strategies and industrial roadmaps have created a new global quantum revolution, driven by initiatives such as the EU Quantum Flagship, US National Quantum Initiative, Chinese national quantum strategy, and analogous programs in the UK, Japan and Australia.[2] At the same time, artificial intelligence technologies are rapidly reshaping the technological landscape. As a result, attention has begun to focus upon the ethical implications of machine learning technology, resulting in the emergence of a burgeoning multidisciplinary field dedicated to the ethics of emergent technologies. For example, the ethics of automation and artificial intelligence covers diverse fields, including fair machine learning,[3] distributive justice, representational justice and jurisprudence. While ethical analyses are advanced or advancing rapidly in many such disciplines, one omission is the absence of a dedicated research program into the ethics of quantum information processing technologies more generally. Some recent scholarship has sought to address this gap, including work on high-level legal frameworks for

[1] Watrous (2018).

[2] European Commission (2021), Atladóttir et al. (2025).

[3] Caton and Haas (2024), Dwork et al. (2012).

E. Perrier (✉)
Centre for Quantum Software and Information, University of Technology, Sydney, Australia

Centre for Law, Medicine and Life Sciences (LML), University of Cambridge, Cambridge, United Kingdom

M. Aboy et al. (eds.), *Quantum Technology Governance II*, Perspectives in Law, Business and Innovation, https://doi.org/10.1007/978-981-92-3768-5_4

quantum technology,[4] legal and ethical implications,[5] overview articles[6] and responsible quantum innovation literature[7] along with earlier high-level work covering societal impacts.[8] Quantum-specific risks such as post-quantum cryptographic disruption, sensing-based surveillance technologies, quantum communication, quantum-internet architectures, and dual-use scenarios have motivated an expansion in the literature on quantum governance and security.[9] Other examples include the World Economic Forum Quantum Computing Governance Principles[10] that set out a more substantive set of guidelines for thinking about the ethics of quantum information processing technologies, which we denote *quantum ethics*.

Yet despite growing research interest in quantum ethics, there is little in the way of a systematic exposition of how quantum ethics as a research program ought to be undertaken. Doing so, we argue, is necessary to address the central question of quantum ethics, namely what is *sui generis*, if anything, about ethical dilemmas raised by quantum technology, by comparison with ethics in general, or other ethical considerations (such as those pertaining to artificial intelligence) in particular. To address this need, we (i) propose a structured roadmap of quantum ethics research and (ii) provide a set of formal taxonomies that connect quantum formalism and ethical theories (and the ways in which unique features of quantum technologies distinguish them from their classical counterpart in ethically relevant ways) in ways we hope are pragmatically useful for researchers.

Our approach is aimed at setting out a relatively comprehensive roadmap for quantum ethics and also connects technical aspects of quantum information processing with ethical formalism—a connection that has to date been missing from the literature. Thus, our intention is as much a call for research as it is an attempt to exemplify one type of ethical research into quantum ethics which we believe will be of benefit in theoretical and applied settings.

We note that many ethical challenges raised by quantum technologies can be understood as an evolution of issues encountered in earlier technological paradigms, including classical computation, the internet, and artificial intelligence. That said, the distinctive features of quantum information processing such as probabilistic computation, superposition, entanglement, and limited observability introduce additional considerations that also warrant quantum-specific ethical analysis. In particular, these features complicate assumptions of transparency and determinism, requiring

---

[4] Perrier (2022), Kop et al. (2021a, b, c, 2023, 2024a, b), Johnson (2018).

[5] Hoofnagle Garfinkel (2021), Aboy et al. (2022).

[6] Kop (2021a).

[7] Ten Holter et al. (2021).

[8] Coenen and Grunwald (2017), Coenen et al. (2022), de Wolf (2017), DiVincenzo (2017), Grinbaum (2017), Vermaas (2017).

[9] Alagic et al. (2024, 2022), Lu et al. (2022), Malia et al. (2022), Neumann et al. (2020), Vermaas et al. (2025), Possati and Vermaas (2025), van der Enden et al. (2024).

[10] World Economic Forum (2022) (note the principles were in part coauthored by this chapter's authors drawing on concepts from early drafts of this chapter).

quantum-specific ethical evaluation to consider not only outcomes but also the processes of computation themselves.

The scope of this chapter is primarily on quantum computation technologies (which we for brevity refer to as 'quantum technologies'), though we also touch upon quantum communication (which can in principle be considered forms of computation, if that term is broadly construed to capture information processing itself).[11] While quantum sensing (covering use of quantum systems for measurement or metrology) is traditionally incorporated within quantum information processing, we do not focus on such technologies in this chapter.

4.1.1 The Sui Generis Question: Why Quantum Ethics?

It is legitimate to ask whether the ethical or moral considerations applicable to quantum technologies are significantly different from those relevant to computational technologies in general. That is, what is *sui generis* about the ethical implications of quantum technology? To motivate research into the ethics of quantum technology, we must ask: is there anything distinct about the ethics of *quantum* computing in particular? Or can the types of ethical analyses applicable to other technologies simply be transferred to the case of quantum technologies? Is quantum ethics well-motivated? Our answer to this question, is yes: while the types of normative considerations applicable to quantum technologies will also apply to other technologies, such as automated algorithmic technologies in general, there are distinct features of both (a) how computing is undertaken in quantum systems and (b) the consequences of quantum computing which distinguish research programs into quantum ethics.

At the technical level, the distinct (by contrast with classical computing) characteristics of quantum computation, including its inherently probabilistic nature, the availability of superposition states and resources such as entanglement have distinct implications for the technical implementation of computational ethical regimes reliant on classical features of computation, including proposals regarding the implementation of algorithmic governance,[12] fair machine learning, cryptography and representational justice. These technical characteristics of quantum technologies are the basis upon which they offer the promise of an exponential increase in computing power, offering the potential to not only solve certain intractable problems in higher-order complexity classes that are unsolvable on any classical computer. They may also render feasible computations which, while theoretically tractable on a classical computer, take such time or inordinate resources that they are effectively intractable, at least by timescales that matter to humans. That said, such claims should be interpreted with care. While quantum algorithms are widely believed to offer substantial speedups for certain problem classes, and in some cases to render previously intractable problems practically solvable, the precise boundaries between quantum

[11] This chapter is a version of previously unpublished work from 2021 that has since been updated.

[12] Johnston (2015).

and classical computational capabilities remain an active area of research. In many cases, quantum advantage is best understood in terms of problems for which no efficient classical algorithms are currently known, rather than problems that are provably unsolvable by classical means.

While much is made of the ability of quantum computers to solve certain exponentially hard problems (such as via the application of Shor's algorithm in cryptographic contexts,[13] a technological feat with possible consequences for geopolitics, privacy and social communication), the more immediate implications of quantum computing may arise through its effective expansion of resources available for classical computation i.e. in enabling classically infeasible computations that directly impact populations (such as simulations of population behavior) to now be undertaken, or to overcome scaling barriers faced by classical computation. Nevertheless, as we discuss below, widespread access to quantum algorithms which may enable both decryption of classically encrypted data and encryption of data in a way that cannot be decrypted (such as by law enforcement) raises serious ethical and moral dilemmas which may, according to some ethical stances, necessitate controls or restrictions upon access to such technology in a way not currently envisaged by stakeholders. It is important to note that the impact of quantum computing on cryptography is not uniform across all encryption schemes. While quantum algorithms such as Shor's pose a significant threat to widely deployed public-key systems (e.g. RSA and elliptic curve cryptography), many symmetric encryption schemes are comparatively less affected, typically requiring only adjustments such as increased key sizes to maintain security. And claims regarding "unbreakable" encryption should be understood in the context of specific protocols and assumptions. While certain quantum cryptographic schemes, such as quantum key distribution, can provide strong or even information-theoretic security under appropriate conditions, their practical security depends on implementation details and threat models. Moreover, there remains considerable uncertainty about precisely what benefits quantum computing will provide by contrast with rapidly scaling classical computing.

To this end, we set out a roadmap for ethical quantum computing. Our aim is to contribute to development of this important and we believe imminently significant field of multidisciplinary research by situating the emergence of quantum computation and its consequences within the broad nexus of ethics, moral philosophy, economics and discourses on ethical computation and algorithms. We aim to provide an overview of key technical features of quantum technologies of relevance to ethical approaches and theories. Of course, any such list cannot be comprehensive given the multidimensional nature of quantum computing and quantum information processing as a discipline.

We hope to provide researchers across the multiplicity of relevant domains, including quantum science, computer science, ethics, philosophy, social sciences, economics and policy a way to understand the ethics of quantum computing in a cross-disciplinary way, providing a point of entry of researchers in one field, such as quantum science, to another, such as algorithmic ethics and moral philosophy.

[13] Shor (1994, 1997).

By doing so, we hope to outline not just why ethical quantum computing is necessarily a multi-disciplinary process, but why understanding and, to the extent possible, managing or even solving ethical dilemmas arising from the use of quantum technologies is necessarily a cross-disciplinary endeavor, where no one field has a monopoly on normative conclusions and where collaboration across the disciplinary aisle is essential.

This chapter advances several core contributions to the emerging field of quantum ethics. First, we argue that quantum technologies give rise to sui generis ethical challenges, grounded in their distinctive computational features, including probabilistic evolution, superposition, entanglement and limited observability. These features necessitate a shift from purely outcome-based ethical analysis to frameworks that also evaluate the processes of computation themselves. Secondly, we propose a structured research roadmap spanning technical foundations, governance and stakeholder responsibility, and risk management, aimed at providing a coherent basis for interdisciplinary research. Thirdly, we demonstrate how ethical constraints must be embedded within the design and control of quantum systems, rather than treated as external constraints, and introduce the "four C's"—computability, complexity, consistency and controllability—as a framework for assessing the feasibility of ethically constrained quantum computation. Finally, we illustrate how quantum technologies reshape existing domains of ethical inquiry, including fairness in machine learning, privacy and cryptography, and distributive justice, highlighting the broader societal and geopolitical implications of quantum technological development.

4.1.2 Contributions

In concrete terms, the contributions of this chapter are as follows.

4.1.2.1 Overview of Quantum Ethics

An overview and roadmap of research into the ethical considerations and consequences of quantum technologies.

4.1.2.2 Quantum Ethics' Taxonomy

A taxonomy for quantum ethics, detailing how the unique characteristics of quantum information processing give rise to distinct ethical consequences for how ethics of quantum computing are characterized, measured and audited (e.g. via quantum fair machine learning).

4.1.2.3 Research Program Mapping

A mapping of potential research programs into the ethics of quantum simulations, privacy in quantum contexts and networked quantum systems.

4.1.2.4 Comparative Ethics Analysis

Situating quantum technologies within existing cross-disciplinary ethical frameworks within moral philosophy, economics and computer science.

4.1.3 Structure

The structure of this chapter is as follows. In Sections 2–4, we set out a high-level proposal for a sequential roadmap of quantum ethics' research covering foundational, technical and governance topics together with features of theoretical and empirical program design. The remaining parts of the chapter then explore specific elements of quantum computing and ethics of relevance to particular limbs of the roadmap.

Section 5 of the chapter provides a short overview of the key technical characteristics of quantum computation relevant to quantum ethics' research and the programs laid out in the previous section, providing a short synopsis of quantum postulates, quantum information processing and related fields including quantum cryptography. The section focuses in particular on key differences between classical and quantum computing in order to provide a basis for understanding how the unique nature of quantum computation potentially impacts the use and governance of computational systems in a way that differs from current (and often well-established) approaches in the classical sphere.

In Sect. 6, we introduce key concepts in ethical computational science, including algorithmic consequentialism and deontology and frame these within the context of quantum science. Sections 7 and 8 examine how the technical differences of quantum computing, as distinct from classical, lead to differences in algorithmic and computational framings, solutions and require consideration of ethical principles dependent upon the structure of computation itself (rather than just the outcome). The focus of this part is on how approaches to fairness in computation and machine learning vary or are impacted by the use of quantum data or quantum algorithms.

Section 9 considers individualized ethics and issues arising from the cryptographic consequences of quantum computing, networked quantum computers and the rapidly evolving plans for a quantum internet. In Sect. 10, we discuss a number of economic and distributive aspects of quantum computing, including geopolitical, economic and social welfare (access to resources) questions. Section 11 sets out a summary of our proposal for a roadmap for the development of quantum ethics, offering recommendations for priority research areas.

4.2 A Quantum Ethics Roadmap

4.2.1 Existing Literature

Work on the impacts of quantum technology has typically not included a systematic exposition of (i) how and why unique features of quantum information processing may give rise to unique ethical concerns and (ii) how such research into quantum ethics should be systematically undertaken or the types of taxonomies of use in such research. In particular, scant attention has been paid thus far to synthesizing formal technical features of quantum information processing with formal elements of ethical theories (such as establishing concepts of duties, responsibilities, rights etc. and then articulating how quantum technologies may affect or alter such normative claims or how ethical constraints might be encoded within quantum information processing protocols themselves).

4.2.1.1 Early Socio-Technical Analysis

Early attempts to address quantum ethics tended to examine potential societal impacts of quantum technology development primarily from high-level policy perspectives (such as work by Vermaas[14]) or brief canvassing of potential quantum technological impacts (e.g. DiVincenzo[15]) but with no engagement with technical literature of either ethics or quantum information processing. Other work of a more technical nature by Möller and Vuik examined the impact on scientific computing arising from the expansion of computational frontiers on computation that quantum technologies potentially afford[16] yet offered little in the way of systematic methodology or consideration of the ethical dimensions of such technological developments. Somewhat more germane work on the impacts of quantum information processing was offered by de Wolf,[17] where three key impacts of quantum computing on cryptography, search and simulation were examined. The primary concern raised in that paper regarded the potential distributional impacts of such technologies, but this was only addressed in a cursory way with no engagement in formal distributional ethics (or related work in economics) and as such lacked methodological utility beyond merely raising the prospect of unequal distribution of resources (something not unique or specific to quantum technology per se). Other research, such as work by Coenen and Grunwald[18] set out analyses of responsible research innovation practices for quantum technologies.

[14] Vermaas (2017).

[15] DiVincenzo (2017).

[16] Möller and Vuik (2017).

[17] de Wolf (2017).

[18] Coenen and Grunwald (2017).

Most of these early works provided mostly high-level analysis of where research and governance policy relating to quantum technological development fits within the broader field of technology policy more generally together with a discursive analysis of the framing and narratives of quantum technology by comparison with nanotechnologies. The result of that work is a prescription for research programs focused on (i) avoiding technological hype, (ii) taking care with respect to narrative framing of quantum technological development. While the discursive treatment of quantum technology is an important feature of the ethical governance of such technology, its conclusions are generic (i.e. they could apply to any technology and indeed are mostly drawn from applying experiences in nanotechnology discourse to quantum), rather than offering anything that may be regarded as a systematic research program, engagement with formal ethical theories or pragmatic guidance for how one conducts ethical calculus in a quantum setting. Related work has also considered how concepts and technological impacts from quantum information processing may be communicated pedagogically and to broader audiences (e.g. Grinbaum[19]), yet only tangentially touches on how such discursive reframings may or may not relate to ethical questions.

4.2.1.2 Quantum Governance Frameworks

A more recent second wave[20] of research on the ethical implications of quantum technology has focused on governance protocols and situating quantum ethics within technology ethics more broadly. An example is Kop's work on situating quantum ethics within broader principles applicable to related technology (such as artificial intelligence)[21] which has seen an explosion of interest and governance. Ten Holter et al.[22] approached the question of quantum governance pragmatically, setting out recommendations for how to (empirically) engage stakeholders across the quantum sector when developing responsible research practices in the area. Other work in the governance context[23] examined impacts upon intellectual property principles of quantum technology[24] which, while not directly related to ethics, would indirectly affect ethical matters of concern, such as property rights and distributional/access issues surrounding quantum technology. Johnson[25] provided a useful overview of how 'soft governance' instruments, such as frameworks, principles and the like, may be of use for quantum governance.

---

[19] Grinbaum (2017).

[20] Kop et al. (2024a).

[21] Kop (2021a).

[22] Ten Holter et al. (2021).

[23] Kop (2021b).

[24] Aboy et al. (2022).

[25] Johnson (2018).

More jurisprudential analysis, such as that of Hoofnagle and Garfinkel,[26] provided a comprehensive treatment of quantum-era privacy, cybersecurity and regulation. Recent legal scholarship has also analyzed intellectual property and legal adaptation for quantum technologies.[27] The impact of government and institutional initiatives, such as the NIST PQC standardization effort[28] and legislation such as the US *Quantum Computing Cybersecurity Preparedness Act* has also been assessed for its impact upon the global cybersecurity landscape, raising ethical questions around transition timelines, equitable access and global security asymmetries.[29] The landscape of post-quantum cryptography is evolving rapidly, with recent standardization efforts formalizing candidate algorithms and shaping transition timelines, underscoring the dynamic nature of quantum-related cybersecurity risks. Recent research at the time of writing, for example, has seen extraordinary progress in the potential for the implementation of Shor's algorithm using several orders-of-magnitude reduction in qubit resources, bringing the reality of quantum decryption much closer.[30] Research has also included the extent to which national governance frameworks related to quantum technology have integrated ethical principles,[31] the importance of public trust in quantum governance[32] and ethical considerations regarding networked quantum internet infrastructure.[33] Other work, including comparative analysis against AI regulation and nanotechnology governance has started to bridge the technical divide to some degree.[34] These approaches provide an example of somewhat more engagement with the technicalities of quantum technology in their normative analysis of quantum networks.[35] In addition, the development of structured assessment tools such as the EQTA, the QTIA framework, and the Rathenau Institute's 2023 survey of quantum technology in society[36] reflects a broader shift toward systematic, anticipatory evaluation of the societal and ethical dimensions of emerging quantum technologies.

While these recent and earlier attempts at exploring quantum ethics are important in canvassing a number of issues, they have generally not emphasized any systematic consideration of how and where quantum ethics as a field should evolve. There has in general also been a lack of integration with formal normative theories (e.g. little mention of consequentialism versus deontology for example), the expansive literature on technology governance and jurisprudence (with some exceptions) or risk-management literature (which is of particular relevance to how one operationalizes

[26] Hoofnagle Garfinkel (2021).

[27] Aboy et al. (2022).

[28] Alagic et al. (2024; 2022).

[29] Rand (2023).

[30] Cain et al. (2026), Babbush et al. (2026).

[31] Atladóttir et al. (2025).

[32] Vermaas et al. (2025).

[33] van der Enden et al. (2024).

[34] Vermaas et al. (2025), Possati and Vermaas (2025), Marchant et al. (2024).

[35] Chiribella et al. (2009).

[36] Rathenau Instituut (2023).

ethical constraints). In general, the literature on quantum governance exhibits limited consideration of or engagement with formal computational science approaches on encoding ethical criteria within the functioning of technology itself (as we discuss below). It is clear that as a cross-disciplinary field, the ethics of quantum information technologies has thus far lacked any cohesive framework for how research into the area should be conducted and any conceptual exploration of how ethical constraints would or could actually be encoded within the design of quantum technologies themselves.

4.2.2 Roadmap

As an emerging cross-disciplinary field at the intersection of a raft of expansive fields, quantum ethics as a discipline faces considerable definitional challenges from its inception. Any research program seeking cover under the flag of such polysemous terminology must provide, if it is to develop with theoretical rigor and practical utility, a well-defined and bounded set of concepts and methods. In this chapter, we do not lay claim to any canonical formulation of quantum ethics. But we do seek to provide introductory structure, concepts and methods to such a field by setting out a strategic roadmap and guideposts for quantum ethics research programs (**QEP**). The aim of the roadmap is to propose for researchers and stakeholders in quantum technology, governance and ethics a set of research imperatives that will facilitate scholarship and thinking around the ethics and governance of quantum computation.

The roadmap is set out in a loosely sequential manner. We argue that for QEP to contribute meaningfully to debates over quantum ethics and regulation, firstly what we denote the 'technical foundations' of such programs must be fleshed out. Such an initial research program would be driven by ethical design principles and therefore necessitate an understanding of the ways in which quantum technologies technically differ from their classical counterparts with respect to properties such as system control, information processing and output when it comes to imposing ethical constraints upon such systems. Placing this program at the beginning, as it were, then enables researchers to situate quantum technologies within the expansive landscape of technological ethics and governance literature in order to facilitate the development of the second part of the roadmap, research into quantum governance models.

With a solid understanding of the similarities and differences of quantum technology with respect to ethical design and control, QEP can then proceed to analysing the extent that (a) existing governance regimes are suitable for managing quantum technologies or (b) new or novel governance or institutional frameworks are needed to manage quantum technologies. For example, quantum communications technology may or may not give rise to new considerations outside the current remit of communications governance. A third part of our roadmap then proposes research into risk-management techniques specifically tailored for quantum technologies and the roles, duties and responsibilities, guided by existing risk theory. The objective of such

Table 1 A taxonomy of quantum ethics research program components

Pillar	Detail
Technical foundations	• **Foundational theory:** o Formalising ethical constraints in terms of quantum information-processing mechanisms o Devising theoretical models to represent ethical classification of quantum procedures and outcomes • **Ethical quantum design:** o Design of quantum systems or algorithms to implement ethical or moral constraints o Design of interfaces with quantum technologies in order to satisfy moral or ethical criteria
Ethical governance	• **Quantum governance:** o Research into applicability of existing technological governance frameworks to quantum technologies o Development of new institutional and governance practices to cater for unique ethical or moral consequences of quantum computation • **Quantum stakeholders:** o Research into ethical duties, obligations and responsibilities of different stakeholders in quantum sectors (e.g., governments, corporations)
Ethical risk management	• **Quantum risk protocols:** o Research into upside and downside risks of quantum computing and related technologies o Research regarding adaptation of existing risk protocols and standards for quantum technologies and institutions • **Quantum transformation management:** o Research into likely transformational impacts of quantum technologies on different constituencies o Research regarding optimal ways to manage such transformational impacts balancing opportunities and risks

research is to provide more granular and useful research for the diverse array of quantum stakeholders involved in the technology's development and use, such as governments, corporations, academia and the public and private sectors. A more detailed example of this analysis is set out via the governance stack model.[37] We summarize our roadmap taxonomy in Table 1 below and elucidate details of such programs below.

4.2.3 *Contextualizing Quantum Ethics*

Any QEP undertaking should situate itself within and draw upon existing approaches to technological ethics. It is important therefore that each limb of any QEP clearly identify the extent to which (i) existing theory or practice can be applied to research into and solving ethical dilemmas arising from quantum technologies; and (ii) novel

[37] Perrier (2022).

approaches to theory, practice or governance are required. The world abounds with technology ethics' theories, frameworks, practices and norms of institutional governance. QEP should where possible avoid 'reinventing the wheel' and instead draw upon existing approaches. For example, the rich body of national and international jurisprudence regarding the governance of technology provides a ready-made basis upon which governance practices for quantum stakeholders and institutions may be based. Conversely, it is important that research into quantum ethics does not simply treat quantum technologies as equivalent to other computational or engineering technologies where to do so would be inappropriate. As we argue below, there are unique characteristics of quantum computation, quantum information processing and certain quantum technologies which motivate the development of quantum-specific ethical epistemology.

QEP are necessarily cross-disciplinary. And as with any cross-disciplinary project, a considerable part of any QEP will involve a process of translation between concepts in one field, such as theoretical quantum computation, to others, such as ethics. At a pragmatic level, this will involve, as is common within quantum-related subdisciplines, extracting 'quantum equivalents' of classical results, such as in quantum communications theory or indeed quantum computing itself. Thus, a fruitful line of research for researchers interested in QEP is to consider how to map the epistemology of ethics to an applied quantum context. Quantum computation has the benefit of being able to draw upon extensive fields at the crossroads of computer science, ethics and decision-theory.

Moreover, when seeking to undertake cross-disciplinary work in computational ethics, it is incumbent on researchers to be aware that the field of ethics itself contains a rich set of decision-procedures and resources for reasoning through ethical dilemmas. A myriad of disciplines from formal ethics to moral philosophy, to economic sciences to name a few provide well-established techniques for systematically defining and resolving (or at least going some way to resolving) such dilemmas. So too do jurisprudential disciplines which, for example, provide often canonical examples of applied deontological reasoning, from the establishment of duties to important concepts of responsibility, standards of care and liability.

4.3 Technical Foundations

The first element in a QEP roadmap involves establishing the technical basis of quantum ethics. Such a *technical foundations* branch would consist of laying out the foundational theorems and framing of quantum computational ethics.

4.3.1 Foundational Theory

The first part of QEP requires the translation of concepts from ethics into a formalism applicable to quantum computation. As we argue below, a number of the unique features of quantum computation, as distinct from classical computation, may lead to distinct ethical consequences. For example, the nature of quantum computation differs from classical computation in significant ways, such as: (i) in how information is encoded in quantum states (such as in superposition states and via basis and phase encoding); (ii) in how quantum systems evolve in the presence or absence of noise; (iii) in the inherent ontological stochasticity of quantum systems (as distinct from their classical counterpart); (iv) in how quantum systems may be measured, controlled or audited; (v) in the availability of certain resources such as entanglement which in turn give rise to novel information architectures unavailable in the classical setting; and (vi) in the unique consequences arising from the quantum nature of such computation, including the capacity to undertake computations that are inefficient or even intractable on classical computers. However, the interpretation of quantum probability remains a matter of ongoing debate within the philosophy of physics. While quantum theory is operationally probabilistic, differing interpretations attribute this either to intrinsic indeterminacy or to epistemic limitations, and our analysis does not depend on resolving these foundational questions.

Each of these distinguishing features potentially carries with it consequences for ethical analysis of quantum computation and quantum systems generally. This is most apparent when the ethical imperatives in question relate directly to the manner in which computation is undertaken itself. A motivating example which we discuss in some detail below is the case requirements for algorithms to meet certain ethical fairness criteria or the proscriptions on the inclusion or combination of certain features (such as protected attributes on the basis of race or ethnicity).

Classically, compliance with ethical requirements, such as those imposed by anti-discrimination principles or even legislation, can take the form of constraints upon inputs (e.g. certain inputs are proscribed), constraints upon form of a program and upon how computation unfolds (for example, prohibitions on combining sensitive confidentialized datasets in ways that allows individuals to be identified - a requirement typical when using Census microdata provided for academic research by government agencies), or constraints upon outputs, such as ensuring classification criteria (such as statistical parity or Lipschitz fairness) are met within certain tolerances.

In a quantum setting, in which quantum algorithms are utilized instead of (or in conjunction with) classical algorithms, the ways in which such ethical criteria are met will differ: the form of quantum computation is governed by Hamiltonian formalism; a quantum algorithm is stochastic, outcomes occur probabilistically rather than deterministically (for example, running the same program over and over again will not necessarily lead to identical output); the manner in which the computation may be controlled also differs; and overall there is much less certainty and because in order to undertake quantum computation, interactions with the quantum system must be kept to a minimum (e.g. only via measurements or control); in order to preserve quantum coherences, tomographic information about the exact nature of the execution of a quantum algorithm and its true evolution will usually remain limited. We expand on these foundational details in Sect. 5 (providing an overview of distinguishing features of quantum as distinct from classical computation) and Sect. 6 (covering ethical framing of computation itself).

4.3.2 Ethical Quantum Design Principles

An important initial focus of our roadmap and any QEP is to connect with the literature on 'ethical design', which considers pragmatic ways in which ethical constraints or criteria may be incorporated into the design of systems, institutions and technology themselves.[38] Examples in ethical research include the study of how institutional design mechanics can facilitate the realization of particular normative imperatives (e.g. Rawlsian principles of justice), encoding moral principles into system mechanics. As ethical design research notes, top-down, deductive, approaches where ideal moral or ethical actions are chosen and systems are then engineered in response suffer from a lack of specificity to be actionable, leading variously to exploration of reflective equilibrium or action-guiding methods. Moreover, given the ubiquity and increasing role of technology as the primary medium for human interactions (such as via social media or designed environments), ethical imperatives require consideration of the design interfaces between technologies and their users.

Specific research questions relevant to QEP from a design perspective include (i) technical specifications regarding how to encode ethical criteria within quantum algorithms (such as phase or basis encoding within Hamiltonians); (ii) research into different techniques for the control of quantum systems affects the degree of control that can be exerted on quantum algorithms to ensure ethical criteria are met; and (iii) understanding how the stochastic aspects of quantum computation may affect the degree of certainty required by normative or jurisprudential criteria. Section 8 in particular provides specific technical examples of how the design of quantum algorithms could be shaped by ethical considerations, drawing on, among other things, examples in classical computational planning literature.

The challenge of any ethical reasoning is to justify *why* a particular ethical constraint, theory or practice should be chosen out of many (to the extent distinct). While QEP should restrain consideration of such meta-ethical questions to remain useful, interrogating such foundational issues is in part unavoidable. For example, the types of concepts of fairness or equality, the types of rights or meaning of rights, according to which quantum systems should be managed is itself usually going to be contested: the values embodied in one set of ethical principles may not be acceptable to other constituencies or appropriate in other contexts.

---

[38] Hoven (2005), Hoven et al. (2015).

The challenge in part with computational technologies is that they in some sense 'put to proof' implicit assumptions or requirements about *how*, for example, an ethical decision-procedure should unfold because of the necessity to encode and design for that procedure within algorithms themselves. That is, the formal requirements of algorithms, which must be designed using logic, can force clarity or form upon ethical discussion which can reveal the inherent tensions (or vagueness) in ethical positions. Rudimentary examples from the world of classical machine learning, for example, include results demonstrating the intuitively obvious fact that ethics usually involves trade-offs, such as the intractability of sub-group statistical parity for arbitrary groups.[39] Other results from quantum logic show how classical principles such as correctness protocols (which may be required to satisfy computational audit requirements, for example) may differ in the case of quantum systems.[40] Ethical design must also contend with the appropriate way to reason through ethical or moral values when considering how to functionally or operationally embed them within quantum systems.

4.4 Quantum Governance and Responsibility

Together with more philosophical or formal theoretical ethical matters, pragmatic considerations regarding the governance and regulation of quantum technologies represent a key feature of QEP. While still nascent, there is now an emerging literature (and set of governance instruments) that examines the ways in which existing governance methodologies would apply to prospective quantum technologies and ways in which new or novel governance approaches may be needed as a result of the unique aspects of quantum systems (as discussed below). For example, national strategies, international standards, PQC migration frameworks, export-control regimes, dual-use sensing policies and quantum-internet roadmaps are emerging across different jurisdictions.[41] Kop et al. (2024a, b) emphasize this as a form of *anticipatory* and *adaptive* governance rather than reactive regulation. On the theoretical front, a governance-stack[42] based approach is being explored in a number of contexts as a means of providing a layered framework—from hardware and protocols to applications and societal structures—for mapping governance instruments to technological strata.

[39] Kearns et al. (2019).

[40] Yuan and Ying (2021).

[41] Atladóttir et al. (2025), Kop et al. (2023), Johnson (2018).

[42] Perrier (2022).

4.4.1 Quantum Governance

The quantum governance branch of QEP should aim to provide research into jurisprudence and governance. As with any technology, governance is a two-way street: quantum technologies, their design, use and distribution, must as with any technology be subject to the rules and conventions. Similarly, laws, regulations and ethical frameworks must be tailored to and fit for purpose with respect to quantum technologies. This may mean, for example, updating laws governing the use, combining or distribution of data containing protected or sensitive information in ways that take into account the unique characteristics of quantum computation (to combine information into superposition states, or limitations on accessing quantum information) directly within legislative regimes.

A potentially useful line of research for QEP concerns an auditing and accounting of the extent to which technology ethics and jurisprudence are fit for the distinct features of quantum technologies. Recent work in this direction aims to provide a high-level legal framework that proposes certain ethical design principles.[43] Other work considers the ways in which intellectual property jurisprudence, such as copyright, patent and trademark regulation, would apply to quantum technologies.[44] As with other fields of technology ethics, QEP can inform how to integrate various ethical considerations into competing objectives related to quantum technology. For example, while much technology ethics is concerned with downside risks, there are also costs and risks from overly constraining or shackling the development of quantum technologies in the name of moral virtue. Understanding the technical trade-offs or compatibility of mooted moral values with the need to foster innovation in quantum technologies is an example where QEP can add value to debates over governance.

4.4.2 Quantum Stakeholders

Reasoning about rights, duties and obligations of stakeholders is a cornerstone activity of many fields of ethics, especially deontological and jurisprudential ethical subdisciplines. In an applied and pragmatic setting, the regulation and governance of quantum technologies will necessarily involve conforming quantum governance regimes into existing jurisprudential frameworks which ascribe rights, duties and responsibilities upon a variety of persons, including individuals, associations, governments and corporations. As discussed in ethical design literature, the design of institutions that will not only govern quantum technologies, but also be involved in their development and deployment, should factor in the particular ethical and moral outcomes that are sought. As such, an important feature in QEP focused on quantum governance will involve an initial mapping of 'quantum stakeholders,'

[43] Kop (2021a).

[44] Aboy et al. (2025).

those constituencies, institutions and agents involved in quantum technological ecosystems.

Such stakeholders include governments, multinational institutions, academia, corporations and individuals, the rights, duties and responsibilities of which in relation to quantum technology will differ depending on context. One such approach that reckons with differences in stakeholder interests and which has influenced subsequent approaches[45] to quantum governance is the governance stack model.[46] Under this model, governance as a process involves mapping the technical stack (in this case, of quantum technology) to the rights and interests of stakeholders. Governance instruments—such as legislation, regulation, policy and so on—are then identified which appropriately mediate the relationships between stakeholders. For example, legislation as an instrument regulating behavior between government and corporations may suit certain requirements (e.g. dual use policy objectives), while other instruments, such as contracts or even soft-governance policy may be more appropriate for regulating interactions among stakeholders during the early-stage of quantum technology innovation.

4.4.2.1 Governments and Multinational Institutions

The regulatory, policy and economic power of nation States makes them the primary stakeholders in any quantum governance regime both at the intranational level (via municipal laws and regulations) and internationally, via treaties, concordats and other multilateral and bilateral instruments. Governments have also to date been the primary economic investors and drivers in the development of quantum technologies and quantum computation, such as via direct programs and, in particular, national defense institutions (such as DARPA). QEP programs could focus upon a fine-grained ethical analysis of the types of duties governments would owe and other normative responsibilities towards their constituencies and how these in turn would shape governmental policy and legislative responses.

Furthermore, given the tight nexus between investment in quantum technology and defense, research programs in this area may also focus on the geo-strategic implications of quantum technologies. Indeed, the fact that the majority of funding for quantum outside academia has largely been via defense-connected institutions and the inclusion of quantum in national strategic outlooks (e.g. China's five-year plans), illustrates how such geostrategic analysis is both timely and relevant to real-world considerations. A similar analysis would also apply, albeit in a different jurisprudential context, regarding multilateral institutions. Comparative analyses reveal that national strategies emphasize competitiveness and security, but may down-weight ethical, social and distributive considerations.[47]

[45] Atladóttir et al. 2025.

[46] Perrier (2022)

[47] Atladóttir et al. 2025

4.4.2.2 Academia

The majority of research and technical expertise in quantum technology has traditionally been situated (and remains) within academic institutions such as universities. Indeed, quantum computation as a discipline emerged out of largely theoretical considerations brought on by the emergence of quantum systems and limitations facing researchers seeking to simulate real-world systems (such as Feynman). Furthermore, government funding of academic quantum programs represents a considerable public benefit. QEP programs may address the types of ethical obligations upon academic institutions to maintain and promote the development of quantum science, but also to meet other moral or ethical constraints. Similarly, QEP can usefully be directed towards guides or even heuristics for the types of ethical considerations that may be relevant to other research programs. For example, cryptographic research with the potential to impact privacy would be one such area. Indeed, recent proposed constraints upon the export of quantum technologies in the name of national security evidence the importance of establishing ethical and governance protocols for quantum research from the outset. Other examples include integrating ethical components into curricula.[48]

4.4.2.3 Other Stakeholders

Other stakeholders of interest include private corporations (users and developers), together with individual users, civil society groups, specialist technical societies and developers, each having roles in the functioning and development of the quantum sector.[49] From an ethics' perspective, QEP can usefully draw in extensive literature on individual, collective and group deontological ethics in order to reason through the different duties and responsibilities of such stakeholders. For example, what duties do private sector stakeholders involved in the development of quantum technologies have regarding access to, controls for or maintaining standards related to such technology? How might the ethical considerations for a quantum algorithm designer working on cryptography differ from a quantum engineer working in a laboratory, or political decision-maker considering quantum policy?

An early example of proposed quantum governance principles directed towards stakeholder interests that attempts to incorporate values-based ethical design was provided by the World Economic Forum's *Quantum Computing Governance Principles*.[50] The principles set out a framework based upon core ethical values of collective well-being, accountability, inclusiveness, equity, non-maleficence, accessibility and transparency. These in turn form the basis of different themes and topics germane to the ethics of quantum computing, such as development goals, opportunities and risks. The principles aim to provide a taxonomic approach of use to different quantum

---

[48] Arrow et al. (2023).

[49] Perrier (2022), Vermaas et al. 2025.

[50] World Economic Forum (2022).

stakeholders in their deliberations and responses and represent an example, albeit generalized, of the type of frameworks that more in-depth QEP research could build upon.

4.4.3 Quantum Risk Management

Another useful source of research for practical use in both quantum governance and technical approaches to quantum ethics involves the application of well-established risk assurance and management frameworks to quantum technologies. As with all technologies, understanding risks is central to making pragmatic decisions regarding the use of technology and in informing the types of ethical or moral constraints that are deemed acceptable. As we discuss below, quantum computing comes with the promise of extraordinary paradigm-shifts in a number of areas, while also representing a potentially profound disruption to core features of modern integrated societies via its impact on cryptographic and communications protocols.

QEP research applying methods derived from international standards[51] and risk management protocols such as ISO 31000[52] in the development of quantum-specific risk management tools would be of considerable use for stakeholders, such as governments and corporations, familiar with such risk management settings. Research programs in this area would adapt familiar risk management paradigms in terms that are pragmatically relevant for particular quantum stakeholders as risks will depend on the interests, duties and obligations of particular stakeholder groups which vary. For example, governments and government agencies bear a different set of ethical duties and obligations to private corporations or academia involved in quantum technology development. As such, the ways in which those institutions manage risk in general and quantum-specific risk will likely differ and can be informed by research programs tailored towards a quantum context.

More broadly, if the potential of quantum technologies is realized, they are likely to have extraordinary and profound transformational impacts. The heightened computational promise of full fault-tolerant quantum computing[53] has the potential to transform sectors and industries, such as pharmaceuticals, health, medicine and industrial technology. As we discuss further in Sect. 10, the capacity to simulate and model complex systems, solving certain intractable currently inefficiently solvable problems in finance,[54] logistics and other areas all potentially could impact different constituencies and stakeholders. A major branch of QEP would then include identification of upside and downside risks from these technologies and the likely institutions and populations they may impact. In practical terms, this may involve ethics' research into (a) how to measure such risks or (b) institutional frameworks

[51] Aboy et al. (2025).

[52] Purdy (2010).

[53] Gottesman (1998, 2010).

[54] Zafar (2025).

for responsibility and change management within organizations affected by quantum technology impacts. Further details of this type of risk assessment process is specified in recent work on quantum governance,[55] covering ethical considerations around access to quantum technology, innovation, raising awareness, cybersecurity, privacy and sustainability.

4.5 Quantum Computing: A Summary

4.5.1 Overview

Quantum computing is a vast multi-faceted discipline, spanning specializations across mathematics, theoretical and applied computer science, condensed matter physics, quantum mechanics,[56] quantum field theory, communications and information theory and cryptography. In this section, we outline the key technical characteristics of *quantum* computation of relevance when assessing the ethical impact of quantum technologies. We summarize the elementary features of quantum computation relevant for understanding how, for example, quantum algorithms differ in key respects from their classical counterparts. Understanding such differences, we argue, is important for research programs assessing the comparative similarities and differences between the ethics of quantum and classical technologies.

Quantum information processing is characterized by constraints upon how information is represented and processed. Here we briefly summarize the postulates of quantum mechanics as applicable to quantum computing[57] in comparative fashion against similar or analogous concepts in classical computer science.

4.5.2 Postulates

Classical computation is typically represented using stateful paradigms in which a system is represented by a *state*, typically comprising a set of properties represented as an element (vector) characterizing the system in that state. Computation is then presented as transitions among states as per classical Turing machine or finite-state formalism (see Sipser[58] for an introduction). Such transitions may be either deterministic or non-deterministic and are usually represented by a transition operator or stochastic transition matrix which sets out the probabilities of the system transitioning from one state to another under the operation of some computational

[55] Perrier (2022).

[56] Townsend (2000).

[57] Nielsen and Chuang (2011).

[58] Sipser (2012).

process. While the specific transition may not be determinable in advance (e.g. it may be probabilistic) and while the exact information about the classical state may not be practically accessible (due to, for example, limitations in hardware or overly complex system descriptions), *in principle* a classical computational system subsists in a definite *single* state: it is *ontologically* determined. Uncertainty about what state a classical system is in is thus not ontological, but epistemological, a representation of the uncertainty of our knowledge rather than any intrinsic indeterminacy about the system state itself. This underlying *in principle* determinacy of classical computational states underpins much of the design thinking and assumptions behind the use, control and auditing of classical computational systems.[59]

Quantum computation, by contrast, is a fundamentally distinct computational paradigm, though contains within it classical computation as a *limiting* case where ontologically the probability of being in a state is unity (not unlike how classical field theories within physics are considered limiting cases of more general quantum field theories). In standard quantum information practice, a *pure state* represents maximal information about a system (up to global phase), whereas a *mixed state* encodes classical uncertainty over such pure states. These questions are investigated primarily within the field of quantum foundations[60] and the philosophy of science, where debates about the ontological status of quantum systems is at issue, for example, in debates over hidden variables' models (where uncertainty about quantum states is due to epistemological incompleteness or inaccessibility of variables or features of quantum systems which exist but cannot be measured) and certain seminal results (such as Bell's celebrated theorems[61]). While foundational debates about whether the state itself is ontic or epistemic are beyond our scope, they do have relevance to certain ethical formulations which may require degrees of certainty about processes (for auditing or surveillance purposes).

Classical computation's unit of analysis is the bit, a binary value $x \in \{0, 1\}$ which, usually in sequences or set of bits (registers), characterizes a state. Information is sequentially encoded in classical bits, for example via bit-strings $x_1, \ldots, x_n = (x_n) \in \{0, 1\}^n$. The bit-string may only subsist in any one evaluated state at any time t. The evolution of classical systems is then represented by mappings (or Boolean functions defined over) subsets of $\{0, 1\}^n$. Quantum systems are, by contrast, described by more structure owing to the fact that they must obey the laws of quantum mechanics. By comparison with the classical case, quantum systems are completely described by (unit) state vectors within a complex (rather than real) valued vector space called a Hilbert space $\mathcal{H}$, a vector space over $\mathbb{C}$ equipped with an inner product. This description applies most directly to pure states of isolated systems. More generally, quantum systems (e.g., particularly those interacting with an environment) are described using density operators, which capture both quantum and classical uncertainty. As we explicate below, this additional structure is necessitated by the ways in which quantum systems evolve and quantum states interact,

59 Burghes and Graham (2004).

60 Harrigan and Spekkens (2010), Bartlett et al. (2007).

61 Bell (2004, 1964, 1966).

primarily in order to preserve certain symmetry properties and statistical probability measures. The most basic formulation of quantum computation involves analysis of the states and evolution of two-level quantum systems, expressed as elements of two-dimensional Hilbert spaces, named qubits. A qubit $|\psi\rangle$ within such a Hilbert space with basis $|0\rangle$ and $|1\rangle$ is represented as $|\psi\rangle = a|0\rangle + b|1\rangle$ where $a, b \in \mathbb{C}$.

Qubits share in common with bits being represented via the binary-valued basis states. However, they differ ontologically and formally in fundamental ways from classical bits.[62] Firstly, it can be shown that unlike classical bits whose states have mutually exclusive descriptions as 0 or 1, the qubit state is a linear composition of *both* basis states. Secondly, each basis state is accompanied by coefficients $a, b \in \mathbb{C}$, denoted as amplitudes. These amplitudes combine in ways that enable a sequence of amplitudes to be represented via a complex-valued vector space mentioned above. These amplitudes are related to (but not identical with) the probabilities of measuring $|\psi\rangle$ to be in state $|0\rangle$ or $|1\rangle$. Here, $|\psi\rangle$ is in state $|0\rangle$ with probability $|a|^2$ and $|1\rangle$ with probability $|b|^2$. Quantum states are therefore characterized by the probability distributions associated with measuring specific outcomes (and their resultant measurement statistics). This rule is known within the field as the Born rule which fundamentally maps specific properties of quantum states (amplitudes) to the probability of measuring that state as such.

We explicate measurement protocols in a bit more detail below, but it is important to be aware that colloquial phrases such as 'the system is in state' or 'the qubit is in state' are inferences drawn from the measurement statistics that arise (and are conditional upon) repeated measurements of identically prepared initial states. Already, this compositional linearity fundamentally distinguishes quantum from classical states with implications for how information is encoded in such systems, how that information evolves (or is processed) and how such systems may be controlled: all key elements, as we articulate, in any attempt to control or conform quantum systems to particular rules, ethical or otherwise.

Furthermore, unlike the classical case, in which information may only be encoded in the value taken on by a bit, information in qubits may be encoded in two ways: (i) via basis encoding (similar to bits); but also (ii) by relative phase encoding, that is, via encoding the amplitudes *a*, *b* in ways that represent information. The amplitudes *a*, *b* are subject to further constraints, known as normalization constraints, imposed in order to ensure the probability of all measurement outcomes sums to unity (i.e. to guarantee an appropriate probability measure on the space). This is denoted formally via the condition upon unit vectors that $\langle\psi|\psi\rangle = 1$ (that is $|a|^2 + |b|^2 = 1$).

Here $\langle\psi|\psi\rangle$ denotes the inner product of quantum states. The inner product has a rich formal theory associated with it, but intuitively it can be thought of as the degree of 'overlap' between two states and thus is used as a measure of their similarity or difference. All classical bits can indeed be represented as being in either the basis state $|0\rangle$ or $|1\rangle$ with unit probability for either e.g. $|a|^2 = 1$. Note, for completeness, that while such a state would be indistinguishable in terms of measurement outcome from a classical bit with value 0, technically speaking the amplitude $a \in \mathbb{C}$ can take

[62] Brukner (2014), Donoghue and Menezes (2020).

any root of unity in $\mathbb{C}$, so need not be the real number 1 (whereas classically this must be the case). It should be noted that quantum information processing literature distinguishes between physical qubits, which is ostensibly any physical system that exhibits or meets the criteria for being a qubit, and logical qubits, which may include a whole system of physical qubits whose collective state behaves according to qubit criteria.

Quantum systems are also highly sensitive to noise and distortions which can give rise to errors in quantum states (e.g. changing the energy level or valuation from $|0\rangle$ to $|1\rangle$ or interfering with coherences). As a result, the imperative of quantum system design is to achieve what is known as *fault tolerant* quantum computation, a technical term with related theorems that refers to the idea that if physical (qubit) error rates can be reduced below a certain threshold, then logical (qubit) error rates can be reduced arbitrarily. Various theoretical and technical means of error correction, such as encoding quantum information in certain codes which are robust to noise or can self-correct up to acceptable probabilities, are a major focus of quantum computing research and distinguish the field from its classical counterpart, where error correction is relevant but less foundational (owing to the robustness of physical classical computing devices). While quantum systems are particularly sensitive to noise due to coherence requirements, error correction is also a foundational concern in classical computing systems. The distinction lies more in the mechanisms and severity of error processes rather than the presence or absence of error correction as such.

For completeness (for readers who may delve more deeply into quantum formalism), more advanced treatments of quantum computing (and quantum information processing) tend to utilize what is known as density operator formalism, which is ostensibly a useful way of representing probability distribution over which a quantum state $|\psi\rangle$ subsists. In density operator formalism, a quantum system is described via the positive density operator ρ with trace unity acting on the state space of the system. If the system is in state ρ_i with probability p_i then $\rho = \sum_i p_i \rho_i$. Density operators are represented usually via matrices.

4.5.3 Encoding Information

There are four primary methods of encoding data in quantum systems:[63] (a) basis encoding (e.g. encoding a bit-string (001) as qubit basis states $|001\rangle$), (b) amplitude encoding, where information is encoded in the amplitudes of quantum states, together with (c) qsample encoding and (d) dynamic encoding (which we omit). This categorization is not exhaustive, and alternative encoding strategies and taxonomies exist within the literature. The methods described here are best understood as commonly used approaches rather than a definitive classification. Typically, encoded data is then placed into a superposition state in order to leverage quantum advantages as a result.

[63] Schuld and Petruccione (2021).

While considered normatively an unremarkable step, there are potential ethical issues to be explored about the ethics of encoding data (such as from fair representation learning).[64] For example, does placing data into superpositions potentially enable the combining (via quantum interference) of protected attributes into new features in a way that is ethically proscribed (e.g. combining information about individuals to create features responsible for unfair computational outcomes)? While speculative, such questions of representational justice are important within certain fields of ethics and jurisprudence.

4.5.4 Quantum State Evolution

A key feature of any program that seeks to address the technical foundations of quantum ethics is an appreciation of the distinct ways in which quantum computation evolves by comparison with its classical counterpart. Quantum systems are constrained in how they may evolve so as to maintain the uniquely quantum features of the system (such as coherences) that distinguish them from classical systems. For example, quantum state transitions must conform to specific rules designed to preserve probability measures.

Quantum systems are also modelled variously in terms of closed and open systems. Closed systems are toy models which treat a quantum system as self-contained and which disregard the effects of various noise sources or other interaction effects from anything outside the system (denoted the environment). What counts as the system or environment will depend upon context. For example, in typical closed-system quantum control toy models which disregard distortion or noise effects, apparatus by which a quantum system is controlled may be conceived as part of the system as a whole (represented by a set of control Hamiltonians), despite being physically distinct from the physical qubits themselves. Open quantum systems are models that take into account the presence of noise which can interfere with the quantum characteristics of a system (such as coherences or energy of the system) in a way that can give rise to errors or the irreversible loss of information.

Closed quantum systems (which we focus on for simplicity) evolve over time $\Delta t = t_1 - t_0$ via unitary transformations $U = T_+ \exp\left(-\frac{i}{\hbar}\int H(t)dt\right)$. Such unitaries represent solutions to the time-dependent Schrödinger equation of motion governing evolution $i\hbar\frac{d|\psi(t)\rangle}{dt} = H(t)|\psi(t)\rangle$ where $\hbar$ is set to unity for convenience and H represents the linear Hermitian operator (Hamiltonian) of the closed system. The T_+ term is the time-ordering operator. The dynamics of the quantum system are completely described by the Hamiltonian operator acting on the state $|\psi\rangle$ such that $|\psi(t)\rangle = U(t)|\psi(t=0)\rangle$. In density operator notation, this is represented as $\rho(t_1) = U(t)\,\rho(t_0)U(t)^\dagger$. Typically solving the continuous form of the Schrödinger equation is intractable or infeasible, so a discretized approximation represented as a discrete

[64] McNamara et al. (2017).

quantum circuit (where each gate U_i is run for a sufficiently small time-step Δt) is used (and the impact of the time-ordering operator is assumed away).

The Hamiltonian H of a system is the most important tool for mathematically characterising dynamics of a system, encoding the computational processing of data encoded into quantum states and specifying how the quantum computation may be controlled. To the extent that computational processes or outcomes are important to ethical criteria (for example, understanding the dynamics giving rise to bias or discriminatory outcomes, or ensuring fair representation learning in a quantum setting), they must usually be encoded in the Hamiltonian of quantum systems. Such a perspective reflects a control-theoretic or continuous-time formulation of quantum computation. In other models, such as the quantum circuit model, computation is typically described in terms of discrete gate operations, and ethical constraints may be implemented at that level of abstraction. Modifications to computational subroutines in quantum computing must be done indirectly, via adjustments to the Hamiltonian which steer quantum systems towards target states using unitary evolution.

4.5.5 Quantum Measurement

Information about or within quantum systems (which characterizes those quantum systems or object information encoded within) is extracted via quantum measurement and its associated formalism. Quantum measurements are represented as sets of measurement operators $\{ M_m \}$. By operating on a system with a measurement operator, the apparatus, where m indexes the outcome of a measurement (e.g. an energy level or state indicator). The probability $p(m)$ of outcome m upon measuring $|\psi\rangle$ is represented by such operators acting on the state such that $p(m) = \langle\psi|M_m^\dagger M_m|\psi\rangle$ with the post-measurement state $|\psi'\rangle$ given by: $|\psi'\rangle = (M_m|\psi\rangle)/\left(\sqrt{}\langle\psi|M_m^\dagger M_m|\psi\rangle\right)$. The probabilistic nature of measurement outcomes is reflected in distributions over those outcomes for which density operator (matrix) formalism in effect provides a way to represent probability distributions for quantum measurement (and thus state characterization) in the language of operator algebra. As we are interested in probability distributions rather than individual probabilities from a single measurement, we calculate the probability distribution over outcomes via Born rule using the trace $p(E_i) = Tr(E_i \rho)$. This formulation is important to quantum fairness metrics discussed below.

4.5.6 Composite Systems

State vectors $|\psi\rangle$ in the Hilbert space may be composite systems, described as the tensor product of the component physical systems $|\psi_i\rangle$, that is $\rho_i = \sum_j p_{\{ij\}} |\psi_{\{ij\}}\rangle\langle\psi_{\{ij\}}|$. We also mention here the importance of open quantum systems where a total system comprises a closed quantum system H_S and environment H_E such that the full Hamiltonian is ($H = H_S + H_E + H_I$), where the last term denotes an interaction term. This is typically how noise is modelled in quantum contexts. Open quantum systems[65] are modelled usually by master equations (beyond the scope of this introductory paper), but they are relevant to quantum fair machine learning, in particular because modelling the dissipative effects of system/environment interaction, or engineering dissipation so as to simulate dissipative characteristics of neural networks.

Other key concepts necessary to understand the formalism below include: (a) *relative phase*, that for a qubit system, where amplitudes a and b differ by a relative phase if $a = exp\,(i\theta)b$, $\theta \in \mathbb{R}$ (as discussed below, classical information is typically encoded in both basis states and in relative phases); (b) *entanglement*,[66] certain composite states (e.g. EPR or Bell states), may be entangled. For example, for a two-qubit state $|\psi\rangle = \frac{1}{\sqrt{2}}\left(|00\rangle + |11\rangle\right)$ measurement of 0 on the first qubit necessarily means that the second qubit is also in the state $|0\rangle$. Entangled states cannot be written as tensor products of their component states. Such states are crucial to important emerging quantum domains of quantum communication and quantum cryptography; (c) *expectation*, expectation E values of an operator A (e.g. a measurement) can be written as $E(A) = Tr(\rho A)$; (d) *mixed* and *pure* states, quantum systems whose states are exactly known to be $|\psi\rangle$ are pure states, while otherwise we denote it as a 'mixed state' i.e. $\rho = \sum_i p_i \rho_i$ where $Tr(\rho^2) < 1$; (e) *commutativity*, where two measurements are performed on a system, the outcome will be order-dependent if they do not commute, that is, if $[A, B] \neq 0$; and (f) *no cloning*, unlike classical data, quantum data cannot be perfectly copied.[67]

We omit a universe of other characteristics of relevance to quantum ethics, including error-correcting codes (encoding mechanisms designed to limit or self-correct errors to achieve fault tolerant quantum computing) which, while relevant, are beyond the scope of this chapter. The above postulates and characteristics of quantum computing also provide the basis for taxonomic distinctions between (a) *quantum data* and *classical data* (e.g. different state characterization) and (b) *quantum information processing* versus *classical information processing* (by the requirement, for example, of any coherence-preserving quantum process to respect unitary evolution). In the following sections, we explore the direct and indirect ethical consequences of distinct characteristics of quantum computing identified above.

---

[65] Wiseman and Milburn (2010).

[66] Wootters (1998).

[67] Wootters and Zurek (1982).

4.6 Quantum Ethics and Ethical Algorithms

4.6.1 Overview

An important characteristic of prospective ethical quantum computing programs is being able to informatively situate quantum ethics research within the broader fields of ethical inquiry. Research into the ethics of algorithms, computation and technology is a vast enterprise, covering classical ethics, philosophy and computer science, together with emergent cross-disciplinary fields such as fair machine learning, computational population ethics and research into regulatory platforms. In this section, we sketch a number of key landmarks and concepts of relevance to quantum ethics research, with the aim of identifying foundational questions in quantum ethics. Put another way, while specialization in quantum ethics is necessary and inevitable, it is incumbent upon researchers in quantum ethics to be sufficiently aware and engage with existing ethics' literature.

4.6.2 Ethical Computation in Quantum Contexts

What it means for computation (as distinct from the consequences of computation) to be ethical or normatively satisfactory requires an appreciation of the nature of computation itself. This is true also of quantum computing. The classification of a quantum computation itself as ethical or not can usefully be understood according to the following taxonomy of algorithmic computation. We adopt a distinction between the process of computing and its outcomes (though note such a distinction can be reframed in terms of either using typical models of computing, such as via Turing machine formalism). While such a distinction oversimplifies the complexities of normative ethics, it is useful as a first framing for researchers.

4.6.2.1 Ethical Quantum Computation

A quantum computation may be ethical if it consists of (i) *ethical procedures*, a form of algorithmic deontology (concerned with what computational evolutions or pathways are or are not permissible) where the process of computation itself (unitary evolution) satisfies some ethical constraint or requirement or (ii) *ethical outcomes*, a form of algorithmic consequentialism. Each classification depends upon the underlying normative criteria specifying what counts as ethical. Ethically classifying the former may require understanding how system Hamiltonians (which govern unitary evolution) encode ethically relevant computations for example (for example, precluding consideration of protected attributes from the action of Hamiltonians). Assessing ethical outcomes may also require understanding quantum measurement statistics, as the ability to identify or audit an evolving quantum system is ultimately contingent upon probabilistic measurement outcomes (we cannot 'open the black box' of a quantum computer, as it were, to audit its operations in the same way as may be in principle available when using a classical computer). That said, while direct inspection of quantum states is not possible in the same manner as classical systems, a range of indirect techniques can provide partial information about quantum computations, albeit with resource and precision limitations.

4.6.2.2 Accuracy of Measurements

An additional consideration arising from the indirect way in which quantum states and processes are identified is the accuracy with which quantum states and processes must be identified for classification as ethical. For example, state characterization is often performed via tomographic methods, which seek to reconstruct characteristics of quantum states from measurements.[68] However, the resources required to tomographically characterize quantum systems scales exponentially, rendering full characterization of quantum systems largely infeasible (though we note recent proposals for classical shadow tomography[69] go some way to addressing such challenges). As such, researchers seeking to ethically classify quantum states or processes must reconcile with inherent uncertainty and vagueness about the actual states/processes of quantum systems. Reckoning the consequences of such informational incompleteness is not unique to quantum information processing (such incompleteness is a feature when seeking to characterize many classical systems). It does, however, speak to the inherently probabilistic nature of quantum computing which has consequences for the degree of certainty or confidence required for ethical classification of quantum computations.

4.6.3 Ethical Procedures Via Planning and Control

The ethical characterization of quantum computation can draw fruitfully upon the extensive literature on constraint satisfaction problems and planning within computational science and control theory.[70] Such approaches represent a form of design-thinking for ethics (discussed above) in computation that aims to encode ethical behavior in the functioning of algorithmic and autonomous systems.

In planning and control literature, one is concerned with how to model and execute planning procedures. Such classical MDP models have more recently been applied to consider ethical compliance of sequential decision procedures with specific ethical criteria. For example, Svegliato et al. propose an MDP-based model for ethically compliant autonomous systems that aims to decouple ethical compliance from task

68 Greenbaum (2015), Mohseni et al. (2008), D'Ariano and Presti (2001).

69 Huang et al. (2020).

70 Kolobov et al. (2012).

completion.[71] In this model, decision-procedures are subject to moral principles within ethical contexts. Such concepts are formalized within an MDP framework following a typical Bellman-style[72] decision-procedure described by the tuple $\langle S, A, T, R, d\rangle$. The system subsists in a finite state $s \in S$, with an action (decision) $a \in A$ giving rise to a transition among states $s_t \rightarrow s_{\{t+1\}}$. The probability of transitioning is given via T and is conditional in $p(s' \mid s, a)$, with $r \in \mathbb{R}$ a reward function and d a parameter modelling which initial state s_0 the system starts in. Solutions to MDPs are policies which are probability distributions over actions π: $S \rightarrow A$ representing the probability of taking action a given state s.

The unfolding of computation is then modelled stochastically in terms of such stochastic state-transitions, where optimizing consists then of finding an appropriate policy π^* that maximizes an expected discounted cumulative reward satisfying a typical Bellman optimality equation. In this model, moral principles (say utilitarianism) form constraints upon the particular policies with optimal policies being those that maximize the dual objectives of conformity with the moral principle while maximizing the overall objective. Such an approach might be described as a 'stateful' approach to ethical computation where satisfying ethical constraints on how a computation should unfold is equivalent to proscribing states that the computational system should not subsist within.

Of course, not every ethical consequence of computational technology necessarily can or should be framed in such a stateful manner e.g. the distributional ethics of quantum technologies is a distinct question from whether a particular computation transitions to a proscribed state or not. But such an approach is (i) very much consistent with the well-established literature on encoding constraints within computational architecture itself[73] and as a result (ii) useful for thinking about cases where ethical or normative requirements mandate that computations are not carried out in a particular way or do not result in particular outcomes.

In these sorts of models, some choice of ethical standard (e.g. a principle of utilitarianism) becomes encoded in the decision-procedures of such algorithms. Moral and ethical principles manifest in proscriptions or prescriptions upon state transitions and their probabilities. For example, proscribed states are then modelled as 'dead ends', e.g. a moral constraint that requires a zero probability of transitioning to a proscribed state.[74] Thus ethical constraints can be equivalently modelled as either (a) constraints on the types of states $s \in S$ into which a system may transition or (b) constraints upon the transition functions among states.

As the broad field of computational planning attests, the challenge lies in issues such as whether a system is fully *controllable* and the extent to which full information about the system is known or knowable, indeed whether a particular end-state is reachable given an arbitrary or unknown initial state s_0 (for example, it may be technically impossible to reduce the transition to an ethically proscribed 'dead end'

[71] Svegliato et al. (2021).

[72] Bellman (1956).

[73] Mouaddib et al. (2015).

[74] Mouaddib et al. (2015).

state to zero no matter what the policy is). Classical Markov decision procedures (MDP) and control theory provide a well-studied framework within which to model the ethical classification of quantum computational processes.

In the quantum setting, imposing moral principles as constraints on the types of states that a system may subsist within and transition to may manifest formally as constraints within the Hamiltonian H of the quantum system. To the extent the system is controllable, then the imposition of moral or ethical constraints in terms of state transitions would also necessitate specific control architecture, which in turn would be represented via, for example, control terms within the Hamiltonian.

In certain ethical frameworks, judgments by a decision-procedure system may be proscribed: a car running a red light, a classification algorithm breaching certain fairness criteria (see below). Because decisions by such a system are modelled in terms of the *state* that the system is in, then to meet ethical policy criteria, one would in a quantum setting require terms in the Hamiltonian that prohibit the quantum system from evolving into that proscribed state $|\psi'\rangle$. Whether a state evolves to such a proscribed state is then a function of the Hamiltonian H as the Hamiltonian ultimately controls the transition probabilities among states (formally expressed through propagators and the Dyson equation). However, what counts is whether such a system can be controlled or influenced. This depends on the initial state of the quantum system $|\psi(0)\rangle$ and how it evolves according to $|\psi(t)\rangle = U(t) \mid \psi(0)\rangle$. In control theory, this is modelled by partitioning the Hamiltonian into controllable H_c and uncontrollable H_d ('drift') terms such that $\mathrm{H} = \mathrm{H_c} + \mathrm{H_d}$.

Controlling a quantum system, or at least rendering it less likely to transition to proscribed states, then becomes a question of how to fashion the control Hamiltonian $\mathrm{H_c}$ which is effectively the way in which a system is by design controlled to maintain constraints. The probability of transitioning to a particular state can be represented, analogously with the transition matrix T, via a density matrix ρ which acts in effect as a representation of a probability distribution over states. The exact form of a control Hamiltonian required to meet a particular ethical constraint will depend on context, quantum algorithm design and a raft of other factors. Nevertheless, the foregoing provides an example of the type of encoding of ethical constraints in quantum systems of relevance to technical foundations QEP.

The approaches described above are by no means the only models according to which quantum algorithms may be classified as ethical, but they provide a guide (particularly starting from a classical perspective) as to how ethical classification and control may work in a quantum context and an indication of the type of research topics that the technical foundations part of a quantum ethics' roadmap could entail.

4.6.4 *Auditing and Provability of Ethical Quantum Computations*

Methods of auditing or proving that a quantum computation is ethically satisfactory (and that ethical constraints are being complied with) form an important potential area quantum ethics' research as they do for classical systems. Auditing of quantum computation poses distinct challenges compared with the classical case[75] because the computation cannot be measured directly (colloquially, one cannot 'open the black box'). Instead, auditing is dependent upon reconstructing information about the computation via repeated measurements on a quantum system.

First, attempts to measure 'in train' as it were can cause quantum states to collapse or disturb quantum systems in a way that interferes with information about the system in the first place.

Secondly, research into auditing of quantum algorithms involves consideration of proof techniques for quantum computation. The provability of quantum computations[76] requires consideration of different strategies and resources (such as for provers and verifiers, including witness states or entanglement[77]), together with quantum correctness logics.[78]

4.7 Four C's of Ethical Computation

In addition to ethical classification, auditing and provability considerations, the specific nature of quantum computing has implications for the four C's of ethical computation: computability, complexity, consistency and controllability.[79] We briefly sketch the significance of these categories for questions about the ethics of quantum computing below.

4.7.1 *Computability and Complexity*

Computability considerations for the ethics of quantum computing require two questions to be asked: (i) is the proposed ethically constrained quantum computation computable? That is: is it even a type of computation that is possible for a quantum computer?; and (ii) is the computation efficient or ethically feasible given resource constraints? For example, imposing particular ethical constraints on the

[75] Kearns et al. (2019).

[76] Vidick and Watrous (2016).

[77] Ji et al. (2020).

[78] Yuan and Ying (2021).

[79] Perrier (2021b).

unitary evolution of an algorithm may increase the resources required to undertake the computation. Relatedly, as discussed below, ethical constraints can sometimes be considered as restricting the subspaces $\mathcal{H}_i$ of $\mathcal{H}$ within which $|\psi\rangle$ is permitted to lie or evolve within. Other considerations we group within computability include the degree of certainty or precision required of a quantum computation, that is, do ethical criteria impose unrealistic levels of precision on measurement or state reconstruction which would render such ethical constraints on the computation infeasible? Additionally, the complexity classes of certain quantum computations[80] is an important characteristic for assessing their feasibility. Indeed, some authors regard complexity as in practice a more relevant property of algorithmic architecture than computability per se (see Lloyd et al.[81] for example). This is because the computation may be outside the bounds of what is tractable for even a quantum computer or, more practically, the complexity specifications help give an indication of the resources required to actually undertake the computation in an ethically constrained manner.

4.7.2 Consistency and Controllability

Consistency and controllability of quantum computations are two more important features that impact on their ethical framing. The types of considerations relevant here are (i) *process (deontological) consistency*, whether similar decisions ought to follow similar methodologies; and (ii) *outcome (consequentialism) consistency*, whether it is normatively permissible for two different quantum algorithms (or even one algorithm) to come to different output classifications given the same input data (e.g. quantum analogues of Lipschitz conditional fairness[82]). Of the four C's above, controllability is among the most studied. Controllability asks whether an ethical algorithm is sufficiently controllable, both in terms of steering it towards desired end-states, but also the extent to which unitary evolution is itself controllable (e.g. via Hamiltonian controls). Quantum control,[83] namely controlling quantum computations to satisfy ethical criteria, is therefore an important feature of research programs examining technicalities of quantum ethics.

Other issues to consider when analyzing the ethics of quantum computations themselves cover those applicable to ethical algorithmic analysis generally, including the appropriateness of (inevitable in most cases) quantum computational heuristics and the types of ethical trade-offs that particular quantum algorithmic architectures presage.

---

[80] See Aaronson (2013).

[81] Lloyd (2012).

[82] Perrier (2021a).

[83] D'Alessandro (2007).

4.8 Quantum Fair Machine Learning

4.8.1 Overview

In this section, we provide examples of how the distinctly quantum nature of quantum computation impacts technical results in ethical computational science. To illustrate the way in which the different nature of quantum (as distinct from classical) computation affects technicalities of ethical research programs, we focus on how the use of quantum data and quantum algorithms, including quantum machine learning-based algorithms,[84] changes how ethical constraints can or would be imposed on those algorithms. In concrete terms, we summarize how various technical results in the field of fair machine learning (the leading technical discipline at the interface of computer science and ethics), such as parity measures, metrics and auditing, are altered when quantum information is involved. Our synopsis here draws on prior work[85] which presents in more detail quantum analogues of canonical results in fair machine learning (such as the use of amplitude amplification to achieve statistical parity and Lipschitz fairness conditions in quantum algorithmic contexts).

4.8.2 Quantum and Classical Fairness

Fair machine learning is a sub-branch of computer science concerned with how classical algorithmic systems can be assessed against ethical criteria (such as bias or discrimination in data or outcomes) and strategies for imposing ethical standards (such as fair outcomes or representational justice) on such algorithms.[86] Quantum fair machine learning[87] (QFML) is a prospective cross-disciplinary area of applied quantum computing where quantum or hybrid (classical-quantum) algorithms (ranging from traditional quantum algorithms to those designed according to machine learning principles) are subject to fairness constraints at the preprocessing, in-processing (modelling) or post-processing (post-measurement) stage. In this sense, the proposal for QFML represents a more technical approach for analyzing how the unique features of quantum computation interplay with ethical requirements. Our exposition focuses on the use of quantum information processing for solving ethically constrained optimization problems involving classical data encoded into quantum systems (in the classical-quantum hybrid domain).[88]

---

[84] Schuld et al. (2015).

[85] Perrier (2021a).

[86] Caton and Haas (2024), Chouldechova (2017), del Barrio et al. (2016), Dwork et al. (2012).

[87] Perrier (2021a).

[88] Aïmeur et al. (2006).

4.8.3 Parity Measures

Fair machine learning is characterized by the designation of some *fairness criteria* according to which (usually the outcomes of) algorithms are adjudged. There are a multitude of fairness criteria.[89] A simple example is statistical parity which demands fair (equiprobability of) classification by a classifier $Y = 1$ of two or more subgroups (g_1, g_2) of a population i.e. $Pr(Y = 1| g_1) = Pr(Y = 1| g_2)$. As discussed in proposals for QFML,[90] parity in a quantum context can be framed in the following way: fairness criteria effectively partition the Hilbert space $\mathcal{H}$ into direct sums $\mathcal{H} = \oplus_i \mathcal{H}_i$ such that satisfying fairness criteria is realized via the equiprobability of $|\psi\rangle$ residing in an arbitrary subspace $|\psi_i\rangle = \left\{ |\psi\rangle \,|\, |\psi\rangle \in \mathcal{H}_i \right\}$. The fairness criterion is then expressed with respect to a suitably chosen (POVM) measurement operator M_i that partitions $\mathcal{H}$ into subspaces $\mathcal{H}_i$ as (quantum fairness):

$$\langle \psi_i | M_i^d M_i | \psi_i \rangle = \left\langle \psi_j \middle| M_j^d M_j \middle| \psi_j \right\rangle$$

$$Tr(\rho_i M_i) = Tr\left(\rho_j M_j\right).$$

where ρ_i corresponds to $|\psi_i\rangle$. That is, the probability of measuring the state $|\psi\rangle$ in $\mathcal{H}_i$ is equal for each subspace. In addition, distance metrics on quantum computers differ in ways that lead to modification of classical fairness constraints. One example is for Lipschitz conditioned fairness (where similar individuals normatively should be subject to similar outcomes), where classical states metrics are replaceable by density operators and quantum metrics, such as trace distance and fidelity, as ways of assessing state similarity.

4.8.4 Mitigating Unfairness

Classical techniques for mitigating unfairness have mixed transferability to quantum computational settings. Strategies for ensuring this in a classical context often involve preprocessing data (redacting data, or sampling to adjust training data composition or regularization). Undertaking quantum computations satisfying such fairness criteria is framed somewhat differently due to the unique aspects of quantum computing discussed above. For example, quantum data and processes cannot be inspected directly, rather one is limited to a probabilistic distribution over measurement outcomes i.e. classification is inherently probabilistic. Moreover, one usually can only sample a portion rather than the entirety of $\mathcal{H}$, thus even the distribution is an

[89] Caton and Haas (2024), del Barrio et al. (2016).

[90] Perrier (2021a).

estimate. Furthermore, there are no guarantees that quantum states (upon which fairness measures depend) are reliably distinguishable in general. One remedial approach is to leverage quantum algorithms to satisfy fairness constraints. An example of this is the application of Grover's amplitude amplification algorithm which can be shown[91] to evolve a quantum system in order to achieve statistical parity (i.e. equiprobability of measuring $|\psi\rangle \in \mathcal{H}_i$) via rotating $|\psi\rangle$ within $\mathcal{H}$.

The discussion above only touches upon a few ethical issues relevant to research programs into quantum fair machine learning. QEP research directions include (a) developing quantum analogues of classical fair machine learning techniques, (b) exploring prospective QFML methods in the presence of noisy or decohering systems (including, for example, leveraging the dissipative characteristics of such systems to simulate the dissipative characteristics of neural networks[92]), (c) a detailed study of how specifically quantum computational resources, such as entanglement, affect fair machine learning techniques and (d) the application of privacy and quantum cryptographic protocols in ethical contexts. In the remainder of this work, we examine normative and ethical considerations arising from quantum computation including for privacy, distributional ethics and geopolitics.

4.9 Privacy and Cryptography

4.9.1 Overview

Quantum computing has significant implications for privacy on the technical, ethical and legal fronts. Construed broadly, research programs considering how quantum technologies impact privacy have the benefit of expansive literature on quantum cryptography. Research programs into ethics of quantum privacy should factor in results from the vast ethical and philosophical work on privacy.[93] For example, within the philosophical literature, a distinction is often drawn[94] between (a) *reductionists* who argue that there is no normatively distinct privacy interests per se because all privacy concerns ultimately are derivative from supervening concerns around utility or other types of wrongs (such as distress); and (b) *coherentists*, in which privacy is viewed as a distinct and normatively valid interest. Here, we examine some of the ethical implications for privacy, encryption and information accessibility arising from quantum technologies.

---

[91] Perrier (2021a).

[92] Schuld et al. (2014).

[93] DeCew (2018).

[94] Schoeman (1984).

4.9.2 Differential Privacy and Quantum Computing

Differential privacy is a leading proposal within computational science for enabling the public distribution of information while retaining as confidential protected or sensitive classes of information (such as individual information). The modern canonical treatment of differential privacy lies in seminal work by Dwork[95] who defined a randomized algorithm $Q(X_i)$ as satisfying ϵ-differential privacy if, given two datasets X_1, X_2 differing by certain sensitive elements, for all subsets R with the image $Q = img(Q(X_i))$, the following relation is satisfied:

$$\Pr(Q(X_1) \in R) \leq \exp(\epsilon) \Pr(Q(X_2) \in R)$$

Intuitively this result says that the ability to distinguish whether a calculation involved the sensitive data (thus being able to estimate how the calculation changed as a result and infer features of the sensitive data) reduces asymptotically to zero in the limit in the presence of sufficient noise. Practically, differential privacy then provides an estimate of the noise or randomness needed to guarantee differential privacy thresholds. What does privacy mean in a quantum context?

One of the advantages of the inherently probabilistic nature of quantum data and quantum information and the no cloning theorem is that it is much more difficult to extract information such that the problems of maintaining privacy in quantum settings while being able to utilize quantum information converge on a similar point. One candidate for addressing privacy in a quantum context is on *gentle measurement*, where parallels are drawn between the need to retain the confidentiality of sensitive information while utilizing that information with the need, in a quantum context, to retain quantum coherence in quantum data while being able to perform informative measurements on the quantum system.[96] Gentle measurement regimes can in principle facilitate the utility of quantum data while retaining quantum coherence and preserving ethically mandated confidentiality. Thus, to the extent that normative privacy concerns drive ethical criteria regarding the use of quantum algorithms, existing quantum methodologies themselves may provide means of satisfying or addressing those concerns.

4.9.3 Quantum Cryptography Ethics

A significant field of quantum computing is the broad field of quantum cryptography, including emerging disciplines such as quantum key distribution and elements of quantum communications. Cryptographic results in quantum information science have provided significant motivation to expansive research into the role and possibilities of encryption in the presence of scalable fault-tolerant quantum computers.

[95] Dwork (2008).

[96] Aaronson and Rothblum (2019).

Much interest in this area - and quantum computing generally - has been driven by Shor's seminal result on the ability of quantum computers to efficiently factor prime numbers in a way that could, under certain conditions, enable breaking of classically-based encryption protocols.[97] That result in itself illustrates the significant potential ethical and indeed geopolitical consequences of quantum computing.

While still technically under development, the potential to decrypt classically encrypted communications holds enormous implications for not just individual privacy concerns, but also the confidentiality upon which economic activity is undertaken across networked communication systems. Similarly, the ability to crack the codes of adversaries has profound strategic implications on the cybersecurity front and for direct armed conflict (as the role of code-breaking during WWII demonstrates). Since those results, extensive work has been undertaken into quantum cryptography with its own set of ethical consequences, these include, for example, the potential for encryption regimes that are effectively non-decryptable even on quantum computers.

The availability of technology to enable effectively unbreakable cryptography also raises a host of ethical questions that research programs into quantum ethics may consider. We sketch a few below.

4.9.4 Distributional Issues

In a similar vein to distributional ethics questions about who may access quantum computational resources, the potential of quantum technologies to decrypt and encrypt data can also be framed in terms of population ethics and distributive justice. That is, if access to quantum technologies provides an advantage to some (by way of unbreakable encryption) and disadvantage to others (by rendering their data potentially subject to decryption), then the availability and distribution of cryptographic resources becomes an ethical question. To this end, the types of considerations we explore in the following section (on distributional ethics of quantum computing generally) will apply to the case of cryptographic resources. For example, research may wish to explore whether the distribution and extent of encryption of data can be modelled via social welfare or expected utility means: what are the consequences, for total social welfare, of ubiquitous access to encryption? Should encryption resources be constrained by pricing systems or other regulatory frameworks?

4.9.5 Decryption Ethics

While much privacy research in computational sciences is directed towards the ethical imperatives of protecting privacy from data breaches or decryption, there are many

[97] Shor (1997).

theoretical and practical cases where it may be ethically desirable or imperative to deprivatize or decrypt. For example, normative Rawlsian arguments[98] can be made that unbreakable encryption is itself unethical, undermining other types of normative requirements and claims regarding social cohesion and ordering. Thus, it is important for research programs in cryptography and privacy to also factor in how technologies can be used to deprivatize data, break codes or interfere with quantum and classical communications.

4.10 Distributive Ethics, Strategy and Quantum Simulations

4.10.1 Overview

The distributional ethics of quantum computing resources is an important research program for quantum ethics. The computational capacities and impact of quantum computing on economic modes of production and communication have the potential for profound structural impact. Quantum computing can properly be construed as an economic resource. The distribution of quantum computing technologies, including who may access them, how access may be mediated (or restricted) and the types of economic (and social) activities for which quantum computers are available is an inherently normative question. Decisions about distribution of quantum technologies involve technical, economic, political and geopolitical questions. For example, establishing networked quantum systems, such as is envisaged via proposals for the quantum internet[99] will be affected in part by distributional questions about access to such technologies (and even moreso, geopolitical questions).

In this sense, because the distribution of networked quantum technologies intrinsically affects both the technicalities of quantum communication and social welfare, the ethics of the distribution of quantum systems is somewhat distinct from other technologies whose distribution does not impact the actual functioning of the devices (that is, distribution correlates with both functionality and social welfare utility in the case of networked systems). From one perspective, it is understandable that quantum researchers have not turned their mind to the ethics of distributing quantum technologies, in a sense one needs to build the technologies first. However, the normative impact of such technologies does presage the study of their distributional consequences. Research programs into these questions will require cross-disciplinarity from the beginning. To this end, we outline a number of ways in which well-developed normative and ethical theories (and debates) may usefully inform such research.

In this section, we outline how results and frameworks from subfields of ethics and economics can help guide research into distribution of quantum technologies.

[98] Bay (2017).

[99] Wehner et al. (2018), Kimble (2008), Simon (2017), Lloyd et al. (2004).

4.10.2 Social Choice Theory and Welfare Axiology

Welfare axiology covers how the ordering of preferences among populations affects the types of distributional systems (such as distribution of economic resources) which are normatively preferable or possible. Conceptually, it is a broad term covering population ethics, the economics of social welfare and public financing, along with social choice and decision-theoretic social sciences. The underlying question of such approaches lies in how to order populations in order to maximize some measure of total social welfare, relying upon an ordering of preferences and method of aggregating them (such as a type of expected utility). Work in this area involves considering how the networked distribution,[100] say of individuals, affects welfare aggregation functions, including cluster analysis[101] along with graph-theoretic methods.[102] The network-theoretic aspect of both distributional ethics and quantum network engineering provides a basis through which to study the ethics of quantum technological distribution. In concrete terms, the task can be framed as a multi-constraint optimization problem, where utility $S(I_i, Q_i, A_{\{I,Q\}})$ is presented as a function of individual utilities I_i (of the population) and desirable quantum measures of utility Q_i of quantum network assets (for example, channel fidelities), along with an adjacency matrix $A_{\{I,Q\}}$ that encodes a graph detailing connection information among individuals, quantum network assets (where they are located) i.e. $\max_A E\left(S\left(I_i, Q_i, A_{\{I,Q\}}\right)\right)$. The output of such research would be an optimal (or more optimal) understanding of how to distribute quantum network technologies to improve social welfare while meeting minimum technical requirements. Moreover, research at the intersection of social choice theory and quantum technology can draw on the emerging field of computational social choice which covers computational paradigms involving social choice mechanisms, such as multi-agent systems.[103]

4.10.3 Impossibility Theorems

Population ethics and social welfare economics are also characterized by in-depth study of impossibility results which ultimately show the impossibility (or inconsistency) of satisfying multiple welfare criteria or obtaining a well-ordering of population ethics satisfying such criteria, including for example optimal distributions of quantum technologies. Examples include seminal work by Arrow[104] and Arrhenius.[105] Practically, expected utility approaches must necessarily be bounded by the

[100] List (2013).

[101] Kleinberg et al. (2023), Barthelemy and Monjardet (1981).

[102] Hammond (1988).

[103] Brandt (2016).

[104] Arrow (1950).

[105] Arrhenius (2000).

resource constraints of calculating such expected utilities (see various critiques[106]). Conversely, it may be that quantum computing does permit the calculation of certain utility functions which would otherwise be infeasible or intractable for classical computing. Put another way, utilizing quantum computers to expand the boundaries of bounded rationality presents an interesting set of QEP (see section in this work on the ethics of quantum simulations and decision-procedures).

4.10.4 Quantum Simulations

One of the motivations for quantum computing has been the capacity of quantum computers to simulate physical systems in a way which is intractable on classical computers or, even if tractable, is practically infeasible (due to spatial or temporal resource constraints). The promise, at least as speculatively put, is that the scalable and exponential computational power of quantum computing devices will expand the frontiers of the types of problems whose solutions which may be feasibly computed, across domains such as finance, economics, multi-agent systems. Such speculations must be contrasted with theoretical and technical realities of quantum computing, including the limited number of problems for which quantum computers are provably superior and considerable difficulties in engineering fault-tolerant scalable quantum devices.[107] Nevertheless, to the extent that quantum computing does offer the promise of, for example, simulating classically complex interacting systems, such as dynamic social or economic systems, then the ethics of such quantum simulations should be a matter of research and debate.

Two proposed research program topics in particular are worth mentioning in this context: (a) *individual simulation* that is, to what extent could the scalable resources of full fault-tolerant quantum computing enable highly precise or accurate simulations of individuals, including their preferences, psychology and behavior? This is not a uniquely quantum question (as classical simulations of individual behavior have a long history as does the emergent use of large language models) but does become a question for quantum ethics if it is the unique aspects of quantum computation that render such simulations feasible. The ethical consequences of such simulation capacity are of course profound and worth exploring; and (b) *multi-agent simulations*, which similarly asks the question of how quantum computing power may push the frontiers of the simulation of multi-agent systems.[108] For example, the ability to more precisely model larger numbers of interacting agents has potential consequences across a range of social, economic and geostrategic contexts. At a practical level, it entails consequences for modelling the interaction of driverless cars, including driverless cars with distinct ethical subroutines (e.g. two car algorithms may have

---

[106] McGee (1991), Simon (1955), Klaes and Sent (2005).

[107] Preskill (2018, 2021).

[108] Drogoul et al. (2002), Parsons and Wooldridge (2002).

different conclusions about how to react to an imminent accident) and multi-agent reinforcement learning contexts.[109]

4.11 Discussion and Conclusion

Quantum information technologies are increasingly transitioning from theoretical constructs to practical systems, bringing with them a range of ethical considerations that intersect with, and extend, existing debates in technology ethics. As contributions in this volume have argued, many of the ethical issues raised by quantum computing (e.g., fairness, privacy, governance, and distributional justice) can be understood as part of an evolution of challenges already encountered in earlier technological paradigms, including classical computation, the internet, and artificial intelligence. These prior domains provide a rich foundation of ethical theory, regulatory practice, and technical approaches that remain highly relevant to quantum technologies.

That said, the distinctive technical characteristics of quantum information processing introduce features that complicate or, in some cases, may reshape these established frameworks. Properties such as probabilistic computation, superposition, entanglement, and limited observability challenge assumptions of determinism, transparency, and auditability that underpin much of classical computational ethics. As a result, ethical analysis and reflection in quantum contexts may need to place greater emphasis not only on outcomes, but also on the processes by which computation is carried out, and on the constraints imposed by the physical realization of those processes. In this sense, quantum ethics is neither wholly novel nor merely derivative, but reflects a continuity with, and refinement of, broader approaches to technology ethics, alongside a set of more distinctive considerations that warrant focused attention.

To provide a foundation for this emerging field, we have proposed a structured research roadmap spanning technical foundations, governance and stakeholder responsibility, and risk management. This roadmap is intended as a set of guideposts for interdisciplinary inquiry, emphasizing the importance of translating concepts across quantum science, ethics, law, and policy. Within this framework, the need to embed ethical constraints within the design and control of quantum systems highlights a closer integration between normative reasoning and technical implementation than is often required in classical settings. Similarly, the introduction of the "four C's" (i.e., computability, complexity, consistency, and controllability) illustrates how ethical aspirations are shaped, and sometimes limited, by the physical and computational properties of quantum systems.

The chapter has also highlighted ways in which quantum technologies may reshape established domains of ethical inquiry. In the context of fair machine learning, the probabilistic and high-dimensional structure of quantum systems necessitates reconsideration of how fairness criteria are defined, implemented, and audited. In

[109] Barton et al. (2019).

privacy and cryptography, quantum capabilities simultaneously threaten existing encryption regimes while enabling new forms of secure communication, giving rise to familiar but reconfigured tensions between confidentiality, access, and governance. More broadly, the potential societal, economic, and geopolitical impacts of quantum technologies underscore the importance of distributional analysis and institutional design, particularly with respect to access to quantum resources and the global asymmetries that may arise from their deployment.

Taken together, these considerations suggest that quantum ethics is best understood as an emerging, cross-disciplinary field that both builds upon and extends existing approaches to technology ethics. Its development will depend on sustained engagement across disciplines, as well as a careful balance between leveraging established ethical frameworks and attending to the genuinely distinctive features of quantum information processing. Rather than requiring a wholesale reinvention of ethical theory, quantum ethics calls for a process of adaptation, integration, and, where necessary, innovation in response to the specific technical and societal characteristics of quantum technologies.

It is our hope that this chapter contributes to that process by providing both a conceptual foundation and a practical roadmap for future research, and by highlighting areas where further work is needed to ensure that the development and deployment of quantum technologies proceeds in a manner that is ethically informed, socially responsive, and attentive to both continuity and change in the landscape of technological ethics.

Acknowledgment This work was made possible through the generous support of the Novo Nordisk Foundation (NNF) via a grant for the scientifically independent Collaborative Research Program in Bioscience Innovation Law (Inter-CeBIL Program—Grant No. NNF23SA0087056). Any use of AI in this manuscript adheres to ethical guidelines for use and acknowledgement of AI in academic research. Each author has made a substantial contribution to the work, which has been thoroughly vetted for accuracy, and assumes responsibility for the integrity of their contributions in accordance with the ethical guidance on AI use and disclosure set out by Porsdam Mann et al.[110]

[110] Porsdam Mann et al. (2024).

References

Aaronson S. (2013) *Quantum Computing Since Democritus*. (Cambridge University Press, USA).
Aaronson S, Rothblum GN. (2019) Gentle measurement of quantum states and differential privacy. *In: Proceedings of the 51st Annual ACM SIGACT Symposium on Theory of Computing (STOC 2019)*. Association for Computing Machinery. 322–33.
Aboy M. et al. (2022) Mapping the patent landscape of quantum technologies: Patenting trends, innovation and policy implications. *IIC-International Review of Intellectual Property and Competition Law* 53(6): 853–882.
Aboy M., et al. (2025) Quantum technology governance: A standards-first approach. *Science* 389(6760): 575–578.
Aïmeur E. et al. (2006) Machine learning in a quantum world. In: Lamontagne L., Marchand M. (eds) *Advances in artificial intelligence. Lecture Notes in Computer Science*. 4013:431–442.
Alagic G., et al. (2022) *Status report on the third round of the NIST post-quantum cryptography standardization process*. National Institute of Standards and Technology.
Alagic G., et al. (2024) *Status Report on the First Round of the Additional Digital Signature Schemes for the NIST Post-Quantum Cryptography Standardization Process*. National Institute of Standards and Technology.
Arrhenius G. (2000) An impossibility theorem for welfarist axiologies. *Economics & Philosophy* 16(2):247–266.
Arrow, E. et al. (2023). A Holistic Approach to Quantum Ethics Education. https://arxiv.org/abs/2306.00027.
Arrow KJ. (1950) A Difficulty in the Concept of Social Welfare. *Journal of Political Economy* 58(4):328–46.
Atladóttir, D. et al. (2025) A Quantum of Responsibility? A Comparison of National Quantum Governance Frameworks and Expert Views. *Digital Society* 4:54.
Babbush, R. et al. (2026). Securing Elliptic Curve Cryptocurrencies against Quantum Vulnerabilities: Resource Estimates and Mitigations. https://arxiv.org/abs/2603.28846.
Bartlett SD., et al. (2007) Reference frames, superselection rules, and quantum information. *Reviews of Modern Physics* 79(2): 555–609.
Barthelemy PJ., Monjardet B. (1981) The median procedure in cluster analysis and social choice theory. *Mathematical Social Sciences* 1(3):235–67.
Barton SL. et al. (2019) Measuring collaborative emergent behavior in multi-agent reinforcement learning. In: Ahram T., Karwowski W., Taiar R. (eds) *Human Systems Engineering and Design. IHSED 2018. Advances in Intelligent Systems and Computing*. 876:501–507.
Bay M. (2017) The ethics of unbreakable encryption: Rawlsian privacy and the San Bernardino iPhone. *First Monday* 22(2).
Bell JS. (1964) On the Einstein Podolsky Rosen paradox. *Physics Physique Fizika* 1(3): 195–200.
Bell JS. (1966) On the Problem of Hidden Variables in Quantum Mechanics. *Reviews of Modern Physics* 38(3):447–452.
Bell JS. (2004) Speakable and Unspeakable in Quantum Mechanics, 2nd. (Cambridge University Press, Cambridge).
Bellman R. (1956) Dynamic Programming and Lagrange Multipliers. *Proceedings of the National Academy of Sciences of the United States of America*. 42(10):767–9.
Brandt F. et al (eds). (2016) Handbook of Computational Social Choice, 1st. (Cambridge University Press, USA).
Brukner Č. (2014) Quantum causality. *Nature Physics* 10(4): 259–263.
Burghes DN., Graham A. (2004) *Control and Optimal Control Theories with Applications*. (Woodhead Publishing Limited, England).
Cain, M. et al. (2026). Shor's algorithm is possible with as few as 10,000 reconfigurable atomic qubits. https://arxiv.org/abs/2603.28627.
Caton, S., Haas, C. (2024) *Fairness in Machine Learning: A Survey*. ACM Comput. Surv. 56(7):166.

Chiribella G., et al. (2009) Theoretical framework for quantum networks. *Physical Review A—Atomic, Molecular, and Optical Physics* 80(2):022339.
Chouldechova A. (2017) Fair prediction with disparate impact: A study of bias in recidivism prediction instruments. *Big Data* 5(2):153–163.
Coenen C., Grunwald A. (2017) Responsible research and innovation (RRI) in quantum technology. *Ethics and Information Technology* 19(4):277–94.
Coenen C. et al. (2022) Quantum Technologies and Society: Towards a Different Spin. *NanoEthics* 16:1–6.
D'Alessandro D. (2007) *Introduction to Quantum Control and Dynamics.* (Taylor & Francis, New York).
D'Ariano GM., Lo Presti P. (2001) Quantum Tomography for Measuring Experimentally the Matrix Elements of an Arbitrary Quantum Operation. *Physical Review Letters* 86(19):4195–4198.
DeCew J (2018) Privacy. In: Zalta EN. (ed) *Stanford Encyclopedia of Philosophy.* Stanford University.
del Barrio E et al. (2016). Review of Mathematical frameworks for Fairness in Machine Learning. arXiv:2005.13755 [cs, stat].
de Wolf R. (2017) The potential impact of quantum computers on society. *Ethics and Information Technology* 19:271–6.
Donoghue JF., Menezes G. (2020) Quantum causality and the arrows of time and thermodynamics. *Progress in Particle and Nuclear Physics* 115: 103812.
DiVincenzo DP. (2017) Scientists and citizens: getting to quantum technologies. *Ethics and Information Technology* 19:247–51.
Drogoul A. et al. (2002) Multi-agent based simulation: Where are the agents? In: Sichman JS., Bousquet F., Davidsson P. (eds) *Multi-agent-based Simulation II* 89–104.
Dwork C. (2008) Differential Privacy: A Survey of Results. In: Agrawal M., Du D., Duan Z., Li A. (eds) *Theory and Applications of Models of Computation. Lecture Notes in Computer Science* 4978:1–19.
Dwork C. et al. (2012) Fairness through awareness. In: *Proceedings of the 3rd Innovations in Theoretical Computer Science Conference (ITCS '12).* ACM. 214–226.
European Commission. (2021) *Quantum Flagship Strategic Report.* (European Commission, Brussels).
Gottesman D. (1998) Theory of fault-tolerant quantum computation. *Physical Review A* 57(1): 127–137.
Gottesman D. (2010) An Introduction to Quantum Error Correction and Fault-Tolerant Quantum Computation. *Quantum information science and its contributions to mathematics, Proceedings of Symposia in Applied Mathematics* 63: 13–58.
Greenbaum D. (2015) Introduction to Quantum Gate Set Tomography. https://arxiv.org/abs/1509.02921.
Grinbaum A. (2017) Narratives of quantum theory in the age of quantum technologies. *Ethics and Information Technology* 19(4): 295–306.
Hammond PJ. (1988) Consequentialist Foundations for Expected Utility Theory. *Theory and Decision.* 25:25–78.
Harrigan N., Spekkens RW. (2010) Einstein, Incompleteness, and the Epistemic View of Quantum States. *Foundations of Physics* 40(2): 125–157.
Hoofnagle CJ., Garfinkel S. (2021) *Law and Policy for the Quantum Age.* (Cambridge University Press, Cambridge).
Hoven MJ. (2005) Design for values and values for design. *Information Age.* 4:4–7.
Hoven MJ., Vermaas, P., van de Poel, I. (eds) (2015) *Handbook of Ethics, Values, and Technological Design: Sources, Theory, Values and Application Domains.* (Springer, Netherlands).
Huang HY. et al. (2020) Predicting many properties of a quantum system from very few measurements. *Nature Physics.* 16(10):1050-7.
Ji Z. et al. (2020) MIP* = RE. https://arxiv.org/abs/2001.04383.

Johnson WG. (2018) Governance Tools for the Second Quantum Revolution. *Jurimetrics* 59(4): 487.

Johnston EW. (2015) *Governance in the Information Era: Theory and Practice of Policy Informatics.* (Routledge, New York).

Kearns M. et al. (2019) An empirical study of rich subgroup fairness for machine learning. In: *Proceedings of the Conference on Fairness, Accountability, and Transparency (FAT'19).* ACM:100–109.

Kimble HJ. (2008) The Quantum Internet. *Nature* 453(7198): 1023–1030.

Klaes M., Sent EM. (2005) A Conceptual History of the Emergence of Bounded Rationality. *History of Political Economy* 37(1):27–59.

Kleinberg J. et al. (2023). Inherent Trade-Offs in the Fair Determination of Risk Scores. In: Raghavan, M. (ed) *The Societal Impacts of Algorithmic Decision-Making.* (Association for Computing Machinery, New York).

Kolobov A. et al. (2012) A theory of goal-oriented MDPs with dead ends. In: Freitas N., Murphy K. eds) *UAI'12: Proceedings of the Twenty-Eighth Conference on Uncertainty in Artificial Intelligence.* (AUAI Press, USA).

Kop M. (2021a) Establishing a legal-ethical framework for quantum technology. *Yale Law School, Yale Journal of Law & Technology (YJoLT), The Record.*

Kop M. (2021b) Ethics in the quantum age. *Physics World* 34(12): 31.

Kop M. (2021c) Quantum Computing and Intellectual Property Law. *Berkeley Technology Law Journal* 35(3)

Kop M., et al. (2023) *Towards responsible quantum technology.* Harvard Berkman Klein Center for Internet & Society Research Publication Series.

Kop M., et al. (2024a) Ten principles for responsible quantum innovation. *Quantum Science and Technology* 9(3): 035013.

Kop M., et al. (2024b) *How Quantum Technologies May Be Integrated Into Healthcare, What Regulators Should Consider*. Stanford Law School.

List C. (2013) Social Choice Theory. In: Zalta EN. (ed) Stanford Encyclopedia of Philosophy. Stanford University.

Lloyd S. et al. (2004). Infrastructure for the quantum Internet. *ACM SIGCOMM Computer Communication Review* 34(5):9-20.

Lloyd S. (2012) A Turing test for free will. *Philosophical Transactions of the Royal Society A: Mathematical, Physical and Engineering Sciences* 370(1971):3597–610.

Lu CY., et al. (2022) Micius quantum experiments in space. *Reviews of Modern Physics* 94(3): 035001.

Malia BK., et al. (2022) Distributed quantum sensing with a mode-entangled network of spin-squeezed atomic states. https://arxiv.org/abs/2205.06382.

Marchant GE., et al. (2024) Learning From Emerging Technology Governance for Guiding Quantum Technology. *Rich JL & Tech* 31:266.

McGee V. (1991) We Turing machines aren't expected-utility maximizers (even ideally). *Philosophical Studies.* 64(1):115–23.

McNamara D. et al. (2017) Provably Fair Representations. arXiv:171004394.

Mohseni M., et al. (2008) Quantum-process tomography: Resource analysis of different strategies. *Physical Review A—Atomic, Molecular, and Optical Physics* 77(3):032322.

Möller M, Vuik C. (2017). On the impact of quantum computing technology on future developments in high-performance scientific computing. *Ethics and Information Technology*. 19(4):253–69.

Mouaddib AI. et al. (2015) Handling Advice in MDPs for Semi-Autonomous Systems. *ICAPS Workshop on Planning and Robotics (PlanRob).* 153–60.

Neumann NMP., et al. (2020) Quantum Communication for Military Applications. https://arxiv.org/abs/2011.04989.

Nielsen MA., Chuang IL. (2011) *Quantum Computation and Quantum Information: 10th Anniversary Edition.* (Cambridge University Press, New York).

Parsons S., Wooldridge M. (2002) Game Theory and Decision Theory in Multi-Agent Systems. *Autonomous Agents and Multi-Agent Systems* 5(3):243–254.
Perrier E. (2021a) Quantum Fair Machine Learning. In: *Proceedings of the 2021 AAAI/ACM Conference on AI, Ethics, and Society*.843-853.
Perrier E. (2021b) Computability, Complexity, Consistency and Controllability: A Four C's Framework for cross-disciplinary Ethical Algorithm Research. https://arxiv.org/abs/2102.04234.
Perrier E. (2022) The Quantum Governance Stack: Models of Governance for Quantum Information Technologies. *Digital Society* 1(3): 22.
Porsdam Mann S. et al. (2024) Guidelines for Ethical use and Acknowledgement of Large Language Models in Academic Writing. *Nature Machine Intelligence* 6:1272–1274.
Possati, L.M., Vermaas, P. (2025) The rationality and morality of connecting quantum computers. *Ethics and Information Technology* 27(30).
Preskill J. (2018) Quantum Computing in the NISQ era and beyond. *Quantum* 2: 79.
Preskill J. (2021). Quantum computing 40 years later. https://arxiv.org/abs/2106.10522.
Purdy G. (2010) ISO 31000:2009—setting a new standard for risk management. *Risk Analysis: An International Journal* 30(6):881–6.
Rand LE. (2023) *Schrodinger's Technology Is Here and Not: A Socio-Technical Evaluation of Quantum Sensing Implications for Nuclear Deterrence.* (University of Maryland, United States).
Rathenau Instituut. (2023) *Quantum technology in society.* (Rathenau Instituut, The Hague).
Schuld M. et al. (2014) The quest for a Quantum Neural Network. *Quantum Information Processing* 13(11):2567–86.
Schuld M., Petruccione F. (2021) *Machine Learning with Quantum Computers.* (Springer, Switzerland).
Schuld M., et al. (2015) An Introduction to Quantum Machine Learning. *Contemporary Physics* 56(2):172–185.
Schoeman FD. (1984) *Philosophical Dimensions of Privacy: An Anthology.* (Cambridge University Press, Cambridge).
Shor PW. (1994) Algorithms for quantum computation: discrete logarithms and factoring. In: *Proceedings 35th annual symposium on foundations of computer science.* (IEEE).
Shor PW. (1997) Polynomial-Time Algorithms for Prime Factorization and Discrete Logarithms on a Quantum Computer. *SIAM Journal on Computing* 26(5): 1484–1509.
Simon C. (2017) Towards a Global Quantum Network. *Nature Photonics* 11(11): 678–680.
Simon HA. (1955) A Behavioral Model of Rational Choice. *The Quarterly Journal of Economics* 69(1):99–118.
Sipser M. (2012) *Introduction to the Theory of Computation.* (Cengage Learning, United States of America).
Svegliato J. et al (2021). Ethically Compliant Sequential Decision Making. *Proceedings of the AAAI Conference on Artificial Intelligence* 35(13):11657–65.
Ten Holter C., et al. (2021) Reading the road: challenges and opportunities on the path to responsible innovation in quantum computing. *Technology Analysis & Strategic Management* 35(7):844–856.
Townsend JS. (2000) *A Modern Approach to Quantum Mechanics.* (University Science Books, United States of America).
van der Enden KL. et al. (2024) Advancing a responsible future quantum internet. In: *2024 IEEE International Conference on Quantum Computing and Engineering (QCE)* 15(2):65–70.
Vermaas PE. (2017) The societal impact of the emerging quantum technologies: a renewed urgency to make quantum theory understandable. *Ethics and Information Technology* 19:241–6.
Vermaas PE. et al. (2025) Quantum Internet, Governance, Trust, and the Promise of Secure Communication: On building a Quantum Internet that will be used. https://arxiv.org/abs/2505.15852.
Vidick T, Watrous J. (2016) Quantum Proofs. *Foundations and Trends in Theoretical Computer Science* 11(1–2):1–215.
Watrous J. (2018) *The Theory of Quantum Information.* (Cambridge University Press, Cambridge).

World Economic Forum. (2022). *Quantum Computing Governance Principles.* (World Economic Forum, Geneva).
Wehner S., et al. (2018) Quantum internet: A vision for the road ahead. *Science* 362(6412).
Wiseman HM., Milburn GJ. (2010) *Quantum Measurement and Control.* (Cambridge University Press, Cambridge).
Wootters WK., Zurek WH. (1982) A single quantum cannot be cloned. *Nature* 299(5886): 802–803.
Wootters WK. (1998) Quantum entanglement as a quantifiable resource. *Philosophical Transactions of the Royal Society of London Series A: Mathematical, Physical and Engineering Sciences* 356(1743): 1717–1731.
Yuan, F., Ying, M. (2021) Quantum Hoare Logic with Classical Variables. *ACM Transactions on Quantum Computing* 2(4):16.
Zafar A. (2025) Quantum computing in finance: Regulatory readiness, legal gaps, and the future of secure tech innovation. *European Journal of Risk Regulation.* 1-32.

Chapter 5
Quantum Computing and Ethical Exceptionalism: Lessons from Classical Computing

Sebastian Porsdam Mann, Mateo Aboy, Marcelo Corrales Compagnucci, Peter Alexander Earls Davis, Brian D. Earp, Timo Minssen, and Gabriela Lenarczyk

5.1 Introduction

The ethical stakes of a given technology correlate with the scale of its potential impacts on individuals, societies, and the environment. By any measure, the potential impacts of quantum computing, as it matures, are of extraordinary magnitude. As detailed in previous chapters of this book, fully realized quantum computing has the potential to render tractable some types of computations that are currently infeasible using classical computing approaches, including factoring, certain quantum simulations, and selected optimization or sampling tasks.[1] This has enormous potential upside for scientific, technological, and medical progress, with substantial attendant economic opportunities. However, given both the wide applicability of quantum computing, as well as the strategic importance of specific applications (e.g., factoring of large composite integers for cryptanalytic purposes, or military communication and surveillance), quantum computing has very significant dual-use potential. This

S. Porsdam Mann (✉) · M. C. Compagnucci · P. A. E. Davis · T. Minssen · G. Lenarczyk
Center for Advanced Studies in Bioscience Innovation Law (CeBIL), Faculty of Law, University of Copenhagen, Copenhagen, Denmark

M. Aboy
Centre for Law, Medicine and Life Sciences (LML) and Centre for Intellectual Property and Information Law (CIPIL), University of Cambridge, Cambridge, UK

B. D. Earp
Center for Biomedical Ethics, Yong Loo Lin School of Medicine, National University of Singapore, Singapore, Singapore

[1] See Aboy et al. (2026).

M. Aboy et al. (eds.), *Quantum Technology Governance II*, Perspectives in Law, Business and Innovation, https://doi.org/10.1007/978-981-92-3768-5_5

complicates otherwise clear principles of open science and transparency, and introduces questions related to IP, trade/state secrets, standardization, and export control.[2] More generally, there is a cluster of ethical issues associated with access to the knowledge, funding, and infrastructure needed to operate quantum computing systems. Scholars have begun to identify and probe various ethical opportunities and issues associated with quantum computing technology.[3]

Central to these emerging discussions is whether quantum computing introduces fundamentally novel ethical challenges requiring entirely new frameworks, or whether it primarily replicates familiar dilemmas from previous technological transitions. This question—call it the quantum computing ethical exceptionalism question—is a familiar one. When the Internet emerged, Judge Frank Easterbrook famously argued against treating 'cyberspace' as a distinct legal domain requiring its own specialized doctrines through his "Law of the Horse" analogy.[4] Just as general principles of property, tort, and contract adequately resolve equine disputes without specialized "horse law," Easterbrook maintained that we should first apply existing principles to identify genuine gaps before constructing bespoke frameworks for cyberspace.

Yet Easterbrook's metaphor itself reveals the stakes of getting this judgment wrong. Imagine, as other scholars have, attempting to govern automobiles using only rules designed for horse-drawn carriages.[5] The car's revolutionary impact on speed, scale, and social organization exposed the limitations of incremental legal adaptation. Similarly, treating quantum computing as merely "classical computing but faster" risks overlooking crucial differences that might create genuinely novel ethical challenges or transform familiar issues to such an extent that simple transplantation of existing frameworks is no longer appropriate. In any case, the challenge lies in distinguishing which aspects, if any, represent real novelty versus those that involve recognizable problems in new forms.[6]

Ethicists, too, have grappled with variations of this question. Over the past several decades, claims of unique ethical challenges demanding new frameworks have emerged in relation to several foundational technological advances, from genetics to machine learning.[7] The history of these debates shows that while new technologies often create specific challenges which do require adapting the way ethical frameworks are applied to these new contexts, they rarely necessitate completely new ethical principles, frameworks, or foundations.[8]

[2] Van Daalen (2024a, b).

[3] Possati (2023), Umbrello (2024).

[4] Easterbrook (1996).

[5] Other scholars have made the similar converse point to Easterbrook using other related analogies. See Kim (2023), Lastowka (2011).

[6] Cheung et al. (2025).

[7] Suter (2001), Bærøe et al. (2020), Klein and Morar (2024).

[8] See, e.g., Shevchenko and Zhavoronkov (2024), Cheung et al. (2025) (arguing against exceptionalism in a different context).

Quantum computing is now prompting precisely this debate. Like its technological predecessors, it has divided scholars between those arguing for ethical exceptionalism and those favoring adaptive application of existing frameworks. Some contend that quantum phenomena create ethical puzzles so unprecedented they require "new conceptual tools and methods."[9] Others acknowledge quantum computing's technical distinctiveness while maintaining that established ethical frameworks, thoughtfully adapted, can address its challenges.[10]

As with previous technologies, scholars have sought guidance through analogies. Some compare quantum computing to artificial intelligence, emphasizing shared concerns about opacity and control. Others draw parallels with nanotechnology's dual-use implications or propose regulatory models from pharmaceuticals.[11] Yet surprisingly, the most direct precedent, classical computing, has received comparatively little attention.

This oversight is particularly striking given that classical computing represents not just another technological analogy but the direct historical antecedent. Classical computing underwent its own fierce "uniqueness debate" that shaped computer ethics as a field.[12] Here was a technology that seemed as revolutionary in its time as quantum computing appears today, that grappled with similar questions about computational power becoming concentrated in few hands, and that raised parallel concerns about dual-use applications from cryptography to weapons systems.

This chapter seeks to address the question of ethical exceptionalism by comparing the nascent field of quantum computing ethics with the rich historical precedent of classical computing and its associated body of computer ethics. Section 5.2 explores how ethical lessons from disruptive technologies can inform quantum computing governance, ultimately arguing that classical computing provides the most relevant comparison due to its similar transformative impact, dual-use potential, and geopolitical context. Section 5.3 reviews emerging ethical concerns in quantum computing based on two key studies by Umbrello and Possati. Section 5.4 discusses how historical developments in classical computing can inform the ethical governance of quantum computing across three key domains: security, justice, and governance. Section 5.5 analyzes whether quantum computing ethics requires entirely new frameworks or if lessons from computer ethics can still apply. Section 5.6 concludes.

---

[9] Possati (2023), p. 1.

[10] Perrier (2022).

[11] See, e.g., Kop (2021), Waldherr et al. (2025), Marchant et al. (2024).

[12] Maner (1980), Maner (1996), Johnson (1985), Moor (1985), Tavani (2002).

5.2 Quantum Computing and Classical Computing

Recent scholarship in quantum computing ethics has advanced historical analogies for quantum computing. Kop, for example, proposes a legal-ethical framework that builds on artificial intelligence (AI) and nanotechnology governance.[13] Kop notes, first, the substantial consensus already achieved around principles like transparency, accountability, and fairness in AI governance; and second, the technical reality that many quantum systems are essentially quantum-AI hybrids. He also draws inspiration from nanoethics, because both fields manipulate matter at dimensions where classical physics gives way to quantum phenomena.

Marchant et al.[14] take a more systematic comparative approach, examining lessons from biotechnology, nanotechnology, and AI governance to extract principles applicable to quantum technologies. Their analysis yields fifteen specific lessons organized around eight governance pillars—including soft law versus hard law, stakeholder engagement, transparency, and international coordination. From biotechnology, they identify how regulatory frameworks can become entrenched, exclude smaller players, and create international regulatory and trade barriers. From nanotechnology, they observe how governance can develop alongside rather than after the technology, and how initial promises and fears often prove exaggerated. From AI, they highlight the extreme "pacing problem" where technology advances far outstrip regulatory responses, and how a proliferation of voluntary measures can create confusion rather than clarity.

There is no doubt that these comparative approaches offer valuable insights. However, the strength of any analogy depends on how closely it captures the relevant features of the phenomenon being studied. The more fundamental the similarities between two technologies, the more applicable the lessons learned from one will be to the other. Classical computing shares quantum computing's most fundamental characteristic: both represent revolutionary leaps in humanity's ability to process information which rendered previously infeasible problems solvable. Both technologies found immediate application in scientific modeling (weather prediction and stellar evolution for classical computing; molecular simulation and optimization for quantum computing).[15]

They have other shared features, too. Both have attracted intense military interest, due to their ability to break encryption and model nuclear processes. Both emerged during periods of superpower competition—classical computing during the Cold War nuclear arms race, quantum computing amid today's technological rivalry between the U.S. and China. Both have raised concerns about encryption and communications security, triggering debates about export controls and intellectual property protection. Perhaps most significantly, both represented fundamental transformations in how information could be processed, stored, and transmitted. Given these structural parallels, classical computing, we argue, offers a particularly relevant lens through

[13] Kop (2021).

[14] Marchant et al. (2024).

[15] See, generally, Dyson (2012).

which to examine the emerging field of quantum computing ethics, to which we now turn.

5.3 Quantum Computing Ethics: What Issues Are Emerging?

Given the many structural parallels between classical and quantum computing, it would be surprising if many of the same ethical issues did not arise. We suggest we can learn from the experiences gained in addressing classical computing ethics, at least to a significant extent. However, before drawing those comparisons, it is useful to map the emerging terrain of quantum computing ethics in its own right. This overview clarifies where the points of contact with classical computing lie, and how familiar ethical issues might manifest differently in quantum contexts. To that end, we begin with an outline of quantum computing ethics.

While quantum computing ethics is still a young field, there have been two recent attempts at summarizing the literature. We can rely on these to establish an overview of the state of the debate. The first of these is a scoping review by Umbrello,[16] who found 10 ethical issues spread across 14 included studies. Privacy and security constitute the most frequently mentioned set of issues, appearing in 78% of the reviewed articles with 116 total mentions—a finding Umbrello attributes to widespread anxieties about quantum computing's potential to render some current encryption methods obsolete (i.e., Shor's algorithm). Trust was the second most discussed issue (86 mentions), followed by concerns about equity, diversity and inclusion (53 mentions). Notably, about half the articles addressed accessibility issues, exploring how unequal access to quantum technologies could exacerbate existing social and economic inequalities, potentially undermining democratic participation, and create new forms of the digital divide widely discussed in relation to internet access. Umbrello observes that responsibility and accountability concerns appeared in five studies, and he also includes less-discussed issues of human autonomy, non-maleficence, democracy, well-being, and free expression. Umbrello notes that his review found ecological and sustainability considerations completely absent from the literature. His review also notes the difficulty of accessing military and defense research on quantum technologies, suggesting that parallel discussions with significant ethical implications may be occurring outside public academic discourse. Table 5.1 lists his 10 identified issues.

Possati reviewed 21 studies.[17] Although he does not list the ethical issues he surveys, we can identify several of them based on his description. Central to Possati's contribution is his detailed analysis of data management challenges, where he argues that quantum properties like superposition and entanglement fundamentally alter traditional concepts of identity, privacy, ownership, and traceability. Possati

[16] Umbrello (2024).

[17] Possati (2023), p. 48.

Table 5.1 Summary of key ethical issues in quantum technologies from Umbrello[18]

Issue	Principle	No. of mentions
Privacy and security	Privacy and security must be protected by potential quantum techniques for intrusion and data collection	116
Accessibility	Access to [quantum technologies] is essential as seen by stakeholders	22
Trust	The exchange of information concerning the ethical and social impacts of quantum technologies is essential for trust and therefore adoption of those technologies	86
Responsibility/accountability	Quantum technologies must not promote the abdication but rather support increasing human responsibility/accountability	19
Equity/Diversity/Inclusion	Quantum technologies must be equitably distributed, permit diverse voices and stakeholders, and permit inclusion of often marginalized groups	53
Democracy	Democratic access to technologies is essential for stakeholder participation	3
Well-being	Quantum technologies, when ubiquitous, should support and promote collective well-being	2
Autonomy	Quantum technologies must protect user autonomy	3
Non-maleficence	Those who design and use quantum technologies have a duty to ensure that those technologies do not inflict harm on others	5
Free expression	The architectures of quantum systems should not restrict stakeholders' right to freedom of expression	3

pays special attention to what he terms "process opacity," arguing that quantum computing introduces a new form of opacity that is ontological rather than epistemic. This distinction, he suggests, requires entirely new approaches to transparency and explainability.[19] His review also emphasizes the dual-use nature of quantum technologies, the potential for a "data deluge" as quantum systems generate unprecedented amounts of information, and environmental concerns related to the energy-intensive cooling requirements of quantum computers. Additionally, Possati argues that quantum computing may intensify familiar algorithmic ethics concerns. In particular, the enhanced connectivity and complexity of quantum algorithms could aggravate problems of bias and fairness, while the distinctive ontological opacity

[18] This table presents an abridged version of Table 5.1 from the original scoping review, focusing on the identified ethical issue, its core principle, and the total number of mentions in the literature reviewed. It excludes the detailed examples mentioned in the original table and the count of unique articles discussing each issue for conciseness. See Umbrello (2024).

[19] By "ontological opacity," Possati means that the lack of transparency is rooted in the nature of quantum systems themselves. Quantum phenomena impose limits not because observers lack sufficient information, but because the processes are inherently indeterminate or nonclassically constituted.

Table 5.2 Six additional ethical issues in QC, identified by the authors of this chapter from a review paper by Possati[20]

Issue	Principle
Science communication & public understanding	Quantum principles and technological impacts must be communicated clearly and accessibly to enable informed public discourse and build trust among diverse stakeholders
Dual-use nature	The inherent potential for quantum technologies to be used for both beneficial and harmful purposes, particularly military applications, requires robust ethical oversight and international governance
Data deluge & management	Anticipated exponential growth in data generated by quantum technologies necessitates new strategies for ethical data management, storage, and consideration of associated resource demands
Environmental impact	The significant energy consumption and resource requirements of quantum computing systems and their supporting infrastructure warrant careful assessment and mitigation of their ecological footprint
Explainability & interpretability	The fundamental operational differences in quantum computing, including aspects like "ontological opacity," require novel approaches to ensure algorithmic processes and outcomes are understandable, interpretable, and justifiable
Geopolitical & power dynamics	The strategic importance of quantum technologies can create or intensify global and regional power imbalances, demanding frameworks that promote equitable development, access, and international cooperation to avoid a "quantum divide"

of quantum processes raises deeper challenges for explainability and accountability. Together, Possati argues that these features risk further constraining human autonomy if decisions come to depend on inscrutable quantum-enhanced systems. Summing up, Possati's review adds six ethical issues to the ones identified by Umbrello. These are detailed in Table 5.2.

While a detailed examination of how each of these 16 issues maps onto classical computing ethics would be prohibitive given space and time constraints, many of these issues can be grouped into themes that reflect an underlying or broader type of concern. For instance, anxieties about encryption vulnerabilities, privacy breaches, dual-use applications, data management challenges, and environmental impacts all fundamentally relate to risk of harm or, conversely, *security*—how quantum computing might create new vulnerabilities or help us protect against existing threats. Similarly, concerns about accessibility barriers, equity/diversity/inclusion, democratic participation, the quantum divide, and geopolitical power

[20] Possati (2023).

imbalances center on questions of *justice*—who benefits from quantum technologies and who bears their risks. Finally, issues of trust, responsibility/accountability, epistemic challenges in science communication, explainability, and process opacity cluster around problems of *governance*—how quantum systems can be effectively overseen, understood, and regulated. These three thematic categories provide a pragmatic framework which we can use to compare quantum computing ethics with its classical computing predecessor.

5.4 Classical Computing and Computer Ethics

Given the vast scope of classical computing ethics literature spanning over five decades, attempting a comprehensive survey of how each theme evolved would be neither feasible nor particularly illuminating within our space constraints. Instead, for each thematic area, we draw on canonical overviews and case studies that illustrate key lessons. Our contribution lies not in providing an exhaustive catalog of classical computing ethics (a task already accomplished by scholars like Bynum, Johnson, and Tavani[21]) but rather in demonstrating that the parallels between classical and quantum computing are sufficiently strong to make historical lessons both relevant and instructive.

5.4.1 Security

Among the security-related ethical concerns identified in quantum computing, encryption stands out as the most salient and historically instructive example. In classical computing, the very first large-scale computational projects were driven by cryptanalytic needs, raising concerns about secrecy, surveillance, and the balance between national security and civil liberties. The parallel for our present topic stems from quantum computing's theoretical ability to break asymmetric cryptography through Shor's algorithm, which would render much of today's digital infrastructure, which relies on these encryption algorithms, vulnerable. Encryption, informational privacy, and Shor's algorithm are currently the most frequently mentioned issues in the quantum computing ethics literature.[22]

The parallels between quantum and classical computing's relationships with encryption are striking. Classical computing itself emerged from cryptanalytic necessity during World War II.[23] Prior to the war, Polish mathematicians had already

---

[21] Bynum (2017), Johnson (2009), Tavani (2016).

[22] Umbrello (2024).

[23] The historical context described, concerning the origins of classical computing in World War II cryptanalysis, is well-established. For foundational accounts, see, e.g., Dyson (2012), Hodges (2014), Gribbin (2013), Gleick (2011), Bhattacharya (2022), Soni and Goodman (2017).

broken early versions of the German Enigma cipher using mathematical techniques. These involved significant amounts of computation, and when the Germans later increased the complexity of their encryption devices, carrying out these computations by hand became infeasible. This drove development of the British Bombe, an electromechanical device automating the search for Enigma settings, and later Colossus, widely regarded as the world's first programmable electronic digital computer, was built to crack the even more complex Lorenz cipher used for high-level German communications.

Given that the Allied victory in World War II is often attributed in no small part to the breaking of Enigma,[24] one can immediately appreciate the dual-use and geopolitical implications of computational advances. This mirrors the current attention being paid to quantum computing's potential to break RSA encryption. In both cases, the military and intelligence value of these capabilities led governments to grapple with fundamental questions about secrecy, export controls, and the balance between national security and commercial development.

Three episodes in the history of classical computing illustrate the importance and difficulty of addressing these questions appropriately. They also contextualize contemporary debates relating to encryption and security within which quantum computing is presently emerging. The Data Encryption Standard (DES) controversy (1973–1977) began when IBM, a leading computing company, developed a strong commercial encryption algorithm called Lucifer with a 128-bit key.[25] During the standardization process, the National Security Agency (NSA) conducted a classified review. According to partially declassified NSA documents, IBM and the NSA may have "compromised on a 56-bit key."[26] This reduction, as the National Research Council's 1996 CRISIS report noted, generated suspicion that the government had deliberately weakened commercial encryption to maintain surveillance capabilities.[27] Civilian researchers Diffie and Hellman argued in 1977 that a purpose-built machine could crack DES,[28] and by the late 1990s such attacks became practically feasible.[29] Later scholarship concluded that the lack of transparency about the DES key length led to widespread doubt about its strength.[30]

A second episode occurred during the so-called Crypto Wars of the 1990s. The U.S. government historically classified encryption software as munitions under arms export regulations.[31] When programmer Phil Zimmermann released Pretty Good Privacy (PGP) in 1991, a software that gave individuals access to military-grade encryption, federal prosecutors launched a three-year criminal investigation for

[24] See, e.g., Deutsch (1978).

[25] Sorkin (1984).

[26] Landau (2014), p. 418.

[27] National Research Council (1996).

[28] Diffie and Hellman (1977).

[29] Landau (2014).

[30] Landau (2014).

[31] National Research Council (1996).

illegal arms trafficking.[32] The government's position was clear: encryption was a weapon, and its spread threatened national security by enabling foreign adversaries and criminals to communicate secretly. The investigation ultimately collapsed without indictment, and by the late 1990s, mounting commercial pressure led the government to abandon the most restrictive export controls entirely.[33] The scholarly consensus, crystallized in the National Research Council's 1996 CRISIS report, as well as in the 2001 Congressional Research Service note on the topic, concluded that export controls had damaged U.S. commercial competitiveness, driven development overseas, and proved unenforceable in an interconnected world where mathematical knowledge could not be contained.[34]

The Clipper Chip initiative (1993–1996) represented the Clinton administration's attempt to balance cryptographic security with surveillance capabilities. The proposal would establish the "Escrowed Encryption Standard" (EES) to be implemented in the Clipper Chip and similar devices.[35] The system would use secret encryption keys that would be split and held in escrow (that is, deposited with one or more secure third parties) by two government agencies, enabling law enforcement access under court order.[36] The proposal generated overwhelming opposition—an announcement in the Federal Register generated 320 comments, almost all negative, including formal objections from government agencies like the Department of Energy and the Nuclear Regulatory Commission.[37] The technical vulnerability of this approach was demonstrated when cryptographer Matt Blaze showed that a user could generate a fake 'Law-Enforcement Access Field' the Clipper chip would accept, letting the conversation stay encrypted while blocking any key-escrow access.[38] The market delivered the decisive verdict—while the FBI purchased 9000 Clipper-enabled phones to trigger adoption, fewer than 8000 others were ultimately sold to other customers.[39]

These three episodes from classical computing history presage encryption's role in today's information society, in which it serves as an indispensable and ubiquitous tool that protects fundamental rights and interests, yet simultaneously provides a flashpoint in debates over national security, surveillance, and the balance of power between individuals and institutions. More recent episodes have further shaped understandings of the legitimacy of state access to encrypted data, the responsibilities of technology companies to their users and governments, and the resilience of democratic institutions in the face of both cyber threats and authoritarian drift—including the role of encryption as a tool that rearranges power.[40] The 2013 Snowden revelations exposed the scale of state surveillance, prompting global concern over privacy, and

32 Stay (1997).

33 Lauzon (1998), Grimmett (2001).

34 National Research Council (1996), Grimmett (2001).

35 Froomkin (1995).

36 Froomkin (1995).

37 Landau (2014).

38 Blaze (1994).

39 Landau (2014).

40 Rogaway (2015).

leading to increased availability of privacy-enhancing technologies like end-to-end encryption in consumer products and services.[41] This led, in 2015–2016, to Apple's refusal to unlock an iPhone for the FBI, underscoring the emerging conflict between individual privacy, corporate power, and national security.[42] The remote hacking of journalist Jamal Khashoggi's or his associates' phone(s) using Pegasus spyware, allegedly by a state actor, highlighted the role of encrypted devices and applications in operationalizing freedom of expression, and the considerable stakes at play when encryption is compromised.[43] Proposals for client-side scanning technologies, introduced in the EU in 2022,[44] have raised complex questions about the technical feasibility and legal implications of detecting harmful content without undermining encryption.[45] In 2024, the European Court of Human Rights ruled that mandating indiscriminate access to encrypted data "impairs the very essence of the right to respect for private life".[46]

As these episodes illustrate, encryption provides a nexus for a degree of complex legal and ethical dilemmas. Quantum computing, so far as it disrupts methods of encryption critical to today's information society, stands to substantially expand public and private surveillance capabilities. However, parallel technological developments such as in post-quantum cryptography and quantum key distribution,[47] may lead to a furtherance of the "going dark" wherein cryptography enables secure communication. In any outcome, past and present debates can assist in informing appropriate policy responses. For example, current discussions in the literature exploring or proposing the insertion of backdoors into post-quantum cryptography, controlling quantum technology exports, and restricting quantum development to preserve existing encryption capabilities echo approaches that have proved problematic in the past.[48] Such insights remain relevant as quantum computing prompts renewed debates concerning the balance between (national) security and individual rights, and the technical feasibility of government control of encryption technologies. However, there remains the potential for quantum computing, and other quantum technologies, to disrupt today's security *status quo* so fundamentally that novel approaches will be needed to grasp the issues that emerge.

---

[41] Rozenshtein (2018).

[42] Schulze (2017).

[43] Kotliar and Carmi (2024).

[44] EU (2022).

[45] Abelson et al. (2024).

[46] *Podchasov v Russia* (2024), para 80.

[47] Broadbent and Schaffner (2016).

[48] See Ravi et al. (2024) (discussing backdoor vulnerabilities in quantum-resistant algorithms), Mishra and Nair (2023, p. 16) (discussing scenarios where "governments could protect and severely restrict quantum computing power to limit the possibility of malicious attacks that could compromise national security.").

5.4.2 *Justice*

Justice in quantum computing encompasses concerns about how both the benefits and burdens of this technology will be distributed across society. This includes questions of accessibility, equity, diversity, inclusion, democratic participation, and the potential for new forms of technological divide between and within nations and communities.[49] Within this category, access—that is, who will be able to use, develop, and benefit from quantum computing capabilities as they mature—is one of the most widely discussed issues in the nascent quantum computing ethics literature.[50] A key factor shaping access to any technology is the extent to which this technology is protected by intellectual property law. Here, the history of classical computing may offer instructive precedents.

The history of classical computing shows that the legal choices made at a technology's birth can profoundly influence whether value accrues narrowly to early movers or broadly to society. In classical computing, a series of *deliberate* decisions to forego, and later to dismantle, strong IP barriers created an unusually open innovation system. Empirical work has since shown that this openness accelerated both the *pace* and the *breadth* of downstream invention.[51]

The early history of computing saw various experimental machines developed across multiple institutions in the 1930s and 1940s. Several of the fundamental breakthroughs that would define modern computing, such as the stored-program architecture, came from John von Neumann and his colleagues.[52] During World War II, the atmosphere of national emergency naturally subordinated concerns about intellectual property and individual credit to the broader war effort. As Jan Rajchman, one of the engineers on the project, recalled: "It was all an atmosphere, of course, of great fervor for the war, and nobody worried about patents or priorities."[53]

This collaborative ethos might have dissipated after the war ended. Instead, von Neumann and his colleagues made the deliberate and consequential decision to place their innovations in the public domain. Despite numerous potentially lucrative inventions, von Neumann actively worked to ensure these advances remained freely available.[54] He and his colleagues went so far as to petition the U.S. Patent Office to treat their technical reports as prior publications, explicitly stating that "it is our intention and desire that any material contained therein which might be of a patentable nature should be placed in the public domain."[55] This openness allowed early technical innovations to spread widely and quickly. Within five years, multiple computers based

---

49 See, also, Kop et al. (2024a).

50 Umbrello (2024).

51 Watzinger et al. (2020), Nagler et al. (2022).

52 See Dyson (2012), Bhattacharya (2022).

53 Dyson (2012), Chapter 5.

54 Dyson (2012), Chapter 5.

55 Dyson (2012), Chapter 5.

on the Institute for Advanced Study architecture had been constructed at institutions around the world.[56]

Another example of how early IP decisions shaped subsequent technological diffusion is given by Bell Laboratories' approach to the transistor (a small electronic device that acts as a switch or amplifier for electrical signals), arguably the most consequential electronic invention of the twentieth Century. Partly motivated by antitrust considerations and the understanding that AT&T's monopoly depended on government goodwill, Bell Lab executives made the strategic decision to license transistor technology broadly.[57] Beginning in the early 1950s, Bell Labs hosted multiday symposia where hundreds of scientists and engineers from around the world learned transistor theory and manufacturing techniques. For the modest fee of $25,000, companies gained access to this revolutionary technology.[58] Following antitrust pressures, Bell lab's parent company AT&T agreed to license, royalty-free, its entire existing U.S. patent portfolio on non-exclusive terms.[59] A recent study compared the change in patent citations before and after the 1956 settlement with the change for a matched set of similar, non-Bell patents.[60] Once the whole Bell portfolio was opened, those citations rose by about 12–15% a year.[61] Most of that extra inventive activity came from small, recently formed companies working outside Bell's own telephone business, showing that cheap, non-exclusive access let newcomers build new products and applications on top of Bell's patent portfolio.[62] A later study that zeroed in on the 110 transistor patents found that the number of new patents that cited those transistor patents rose by about 135% once Bell issued the $25,000 license and ran its crash-course symposium in 1952, compared with a matched set of similar patents.[63]

These early patterns of openness established norms that continued throughout classical computing's development. Federal research agencies like the Defense Advanced Research Projects Agency (DARPA) encouraged grant recipients to publish findings and make them widely available.[64] The Internet's core protocols similarly remained unpatented, allowing Transmission Control Protocol (TCP) / Internet Protocol (IP) to spread organically across institutional and national boundaries.[65] Perhaps most dramatically, Tim Berners-Lee and CERN's decision to release

---

[56] Dyson (2012), Chapter 5.

[57] Gertner (2012).

[58] Gertner (2012).

[59] Watzinger et al. (2020).

[60] Watzinger et al. (2020).

[61] Watzinger et al. (2020).

[62] Watzinger et al. (2020).

[63] Nagler et al. (2022).

[64] National Research Council (1999).

[65] Mair (2012, p. 57) (Citing Tim Berners-Lee: "When the Web began, I did not have to obtain permission or pay royalties to use the Internet's own open standards, such as the well-known Transmission Control Protocol and Internet Protocol (TCP/IP)").

the World Wide Web into the public domain in 1993 enabled an information revolution whose impact is still unfolding.[66] The subsequent rise of open-source software demonstrates how robust innovation ecosystems can thrive even without traditional IP protections.[67]

Today's quantum computing landscape presents a stark contrast to this history of openness. Empirical analysis reveals significant scrambling for IP control in the quantum computing industry, with patent applications increasing exponentially—by 42% annually between 2014 and 2021.[68] Analysis suggests there is actually a surprising degree of diversity in patent ownership.[69] Specialized quantum startups like D-Wave and Rigetti have successfully built competitive patent portfolios alongside established players, with D-Wave holding more quantum computing patents than tech giants like Google, Microsoft, and Intel despite vastly smaller market capitalizations.[70] Nevertheless, there is also clear evidence of overlapping intellectual property rights across the quantum stack that warrants attention.[71] This dense web of patents (known as a 'patent thicket') could potentially "denote an inappropriate duration of global exclusive exploitation rights for first movers, result in market skewness and barriers for quantum start-ups and give rise to anticommons concerns including underuse caused by fragmented ownership rights."[72] Unlike classical computing's development, where foundational technologies were deliberately placed in the public domain or broadly licensed, quantum computing is evolving in an era with different intellectual property norms and competitive dynamics.

Classical computing's history offers valuable insights for quantum computing governance. While patents clearly play a valuable role in quantum computing's ecosystem—particularly for specialized startups securing investment—the historical evidence suggests substantial benefits to increasing incentives for openness alongside traditional intellectual property protection. This historical perspective does not provide simple answers, but it suggests that intellectual property decisions made today will profoundly shape whether quantum computing's revolutionary potential benefits society broadly or primarily serves those who already possess technological privilege.

[66] CERN (1993) (declaring that "CERN relinquishes all intellectual property rights to this code…and permission is granted for anyone to use, duplicate, modify and redistribute it").

[67] Hoffmann et al. (2024).

[68] Aboy et al. (2022).

[69] Aboy et al. (2022).

[70] Aboy et al. (2022).

[71] Kop et al. (2022).

[72] Kop et al. (2022), p. 627.

5.4.3 Governance

Governance in quantum computing encompasses concerns about oversight mechanisms, standards development, accountability frameworks, and transparency requirements.[73] Within the quantum computing ethics literature, issues of process opacity, explainability, and trust feature prominently.[74] Governance frameworks typically mature alongside technologies. In early development stages, when trajectories remain uncertain, informal coordination and ad hoc guidelines often prevail. However, as efforts multiply common standards and institutional oversight become necessary to ensure interoperability. Knowing when, how, and what standards and oversights to impose is a difficult task made harder by what is known as the Collingridge dilemma (after David Collingridge, a British scholar who explored the challenges of controlling emerging technologies): If introduced too early, governance mechanisms often fail to predict or address important longer-term implications; yet, if left too late, governance mechanisms likewise fail to prevent harmful practices from establishing themselves.[75]

The history of governance in classical computing may offer several instructive insights for quantum computing. The earliest classical computers were developed in wartime by academic, government, and industrial teams.[76] Thus, de facto governance took place via a combination of security classifications, government Research and Development (R&D) contracts, and institutional policies with minimal commercial regulation. Once computers moved into commercial production in the early-to-mid-1950s, technical governance shifted toward consensus standards crafted by mixed industry–academic bodies such as CODASYL, the American Standards Association (later ANSI), and the Association for Computing Machinery (ACM).[77] Federal intervention during this formative era consisted chiefly of two mechanisms: antitrust decrees that compelled open licensing of dominant portfolios, Defense-Department procurement rules, such as the "second-source" requirement, that pushed suppliers toward compatible designs. Together, these had the effect of keeping patent protection comparatively weak so that new technologies could diffuse quickly.[78]

A good example of this evolutionary, bottom-up pattern is the attempt to tame the early "Tower of Babel" in programming languages. As commercial computers spread in the late-1950s, every vendor shipped its own machine-specific language, so that moving a program from one manufacturer's hardware to another's required substantial rewriting and programmers' skills did not readily transfer across installations.[79] Over the following decades, voluntary consensus-driven processes led by industry users, manufacturers, and standards bodies, with significant federal procurement

[73] Cf. Kop et al. (2024b).

[74] Umbrello (2024).

[75] Collingridge (1980).

[76] Dyson (2012).

[77] Mowery (2011), Sammet (1981).

[78] Mowery (2011).

[79] Backus (1981)

pressure produced common language standards for FORTRAN and COBOL that enabled portability across machines.[80] The first formal FORTRAN standard appeared in 1966 (FORTRAN 66), produced through the American Standards Association's X3.4.3 subcommittee.[81] A parallel process under CODASYL and ANSI produced a corresponding standard for COBOL, originally specified in 1960 and formalized as an ANSI standard in 1968.[82] Procurement standards, such as the Department of Defense's requirement that all general-purpose computers purchased by the military must support COBOL, helped cement these emerging standards.[83] The standards, in turn, led to cost savings by reducing the need for retraining and conversion of code.[84]

Today's quantum computing landscape can learn from these early classical computing challenges. Major companies have developed proprietary quantum programming frameworks—IBM's Qiskit, Google's Cirq, Microsoft's Q#, and others—each with distinct syntax, libraries, and hardware targets.[85] While this diversity reflects healthy experimentation in an emerging field, it creates significant barriers to code portability and knowledge transfer. Early standardization efforts are beginning to address this fragmentation: IEEE Working Group P7130 is developing standard definitions for quantum computing terminology, while OpenQASM has emerged as a potential hardware-agnostic language for quantum circuits.[86] While these initiatives face considerable challenges, they represent crucial steps toward establishing the governance foundations necessary for a thriving quantum ecosystem.

Classical computing's governance evolution offers valuable guidance for quantum computing: voluntary, consensus-driven standards and professional organizations should form the primary governance mechanisms, with targeted government interventions reserved for ensuring competition, security, or critical interoperability.

Yet governance of quantum technologies cannot be confined to national or even regional arenas. The stakes are profoundly global: quantum computing has the potential to reshape communications security, financial infrastructures, and scientific capacity worldwide. As in the nuclear and AI domains, effective governance will require robust international coordination to prevent fragmentation, manage dual-use risks, and avoid a technological arms race. Recent analyses warn of a growing 'quantum divide' between states with the resources to invest in the required infrastructure and those without, raising risks of exclusion, dependency, and geopolitical imbalance. These dynamics underline the importance of inclusive standard-setting processes that incorporate perspectives from the Global South. Equitable access and

---

[80] Marshall (1979), Mowery (2011), Sammet (1981).

[81] Marshall (1979).

[82] Sammet (1981).

[83] Mowery (2011).

[84] Sammet (1981).

[85] Ferreira and Campos (2025).

[86] IEEE (2025), Cross et al. (2017), Cross et al. (2022).

meaningful participation in agenda-setting are crucial if quantum governance frameworks are to avoid reinforcing existing inequalities and instead serve broader goals of global justice and the human right to science.[87]

5.5 Discussion

In this chapter, we have identified several parallels between the ethical challenges accompanying the rise of classical computing and those now emerging with quantum computing. This rests on foundational similarities: both technologies represent revolutionary leaps in information processing; both immediately attracted significant scientific, commercial, and military interest due to their dual use potential (e.g., for decryption and complex simulation); and both emerged within contexts of intense geopolitical and economic competition. As a result, the *types* of ethical issues encountered are remarkably similar across these two computational eras.

There are, however, important differences that prevent a direct application of classical computing experience to quantum computing contexts. One way to understand these issues is to associate them to the layers of their respective technology stacks. As explained in the Introduction to this volume, quantum information technology, including quantum computing, is a complex technological system involving several hardware and software layers. This stack model is a useful analytical tool, as it allows for the mapping of governance instruments to the appropriate technical level, facilitates the identification of the subject matter for regulation, and aids in understanding technological interdependencies and assessing risks.

Just as this layered perspective can enhance the efficacy of governance by ensuring that regulatory instruments are appropriately mapped to the technical stratum where they can be most effective, so too can identifying the primary layer at which a particular ethical issue manifests within a technology stack inform our ethical analysis. To this end, Table 5.3 reproduces the first column of Table 5.1 from the Introduction to this volume and supplements it with the analogous levels of the CC technology stack.

With this overview in mind, we can continue to examine the extent to which the ethical issues map onto analogous layers in the respective technology stacks, as well as to analyze the implications of any differences.

In Sect. 4.1, we focused on classical computing's encryption challenges, such as the DES key length debates. In classical computing, these vulnerabilities typically arose from limitations within the design or parameters of algorithms residing at higher stack levels.[88] The ethical debates centered on the trustworthiness of specific cryptographic software and protocols, while the underlying logic-gate / transistor layer was generally assumed to correctly execute these. In quantum computing, however, the threat to encryption is associated with novel computational capabilities enabled

[87] Hidary and Sarkar (2023).

[88] See Sect. 4.1 and associated footnotes.

Table 5.3 Quantum information-technology layers and their classical computing analogues[89]

Quantum information-technology layer	Classical-computing analogue
Quantum circuit layer	Logic-gate / transistor layer
Measurement & control layer	Clocking, I/O, and signal control (handled in hardware)
Error correction layer	Dispersed (ECC, parity, CRC, etc.)
Logical qubit layer	Reliable bits via hardware design and error correction
Quantum assembly language	Machine-code / ISA
Quantum compiler	Compiler
Quantum intermediate representation	Intermediate representation (e.g., LLVM IR)
Quantum programming language	Classical programming language
Applications layer	Applications layer
Classical interface layer	—Not needed (system is already classical)

by quantum-physical phenomena at the lower layers of the stack, even though operationally these capabilities require the full quantum stack of algorithms, error correction, compilation, and hardware to function. The technical implications of this layer shift relate to the permanence and systemic nature of the resulting vulnerabilities. Because the threat stems from a future capability at the lower layers of the quantum stack that will render some of today's mathematical encryptions obsolete, any data encrypted with quantum-vulnerable public-key schemes intercepted and stored by an adversary today cannot be retroactively re-secured. Once encrypted data has been intercepted and stored, later migration to stronger cryptographic systems may not protect previously captured ciphertext.

This, in turn, informs how we should understand the central lesson from Sect. 4.1—that efforts to weaken or control encryption in the classical computing era generally backfired. That classical lesson often involved resisting active attempts, typically by governments, to undermine specific cryptographic *tools or protocols* operating at higher software or policy layers.[90] In quantum computing, the cryptographic threat emerges from the lower layers of the quantum stack. If similar historical impulses to "control" the cryptographic landscape, perhaps in order to retain advantage or backdoors, were now directed towards the *very source of this new quantum computational power*—for instance, by attempting to restrict global access to, or the development of, advanced quantum computing hardware itself in an effort to "protect" old encryption or maintain a strategic advantage—such efforts have the potential to backfire with even more spectacular unintended consequences than past attempts to control classical cryptographic software. Trying to control encryption by interfering with the development of quantum computing could foreseeably drive development into secretive and unverifiable state programs, create extreme and

[89] This table compares distinct layers within a quantum information-technology stack to their analogous levels in classical computing architectures. It reproduces the first column of Table 5.1 from the "Introduction" to this volume and supplements it with the classical computing analogues.

[90] See Sect. 4.1 and associated footnotes.

dangerous global power asymmetries, stifle the open scientific progress needed for robust defenses (including post-quantum cryptography and broader quantum security research), and ultimately fail to prevent determined actors from acquiring such transformative capabilities.

Attempts to control the spread of strong classical crypto software often spurred clandestine development elsewhere and ultimately failed to prevent widespread access by determined actors[91]; similarly, restricting quantum computing hardware to protect encryption could drive pursuits of this powerful technology into secretive national programs, reducing global transparency and increasing geopolitical uncertainty. The history of the controversies around standards like DES shows a strong pushback against opaque processes or perceived efforts by dominant actors to retain an information advantage, leading to a preference for open and verifiable security alternatives.[92] If the power of quantum computing hardware becomes the exclusive domain of a select few, it would naturally generate widespread suspicion regarding their intentions and capabilities. Such a concentration of power, far exceeding classical information advantages, risks creating extreme global asymmetries and motivating other actors to pursue quantum capabilities urgently, perhaps outside transparent frameworks. Furthermore, the classical era demonstrated that open scientific collaboration strengthens cryptographic security; heavy controls on quantum computing hardware could stifle the broad research needed to understand quantum threats and develop robust defenses like post-quantum cryptography.[93] Ultimately, classical attempts to control powerful information technologies often failed to prevent their proliferation among determined states, and given quantum computing's strategic importance, it is probable that similar efforts to restrict fundamental hardware access would likewise fail to stop key nations from eventually developing these transformative capabilities.[94] Because the "thing to be controlled" in quantum computing is at a more fundamental layer and confers such a transformative advantage, the potential negative repercussions of such control efforts are likely to be far more severe and have more far-reaching knock-on effects than those witnessed when control was attempted at higher layers in the classical era.

Section 4.2 highlighted how transformative periods of innovation in classical computing were often catalyzed by deliberate decisions promoting openness at surprisingly fundamental layers of its technology stack. This included the broad licensing of foundational hardware like the transistor and the public sharing of core system architectures.[95] This deep-level openness provided a fertile ground for widespread experimentation and downstream invention.[96] In quantum computing, while initiatives for openness at higher stack layers, such as open-source software libraries at the applications layer, are valuable and mirror positive classical computing

---

[91] See Sect. 4.1 and associated footnotes.

[92] Landau (2014), National Research Council (1996).

[93] Landau (2014), National Research Council (1996).

[94] Landau (2014), National Research Council (1996).

[95] Gertner (2012).

[96] Watzinger et al. (2020), Nagler et al. (2022).

precedents, the most significant current barriers to broad, equitable access and distributed innovation often lie at the foundational quantum circuit layer and logical qubit layer. These deep layers, encompassing qubit design, fabrication, and error correction, are exceptionally capital-intensive and sites of intense early patenting.[97] This presents a layer shift in the locus of critical access constraints compared to some of classical computing's most impactful periods of open innovation. The ethical implication, illuminated by this layer shift, is that to genuinely foster a broadly innovative and equitably accessible quantum ecosystem akin to the most dynamic phases of classical computing, a primary focus must be on creating stronger incentives and mechanisms for public accessibility and pre-competitive collaboration at these fundamental hardware and core logical layers of quantum computing. While open software is beneficial, the classical lesson, adapted through this layered lens, suggests that the underlying hardware itself needs to be more widely accessible if we are to avoid an entrenched quantum divide with attendant ethical implications.

Section 4.3 highlighted two key aspects from the classical computing era: first, that standardization efforts, like those for programming languages and data formats, were crucial for interoperability and ecosystem growth, typically focusing on higher levels of the technology stack once foundational hardware matured. Second, concerns about system opacity generally arose from the increasing complexity of software at the application layer, prompting demands for algorithmic transparency. In quantum computing, however, analogous governance needs to engage more foundational layers. The drive for standardization, for example, must now address not only high-level programming environments but also fundamental elements like quantum assembly languages, quality metrics for logical qubits, and operational protocols for measurement and control systems and error correction mechanisms. This is a different emphasis from classical computing, where much standardization occurred over more stable, often proprietary, foundational hardware.[98]

It is important to acknowledge several limitations to our analysis. Firstly, quantum computing technology is still in its relative infancy. Many of its applications and consequent societal impacts remain speculative, and as the technology matures and proliferates, genuinely novel ethical dimensions, perhaps not clearly foreseeable from today's vantage point or through the lens of classical computing, may indeed emerge. Secondly, our comparative approach, particularly the use of historical case studies from classical computing, has been illustrative rather than exhaustive. A more granular historical and ethical analysis by specialists in classical computing history and computer ethics would undoubtedly reveal further nuances and deeper lessons applicable to the quantum transition. Our aim has been to highlight the *relevance* of this analogy and to encourage such deeper explorations. Thirdly, our analytical frameworks, including the thematic categorization of quantum computing ethics issues and the layer shift concept, are necessarily simplifications of complex, dynamic realities. While useful for structuring the comparison and drawing out generalizable insights,

---

97 Aboy et al. (2022).

98 See, generally, Dyson (2012).

they do not capture the full intricacy of these interacting technological and social systems.

Our analysis points towards several promising avenues for future research that can build upon the arguments presented here. Further in-depth historical investigations by specialists into specific ethical transitions and governance challenges within classical computing, such as the evolution of software liability or data privacy norms, could yield more precise lessons for analogous developmental stages in quantum computing ethics. As quantum systems begin to be deployed, empirical studies will also be crucial to examine how ethical values are currently being embedded in their design. The layer shift concept itself warrants further theoretical development, perhaps applying it across a broader range of quantum information technologies beyond computing and creating more granular models for how different ethical concerns migrate. Additionally, research should explore how the vastly different contemporary global context, characterized by pervasive digital platforms, advanced artificial intelligence co-evolving with quantum computing, intricate global supply chains, and distinct geopolitical dynamics, might alter the trajectory of ethical and societal responses to quantum computing compared to the classical era. Finally, building directly on lessons from classical computing governance, a critical area for future work is the design, proposal, and testing of proactive, adaptive governance mechanisms for quantum technologies, explicitly informed by an understanding of layer shifts and aimed at fostering responsible innovation while mitigating risks.

5.6 Conclusion

This chapter has explored a central question in the emerging field of quantum computing ethics: does quantum computing present fundamentally new ethical challenges that require the development of novel frameworks, or can we meaningfully apply and adapt existing ethical principles developed for classical computing and other technologies? By comparing quantum computing with its most direct technological predecessor, classical computing, we have argued that while quantum computing introduces significant new technical capabilities and poses distinctive risks, the ethical questions it raises are not without precedent. Rather, they echo long-standing dilemmas around security, justice, and governance that have accompanied previous waves of technological innovation.

Through a thematic analysis of quantum computing ethics literature and historical case studies from the field of classical computing ethics, we have shown that many of the core concerns in quantum computing ethics are variations on problems first confronted in the classical computing era. The richness of the computer ethics tradition, built over decades of grappling with analogous questions, offers a robust foundation for responding to the ethical challenges posed by quantum technologies. Importantly, this approach avoids both the pitfalls of ethical amnesia, that is, ignoring past insights, and the risks of ethical overreach, that is, claiming the need for entirely new principles without sufficient justification.

A key analytical tool introduced in this chapter is the concept of "layer shifts," which captures how similar ethical issues may emerge at different levels of the quantum versus classical technology stacks. For instance, whereas encryption concerns in classical computing often centered on software and algorithm design, in quantum computing the threat is rooted in quantum-physical phenomena at lower layers of the stack and could compromise widely used public-key cryptographic systems. Recognizing such shifts is essential not only for accurate ethical analysis but also for designing effective and proportionate governance strategies.

Moreover, our comparative analysis underscores the importance of maintaining openness, transparency, and broad participation in the development of quantum technologies. Historical precedents from classical computing reveal that policies promoting open standards, shared innovation, and inclusive access helped to democratize technological benefits and mitigate risks of concentration and control. These lessons are highly relevant today, as the quantum landscape becomes increasingly shaped by competitive patenting, proprietary architectures, and geopolitical rivalry.

At the same time, we have acknowledged the limitations of analogy. Quantum computing is still in its infancy, and future developments may introduce genuinely unprecedented ethical challenges that require new conceptual tools. Furthermore, the ethical analysis of quantum phenomena such as superposition, entanglement, and measurement collapse is still developing. Clarifying how such phenomena intersect with questions of human agency, responsibility, and control is a priority for future research. To this end, it is crucial to avoid category errors that confuse physical properties with ethical consequences and instead focus on the systems-level interactions between quantum technologies and human societies.

In conclusion, this chapter has argued that while quantum computing represents a revolutionary technological advance with profound implications, its ethical challenges largely echo familiar patterns, necessitating a thoughtful adaptation rather than a wholesale reinvention of existing ethical frameworks. By recognizing how similar ethical concerns manifest at different layers within the respective technology stacks, and by drawing on the hard-won lessons from classical computing's ethical evolution, the field of quantum computing ethics can develop more effective and grounded approaches.

Acknowledgements This work was made possible through the generous support of the Novo Nordisk Foundation (NNF) via a grant for the scientifically independent Collaborative Research Program in Bioscience Innovation Law (Inter-CeBIL Program—Grant No. NNF23SA0087056). Any use of AI in this manuscript adheres to ethical guidelines for use and acknowledgement of AI in academic research. Each author has made a substantial contribution to the work, which has been thoroughly vetted for accuracy, and assumes responsibility for the integrity of their contributions in accordance with the ethical guidance on AI use and disclosure set out by Porsdam Mann et al. (2024).

References

Abelson, H., et al. (2024) Bugs in our pockets: the risks of client-side scanning. *Journal of Cybersecurity* 10(1): tyad020.

Aboy, M., Minssen, T., Kop, M. (2022) Mapping the Patent Landscape of Quantum Technologies: Patenting Trends, Innovation and Policy Implications. *Int'l Rev. Intell. Prop. & Comp. L.* 53: 853.

Aboy, M., Corrales Compagnucci, M., Minssen, T. (eds.) (2026), Quantum Technology Governance I. Springer Nature.

Backus, J. 1981. The history of Fortran I, II, and III. History of programming languages. Association for Computing Machinery, New York, NY, USA, 25–74. https://doi.org/10.1145/800025.1198345

Bærøe, K., Jansen, M., Kerasidou, A. (2020) Machine Learning in Healthcare: Exceptional Technologies Require Exceptional Ethics. *American Journal of Bioethics* 20: 48.

Bhattacharya, A. (2022) *The Man from the Future: The Visionary Life of John von Neumann.* (W. W. Norton & Co.).

Blaze, M. (1994) Protocol Failure in the Escrowed Encryption Standard. In: *Proceedings of the 2d ACM Conference on Computer and Communications Security*, pp. 59–67. (Association for Computing Machinery).

Broadbent, A., Schaffner, C. (2016) Quantum cryptography beyond quantum key distribution. *Designs, Codes and Cryptography* 78: 351.

Bynum, T.W. (2017) Computer and Information Ethics. In: *The Stanford Encyclopedia of Philosophy* (Fall 2017 ed., Edward N. Zalta (ed.)).

Cheung, K., Earp, B.D., Patch, K., Yaden, D.B. (2025) Distinctive but Not Exceptional: The Risks of Psychedelic Ethical Exceptionalism. *American Journal of Bioethics* 25: 16.

Collingridge, D. (1980) *The Social Control of Technology.* (St. Martin's Press, New York; Pinter, London).

Cross, A.W., Bishop, L.S., Smolin, J.A., Gambetta, J.M. (2017) Open Quantum Assembly Language. *arXiv* 1707.03429.

Cross, A., et al. (2022) OpenQASM 3: A Broader and Deeper Quantum Assembly Language. *ACM Transactions on Quantum Computing* 3: art. 12.

Deutsch, H.C. (1978) The Influence of Ultra on World War II. *Parameters* 8, art. 5.

Diffie, W., Hellman, M.E. (1977) Exhaustive Cryptanalysis of the NBS Data Encryption Standard. *Computer* 10: 74.

Dyson, G. (2012) *Turing's Cathedral: The Origins of the Digital Universe.* (Pantheon Books).

Easterbrook, F.H. (1996) Cyberspace and the Law of the Horse. *University of Chicago Legal Forum* 1996: 207. Available at: https://chicagounbound.uchicago.edu/uclf/vol1996/iss1/7/.

European Union. Proposal for a Regulation of the European Parliament and of the Council laying down rules to prevent and combat child sexual abuse, COM(2022) 209 final, 11 May 2022.

Ferreira, F., Campos, J. (2025) An Exploratory Study on the Usage of Quantum Programming Languages. *Science of Computer Programming* 240: 103217.

Froomkin, A.M. (1995) The Metaphor Is the Key: Cryptography, the Clipper Chip, and the Constitution. *University of Pennsylvania Law Review* 143: 709.

Gertner, J. (2012) *The Idea Factory: Bell Labs and the Great Age of American Innovation.* (Penguin).

Gleick, J. (2011) *The Information: A History, a Theory, a Flood.* (Pantheon Books).

Gribbin, J. (2013) *Computing with Quantum Cats: From Colossus to Qubits.* (Bantam Press).

Grimmett, J.J. (2001) Encryption Export Controls, CRS Rep. RL30273, (Cong. Research Serv).

Hidary, J., Sarkar, A. (2023) The world is heading for a 'quantum divide': here's why it matters. Available at: https://www.weforum.org/stories/2023/01/the-world-quantum-divide-why-it-matters-davos2023/

Hoffmann, M., Nagle, F., Zhou, Y. (2024) *The Value of Open Source Software.* Harvard Business School Working Paper No. 24-038.

Hodges, A. (2014) *Alan Turing: The Enigma.* (Princeton University Press).

IEEE Standards Association. (2025). IEEE P7130 Quantum Computing Nomenclature Working Group. Available at: https://sagroups.ieee.org/7130/ (Accessed 22 May 2025).

Johnson, D.G. (1985) *Computer Ethics*. (Prentice Hall).

Johnson, D.G. (2009) *Computer Ethics*. 4th ed. (Pearson Prentice Hall).

Kim, Y. P. (2023) The Faster Horse Fallacy: How Technology Distorts the Law. Working paper. Available at: https://www.yunsieg-kim.com/publication/the-faster-horse-fallacy-how-technology-distorts-the-law/the-faster-horse-fallacy-how-technology-distorts-the-law.pdf.

Klein, E., Morar, N. (2024) Brain Exceptionalism? Learning from the Past with an Eye Toward the Future. *AJOB Neuroscience* 15: 139.

Kotliar, D.M., Carmi, E. (2024) Keeping Pegasus on the wing: legitimizing cyber espionage. *Information, Communication & Society* 27(8): 1499.

Kop, M. (2021) Establishing a Legal-Ethical Framework for Quantum Technology. *Yale Journal of Law & Technology: The Record* (30 Mar 2021). Available at: https://yjolt.org/blog/establishing-legal-ethical-framework-quantum-technology.

Kop, M., Aboy, M., Minssen, T. (2022) Intellectual Property in Quantum Computing and Market Power: A Theoretical Discussion and Empirical Analysis. *Journal of Intellectual Property Law & Practice* 17: 613.

Kop, M., Aboy, M., De Jong, E., Gasser, U., Minssen, T., Cohen, I.G., Brongersma, M.L., Quintel, T., Floridi, L., Laflamme, R. (2024a) 10 Principles for Responsible Quantum Innovation (12 Apr 2023). *Quantum Science and Technology* 9: 035013. Available at: https://doi.org/10.1088/2058-9565/ad3776.

Kop, M., Aboy, M., De Jong, E., Gasser, U., Minssen, T., Cohen, I.G., Brongersma, M.L., Quintel, T., Floridi, L., Laflamme, R. (2024b) Towards Responsible Quantum Technology: Safeguarding, Engaging and Advancing Quantum R&D. *The UC Law Science and Technology Journal* 15: 63.

Landau, S. (2014) Under the Radar: NSA's Efforts to Secure Private-Sector Telecommunications Infrastructure. *Journal of National Security Law & Policy* 7: 411.

Lastowka, G. (2011) "Foreword: Paving the Path of Cyberlaw," *William Mitchell Law Review* 38(1): Article 13. Available at: http://open.mitchellhamline.edu/wmlr/vol38/iss1/13

Lauzon, E. (1998) The Philip Zimmerman Investigation: The Start of the Fall of Export Restrictions on Encryption Software under First Amendment Free Speech Issues. *Syracuse Law Review* 48: 1307.

Mair, C. (2012) Openness, Intellectual Property and Standardization in the European ICT Sector. *IP Theory* 2: 52.

Maner, W. (1980) *Starter Kit on Teaching Computer Ethics*.

Maner, W. (1996) Unique Ethical Problems in Information Technology. *Science & Engineering Ethics* 2: 137.

Marchant, G.E., et al. (2024) Learning From Emerging Technology Governance for Guiding Quantum Technology. Arizona State Univ. Sandra Day O'Connor Col. L. Paper No. 4923230 (9 Aug 2024). Available at: https://ssrn.com/abstract=4923230.

Marshall, N.H., (1979). An overview of fortran standardization activities. In Proceedings of the 1979 annual conference (ACM '79). Association for Computing Machinery, New York, NY, USA, 164. https://doi.org/10.1145/800177.810058

Mishra, A., Nair, B. (2023) *Quantum Futures: Making Quantum Computing Work for International Development*. (Research Technical Assistance Center, Washington, DC).

Moor, J.H. (1985) What Is Computer Ethics? *Metaphilosophy* 16: 266.

Mowery, D.C. (2011) Federal Policy and the Development of Semiconductors, Computer Hardware, and Computer Software: A Policy Model for Climate Change R&D? In: *Accelerating Energy Innovation: Insights from Multiple Sectors*. (National Bureau of Economic Research, Inc.).

Nagler, M., Schnitzer, M., Watzinger, M. (2022) Fostering the Diffusion of General Purpose Technologies: Evidence from the Licensing of the Transistor Patents. *Journal of Industrial Economics* 70: 838.

National Research Council (1996) *Cryptography's Role in Securing the Information Society*. (National Academies Press).

National Research Council (1999) *Funding a Revolution: Government Support for Computing Research.* (National Academies Press, Washington, DC).
Organisation Européenne pour la Recherche Nucléaire (CERN) (1993) *Statement Concerning CERN W3 Software Release into Public Domain 2* (30 Apr 1993) (CERN Document Server, Record No. CERN-IT-9304003)
Perrier, E. (2022) Ethical Quantum Computing: A Roadmap. *arXiv* 2102.00759 [quant-ph] (20 Apr 2022 version).
Podchasov v Russia, App. No. 33696/19 (ECtHR, 13 Feb 2024).
Porsdam Mann, S., Vazirani, A. A., Aboy, M., Earp, B. D., Minssen, T., Cohen, I. G., Savulescu, J. (2024). Guidelines for ethical use and acknowledgement of large language models in academic writing. *Nature Machine Intelligence* 6: 1272.
Possati, L.M. (2023) Ethics of Quantum Computing: An Outline. *Philosophy & Technology* 36: 48.
Ravi, P., et al. (2024) Backdooring post-quantum cryptography: Kleptographic attacks on lattice-based KEMs. *Proceedings of the Great Lakes Symposium on VLSI,* 216.
Rogaway, P. (2015) The moral character of cryptographic work. *Cryptology ePrint Archive.*
Rozenshtein, A.Z. (2018) Surveillance intermediaries. *Stanford Law Review* 70: 99.
Sammet, J.E. (1981) The Early History of COBOL. In: *Proceedings of the ACM SIGPLAN History of Programming Languages Conference,* 199. (Association for Computing Machinery).
Schulze, M. (2017) Clipper meets Apple vs. FBI: a comparison of the cryptography discourses from 1993 and 2016. *Media and Communication* 5: 54.
Shevchenko, S., Zhavoronkov, A. (2024) The Role of Exceptionalism in the Evolution of Bioethical Regulation. *Cambridge Quarterly of Healthcare Ethics* 33: 185.
Soni, J., Goodman, R. (2017) A Mind at Play: How Claude Shannon Invented the Information Age. (Simon & Schuster).
Sorkin, A. (1984) Lucifer: A Cryptographic Algorithm. *Cryptologia* 8: 22.
Stay, R.J. (1997) Cryptic Controversy: U.S. Government Restrictions on Cryptography Exports and the Plight of Philip Zimmermann. *Georgia State University Law Review* 13: 581.
Suter, S.M. (2001) The Allure and Peril of Genetic Exceptionalism: Do We Need Special Genetics Legislation? *Washington University Law Review* 79: 669.
Tavani, H.T. (2002) The Uniqueness Debate in Computer Ethics: What Exactly Is at Issue, and Why Does It Matter? *Ethics & Information Technology* 4: 37.
Tavani, H.T. (2016) *Ethics and Technology: Controversies, Questions, and Strategies for Ethical Computing.* 5th ed. (Wiley).
Umbrello, S. (2024) Ethics of Quantum Technologies: A Scoping Review. *International Journal of Applied Philosophy* 37: 179.
van Daalen, O. (2024a) Developing a Human Rights Compatible Governance Framework for Quantum Computing. *Rsch. Dirs.: Quantum Tech.* 2: e1.
van Daalen, O. (2024b) *From Encryption to Quantum Computing: The Governance of Information Security and Human Rights.* (Info. Tech. & L. Ser. vol. 38).
Waldherr, A., Cohen, I.G., Kop, M. (2025) Quantum Trials: An FDA for Quantum Technology. Stanford Center for Responsible Quantum Technology Research Series.
Watzinger, M., Fackler, T.A., Nagler, M., Schnitzer, M. (2020) How Antitrust Enforcement Can Spur Innovation: Bell Labs and the 1956 Consent Decree. *American Economic Journal: Economic Policy* 12: 328.

Chapter 6
Quantum Computing and the Right to Science: A Stress-Test and a Test Case*

Sebastian Porsdam Mann, Gabriela Lenarczyk, Timo Minssen, Hannah Louise Smith, and Brian D. Earp

6.1 Introduction

Quantum computing involves harnessing the principles of quantum mechanics, such as superposition, entanglement, and quantum interference, to process information in fundamentally new ways. As a result, it has the potential to solve certain classes of problems far more efficiently than classical computers, including tasks in cryptanalysis, simulation of complex physical and chemical systems, and optimization. Discussions around the governance of quantum computing tend to focus on export controls to protect different nations' interests or technical standards that promote quantum computing's coherent development and interoperability. These have a role to play, but an exclusive focus on such areas may neglect crucial questions about the development of quantum computing. These include how to secure its benefits equitably, how to embed democratic values and fundamental rights that transcend national borders, and what constitutes legitimate limitations on such aims. The relevance of such questions highlights the role of human rights law in the governance of quantum computing.

A range of rights[1] are potentially engaged by the advancement of quantum computing but this chapter will focus on the human right to science. Enshrined in both the Universal Declaration of Human Rights (UDHR) and the International Covenant on Economic, Social and Cultural Rights (ICESCR), the right to science directly

Sebastian Porsdam Mann and Gabriela Lenarczyk are joint first authors and contributed equally to this work.

S. Porsdam Mann (✉) · G. Lenarczyk · T. Minssen · H. L. Smith
Center for Advanced Studies in Bioscience Innovation Law (CeBIL), Faculty of Law, University of Copenhagen, Copenhagen, Denmark

B. D. Earp
Center for Biomedical Ethics, Yong Loo Lin School of Medicine, National University of Singapore, Singapore, Singapore

[1] Van Daalen (2024).

M. Aboy et al. (eds.), *Quantum Technology Governance II*, Perspectives in Law, Business and Innovation, https://doi.org/10.1007/978-981-92-3768-5_6

addresses humanity's relationship with science and technology. Yet, this right has been characterized as a "sleeping beauty" as its profound potential remains largely untapped by States and scholars, in part because the treaty language was vague and lacked interpretive guidance, and in part because institutions charged with implementation treated it as aspirational rather than enforceable.[2] Nevertheless, there are signs of it stirring from this slumber in the context of quantum computing.[3] Such research is still in its infancy and a focus on specific security-related policy questions, such as the threat that Shor's algorithm poses to public-key encryption, the military potential of quantum sensors to detect submarines or stealth aircraft, or the strategic competition driving massive State subsidies, rather than the broader implications of quantum computing, leaves much ground untouched. This chapter examines some of these questions, using the right to science to explore who should participate in quantum development, how quantum benefits should be distributed, what obligations exist to ensure equitable access, and how democratic societies should set quantum research priorities. These wider questions of participation, distribution, and governance are key areas within the wider remit of the right to science and represent promising areas for application of right to science norms beyond their utility in responding to security concerns.

This chapter seeks to develop some of these further lessons. We argue that a historically informed understanding of the right to science can provide a robust normative framework for helping to ensure that quantum computing serves general well-being. To this end, sect. 2 starts out by explaining the basic legal frameworks and the most pressing contemporary challenges to the right to science. Section 3 follows with a description and analysis of what we see as the five main barriers to realizing and reconciling the right to science with some of the dynamics that currently drive advances in quantum computing and the promotion, protection, and sharing of these advances. In sect. 4 we then connect the dots and briefly discuss our findings in light of future challenges and opportunities, which will allow us to draw conclusions in sect. 5.

6.2 The Human Right to Science: Legal Framework and Contemporary Challenges

Before analyzing the interfaces, tensions, and opportunities that arise from recent advances in quantum computing and the right to science, it is important to fully grasp what this right entails. To do so, it is not only important to know the legal framework that applies to it, but also to understand the history of how this right came into existence, how it was interpreted, and what some of the inherent challenges are. In other words, the following sections will provide the foundation for our quantum computing-specific analysis in later parts.

---

[2] Riedel (2012); Porsdam Mann et al. (2020).

[3] Van Daalen (2024); Van Daalen (2025).

6.2.1 Legal Foundations and Core Components

The right to science has firm roots in the international human rights framework, but its language was drafted in highly general terms. This lack of precise definitions has left significant ambiguity about its scope and meaning. That ambiguity is only recently beginning to be addressed through soft-law instruments and interpretive efforts by scholars and UN bodies, which now serve as the most authoritative sources we have for understanding and applying the right.

The right to science finds its legal foundation in two core international human rights instruments: Article 27(1) of the 1948 UDHR recognizes everyone's right to "share in scientific advancement and its benefits."[4] Article 15(1)(b) of the 1966 ICESCR contains a more detailed version of the right, recognizing "the right of everyone to enjoy the benefits of scientific progress and its applications."[5]

This is complemented by related provisions within Article 15 ICESCR that together establish a comprehensive framework for science and culture, including the right to "take part in cultural life"[6] and to "benefit from the protection of the moral and material interests resulting from any scientific, literary or artistic production".[7] Three additional provisions establish obligations on States related to the implementation of these rights: Article 15(2) requires States to take steps "necessary for the conservation, the development and the diffusion of science and culture"; [8] Article 15(3) mandates respect for "the freedom indispensable for scientific research and creative activity"; [9] and Article 15(4) calls for recognition of benefits from "international contacts and co-operation in the scientific and cultural fields."[10] Together with the right to education in Article 13, these rights—to science, to culture, and to education—make up the category of cultural human rights.[11]

Despite its contemporary relevance, the right to science has long been the "most obscure of all international human rights treaty provisions."[12] The abstract language of Article 15, combined with uncertainty about the precise meaning of terms like "scientific progress" and "benefits," discouraged much development of the right.[13] This neglect proved particularly problematic as science and technology's influence on society and individuals has expanded far beyond what the ICESCR's drafters could have envisioned, and marks a missed opportunity for human rights law to shape the development of emerging technologies from an earlier stage. Quantum computing is a case in point: had the right to science been more fully articulated and

[4] UDHR (1948), Art. 27(1).

[5] ICESCR (1966), Art. 15(1)(b).

[6] ICESCR (1966), Art. 15(1)(a).

[7] ICESCR (1966), Art. 15(1)(c).

[8] ICESCR (1966), Art. 15(2).

[9] ICESCR (1966), Art. 15(3).

[10] ICESCR (1966), Art. 15(4).

[11] On science and its relation to cultural rights, see generally Porsdam (2022).

[12] Bishop (2021), p. xi.

[13] Riedel (2012).

operationalized earlier, it might already provide clearer guidance on how to balance openness, security, and equitable access in the governance of this technology.

Notwithstanding the recent proliferation of scholarly commentary on this right,[14] substantive engagement with the right to science in the decades following the adoption of the ICESCR remained largely confined to UNESCO's standard-setting efforts in the scientific and cultural spheres.[15] The awakening did not begin until around the turn of the millennium, when scholars working in the field of intellectual property began to understand the right's relevance to their work, and to incorporate it into their research.[16] The revival was particularly galvanized by a series of meetings hosted by UNESCO, which culminated in the 2009 Venice Statement that is the first document to attempt to lay out the normative content of the right.[17] Most significantly, the Statement identified five main normative challenges that remain central to right to science debates: clarifying the nature of scientific knowledge and progress; ensuring freedom of inquiry; establishing state and private sector responsibilities for scientific capacity building; managing tensions between the right to science and intellectual property regimes; and distinguishing between participation in scientific progress and sharing in its benefits.[18] The Venice Statement also first systematically applied the established human rights framework of tripartite obligations (to respect, to protect, and to fulfill) to the right to science, providing more concrete guidance on State obligations.[19]

The mandate of the Special Rapporteur in the field of cultural rights, established in 2012,[20] monitors implementation of cultural rights under Article 15 ICESCR.[21] In 2012, Farida Shaheed, serving as Special Rapporteur, produced the landmark report "The Right to Enjoy the Benefits of Scientific Progress and its Applications"—the first in-depth UN analysis of Article 15(1)(b).[22] The report applied the AAAQ framework (availability, accessibility, acceptability, quality) to scientific benefits, examined at length the connection between science and culture, and critically examined tensions between intellectual property protection and scientific access. Shaheed emphasized the need to ensure access not only to "innovations essential for a life with dignity", such as essential medicines, but also to "scientific advances likely to have

[14] See e.g. Romano & Boggio (2024); Besson (2023); Porsdam & Porsdam Mann (2021); Plomer (2021); Boggio (2021); Donders & Plozza (2023); Mancisidor (2021); Mazibrada (2022); Massimi (2025); Beiter (2019); Schabas (2024); Haugen (2025).

[15] UNESCO (1974).

[16] See, e.g., Chapman (1998); Green (2000). For systematic reviews of the scholarship, see Porsdam Mann et al. (2020); Porsdam Mann et al. (2018).

[17] UNESCO (2009); Müller (2010).

[18] UNESCO (2009), paras 7–11.

[19] UNESCO (2009), paras 14–16.

[20] Preceded by a mandate for an Independent Expert, 2009–2012: UN HRC (2009), Res 10/23.

[21] UN HRC (2012), Res 19/6.

[22] Shaheed (2012).

a significant impact on human rights, such as [...] information and communication technologies" by all, regardless of background.[23]

However, the most significant development in interpretation came with the UN Committee on Economic, Social and Cultural Rights' (CESCR) adoption of General Comment No. 25 in April 2020. As the treaty body responsible for monitoring ICESCR implementation, the CESCR's General Comments carry considerable interpretive authority, despite their technically non-binding status.[24] The Comment clarified that "benefits" encompass not only material applications (like quantum computing hardware) but also scientific knowledge itself and the development of "critical and responsible citizens who are able to participate fully in a democratic society."[25] Like the Special Rapporteur's report before it, the General Comment articulates the right through the AAAQ framework: scientific progress must be available (with States directing resources to ensure progress happens), accessible (without discrimination), of suitable quality (meeting scientific standards), and acceptable (explained in ways that facilitate understanding across cultural contexts).[26] It also establishes specific obligations for marginalized groups, requiring states to eliminate barriers facing women in science, ensure universal design for persons with disabilities, and prioritize access to technology by those living in poverty.[27]

Most importantly for our analysis, the Committee explicitly situated quantum computing within the broader category of emerging technologies that demand special human rights scrutiny. It dedicated an entire section to "risks and promises of new emerging technologies," explicitly naming quantum computers alongside artificial intelligence, robotics, biotechnology, and big data as technologies that are "blurring the boundaries between the physical, digital and biological worlds".[28] It acknowledged the dual nature of these technologies, that is, their potential to "enhance the enjoyment of economic, social and cultural rights" through productivity gains while also warning that they "might intensify social inequalities by increasing unemployment and segregation in the labor market".[29] The Committee stressed that governance of these emerging technologies must be global in scope, made within a holistic human rights framework, and contain mechanisms for addressing job displacement and data control according to human rights principles.[30] Crucially, the Committee noted that "States parties should establish a legal framework that imposes on non-State actors a duty of human rights due diligence".[31]

For our purposes, the key point is that the right now offers conceptual tools (AAAQ, tripartite obligations), interpretive authority (General Comment No. 25),

---

[23] Shaheed (2012), para. 29.

[24] Mazibrada et al. (2023).

[25] CESCR (2020), para. 8.

[26] CESCR (2020), paras 16–19.

[27] CESCR (2020), paras 26–40.

[28] CESCR (2020), paras 72–76.

[29] CESCR (2020), para. 73.

[30] CESCR (2020), paras 73–76.

[31] CESCR (2020), para. 75.

and explicit recognition of quantum computing as a relevant domain. This provides a foundation for the analysis that follows: assessing how right to science standards can and should guide the governance of quantum computing.

6.2.2 The ICESCR Treaty Framework Applied to QC

How does the normative content of the right to science apply to quantum computing? To answer this, we must first grapple with the treaty framework of the ICESCR as well as the wider interpretive frameworks of international human rights law within which the right operates. Collectively, these frameworks attempt to clarify human rights obligations by answering four fundamental questions: What does the right contain? How must States act? When do obligations mature? And to what extent can rights be enforced and in how far can they be limited?

6.2.2.1 What?—The Availability, Accessibility, Acceptability & Quality (AAAQ) Framework

What does the human right to science contain? The AAAQ framework introduced above has emerged as a central analytical tool for understanding the normative content of economic, social and cultural rights. Katarina Tomaševski, the UN Special Rapporteur on the right to education, introduced this approach for human rights analysis in a 1999 report.[32] She analyzed States' obligations under "4 A's": availability, accessibility, acceptability and adaptability.[33] The framework was adopted for use in CESCR's General Comment 13 on education,[34] and modified to the health context as the AAAQ (with 'quality' replacing 'adaptability') framework in General Comment 14 on health.[35] In this modified form, the framework has been applied by the CESCR, scholars, and others across a wide range of rights.[36]

The Committee elaborated its understanding of these elements as they apply to the right to science in General Comment No. 25. Accordingly, availability requires that scientific progress is "actually taking place," that "applications and benefits are distributed and are available," and that scientific knowledge and its applications are protected and widely disseminated through libraries, museums, Internet networks, and adequate research infrastructure.[37] Accessibility is analyzed along three dimensions: equal access to the applications of science without discrimination, accessible information about risks and benefits, and open opportunities for all to participate in

[32] Tomasevski (1999).

[33] Tomasevski (1999), paras 51–74.

[34] CESCR (1999).

[35] CESCR (2000).

[36] See e.g. CESCR (2009).

[37] CESCR (2020), para. 16.

scientific progress.[38] Acceptability means science should be explained and disseminated in culturally appropriate ways, so long as this does not affect its quality and integrity, and should be conducted according to ethical standards, such as the maximization of benefit and minimization of risk as well as the requirement of informed consent for human subjects research.[39] Finally, quality refers to the most advanced, up-to-date and generally accepted science available, according to the criteria generally accepted in scientific communities, and may include regulation and certification meant to force or acknowledge adherence to ethical standards, where appropriate.[40]

Applied to quantum computing, the AAAQ framework *prima facie* requires at least the following. States must ensure that progress within quantum computing actually happens; as we shall discuss in more detail below, this progress must not be limited to physics, logic, and engineering, but also to ethical, legal, and social issues related to or impacted by quantum computing advances. This information must be disseminated through educational institutions and should not, as a general rule, be hidden behind paywalls, trade secrets, export controls, or other barriers. The benefits resulting from research into and use of quantum computers, such as knowledge, applications, and perhaps even the resulting economic gains, should be shared with all members of society, and not just with those who have invested in or taken part in developing this technology. Both the research itself and the resulting applications should respect generally acknowledged ethical standards, such as those relating to open science principles.

6.2.2.2 How? —Tripartite Obligations

How must States act with respect to the development of quantum computing? If the AAAQ framework is used to conceptualize and describe the normative content of a right, the tripartite typology describes *how* these obligations should be realized. As the name suggests, the tripartite typology consists of three types of obligations: to respect, protect, and fulfill a human right. The tripartite framework emerged in parallel from two distinct disciplinary traditions in the early 1980s. Moral philosopher Henry Shue argued that every basic right involved three correlated duties: to avoid depriving someone of the enjoyment of the right, to protect people from deprivation of their right by third parties, and to aid the deprived in fully realizing their right.[41] In the international human rights law context, Asbjørn Eide, then a Special Rapporteur for the Sub-Commission on Prevention of Discrimination and Protection of Minorities, independently developed a structurally similar account into the now-standard formulation of *respecting, protecting, and fulfilling* human rights.[42] The typology featured prominently in the 1997 Maastricht Guidelines on Violations of

[38] CESCR (2020), para. 17.

[39] CESCR (2020), para. 19.

[40] CESCR (2020), para. 18.

[41] Shue (2020).

[42] Eide (1987).

Economic, Social and Cultural Rights and has been a key feature of CESCR General Comments for roughly 30 years.[43]

In General Comment No. 25, the CESCR applied the framework directly to the right to science. According to this analysis, the obligation to respect requires States to refrain from interfering directly or indirectly in the enjoyment of the right, including eliminating barriers to accessing quality science education, refraining from censorship or arbitrary limitations on knowledge access, avoiding mis- and disinformation, and eschewing obstacles to international scientific collaboration.[44] The obligation to protect demands that States prevent third parties from interfering with the right, for example by ensuring that scientific associations and universities do not apply discriminatory criteria; by protecting people from participating in research that contravenes widely accepted ethical principles; seeing to it that private investments do not infringe on scientific freedom; and preventing private actors from disseminating false or pseudoscientific information.[45] The obligation to fulfill requires positive measures targeted at facilitating scientific progress, including developing national science plans, providing adequate public funding, establishing science education programs, promoting international cooperation, actively protecting scientific freedom, and ensuring that people can actually access, participate in, and benefit from scientific progress and its applications.[46]

The tripartite typology likewise produces several *prima facie* obligations when applied to quantum computing. To respect the right, States must refrain from blocking quantum research or quantum research collaborations; censoring or burying quantum research findings; or creating arbitrary barriers to quantum education and careers. This includes avoiding overly broad export controls that prevent legitimate scientific exchange or restrictions on access to knowledge or to quantum research funding based on researchers' nationality or political views, a point we shall return to below. To protect, States must prevent corporations from monopolizing quantum computing advances to the detriment of public benefit, for example via patenting activity that disproportionately prevents scientific progress; and ensure private quantum research respects ethical standards and human subjects protections. To fulfill, States must invest in quantum education infrastructure; support public quantum research, including associated humanities and social science efforts; facilitate international quantum research exchanges and partnerships; ensure marginalized communities can access quantum information, services, and infrastructure, at least once these mature; provide the infrastructure and conditions necessary to freely conduct scientific research into quantum computing; and create governance frameworks that ensure that the benefits resulting from progress in quantum computing reaches society as a whole.

[43] ICJ (1997); CESCR (1999).

[44] CESCR (2020), para. 42.

[45] CESCR (2020), paras 43–44.

[46] CESCR (2020), paras 45–50.

6.2.2.3 When?—Minimum Core Obligations, Progressive Realization

A further question concerns the timeline for implementing the right to science: are States required to secure its enjoyment immediately, or may obligations unfold gradually over time?

Unlike the International Covenant on Civil and Political Rights,[47] the economic, social, and cultural rights contained in the ICESCR were held, during the drafting of the Covenants, to be of a nature which required progressive, rather than immediate, realization.[48] As a result, Article 2(1) ICESCR requires each State party to the Covenant to undertake "to take steps, individually and through international assistance and co-operation, especially economic and technical, to the maximum of its available resources, with a view to achieving progressively the full realization of the rights recognized in the present Covenant by all appropriate means, including particularly the adoption of legislative measures."[49]

The doctrine of progressive realization recognizes the reality that States possess vastly different levels of resources and capacities to implement their obligations under the ICESCR. This flexibility acknowledges that what might be immediately achievable for a wealthy nation could require years of development for a resource-constrained one. Nevertheless, the Committee has consistently emphasized that resource limitations cannot serve as a blanket justification for inaction.[50] States must demonstrate they are taking deliberate, concrete steps toward full realization using whatever means are available to them.[51]

To prevent the concept of progressive realization from becoming an indefinite deferral of obligations, the Committee has introduced two devices intended to function as safeguards. First, every right is associated with certain "core obligations"—essential minimum standards that must be met immediately, irrespective of a State's economic situation or development level.[52] These represent a floor below which no State may fall, with a view to ensuring that even the most fundamental aspects of rights remain protected. Second, the principle of non-retrogression prohibits States from reducing the level of rights protection they have already achieved.[53] Any backwards movement requires exceptional justification.[54] Together, these requirements are meant to ensure that progressive realization remains a pathway toward expanding rights enjoyment rather than an escape clause from human rights obligations.

Immediate implementation. General Comment No. 25 identifies several core obligations that States must implement immediately regarding the right to science.[55]

---

47 ICCPR (1966), Arts 2–3.

48 See generally, Craven (2002).

49 ICESCR (1966), Art. 2(1).

50 CESCR (1991), para. 9.

51 CESCR (1991), para. 9.

52 CESCR (1991), para. 10.

53 CESCR (1991), para. 9.

54 CESCR (1991), para. 9.

55 CESCR (2020), para. 52.

These include: eliminating laws and practices that unjustifiably limit access to scientific knowledge; ensuring basic science education that respects the best available scientific knowledge; protecting people from harmful consequences of false or pseudoscience-based practices; promoting accurate scientific information while refraining from disinformation; and fostering international scientific cooperation without imposing unjustified restrictions.[56] The Committee emphasizes that retrogressive measures with respect to the right to science, such as the imposition of barriers to access to scientific knowledge or its applications, are presumptively impermissible.[57] When such measures are unavoidable, States must ensure they are necessary and proportionate, remain in place only as long as necessary, do not disproportionately affect disadvantaged groups, and leave intact the enjoyment of the minimal core obligations.[58]

Several of these standards can be directly applied to the quantum computing context. Minimum core obligations that apply immediately include: ensuring legal protection for scientific freedom to conduct quantum research; preventing discrimination in access to quantum information, infrastructure, education, and careers; providing accurate public information about quantum computing to enable democratic participation; ensuring mechanisms aimed at aligning government policies on quantum computing with up to date, high quality scientific evidence are in place; protecting people from fraudulent or harmful claims about quantum technologies; and removing unjustified barriers to international quantum research collaboration.

These obligations apply regardless of a State's level of development or available resources. Progressive obligations encompass more resource-intensive measures: building quantum research facilities and educational programs; ensuring universal access to quantum-enhanced services as they mature; developing comprehensive quantum literacy curricula; creating quantum technology transfer mechanisms for developing countries; and establishing sophisticated regulatory frameworks for quantum applications and the distribution of their downstream benefits. Importantly, non-retrogression means States cannot reduce existing support for quantum research or access to quantum knowledge, for example by reclassifying as secret or controlled information that is currently in the public domain, without compelling justification.

6.2.2.4 To What Extent?—Legitimate Limitations

What about limitations? While human rights are fundamental, they are not absolute. Unlike the International Covenant on Civil and Political Rights, which allows limitations for specific rights and for various purposes including national security, public order, and morals,[59] the drafters of the ICESCR deliberately chose a more restrictive

---

[56] CESCR (2020), para. 52.

[57] CESCR (2020), para. 24.

[58] CESCR (2020), para. 24.

[59] See, for example, ICCPR (1966), Art. 12.

formulation.[60] Article 4 permits limitations only when they are "determined by law," are "compatible with the nature of these rights," and are imposed "solely for the purpose of promoting the general welfare in a democratic society."[61] Various foundational documents, such as the 1986 Limburg Principles and the 1997 Maastricht Guidelines, make clear that the limitations criteria are to be interpreted strictly and are not meant to function as escape clauses for States.[62]

General Comment No. 25 provides specific guidance on how these criteria apply to the right to science. The Committee emphasizes that limitations must be lawful, must not destroy the core content of the right and must be proportionate, meaning "where there are several means reasonably capable of achieving the legitimate aim of the limitation, the one least restrictive to economic, social and cultural rights must be selected" and that the benefits of any limitation must outweigh its burdens.[63] The burden of proof lies with the State to demonstrate that any limitation meets all these criteria.[64]

Applied to quantum computing, this framework significantly constrains permissible restrictions. Export controls on quantum technologies, for instance, must meet all three criteria. They must be established through clear, publicly accessible legal channels. They must not undermine core obligations such as scientific freedom or non-discriminatory access to scientific knowledge—as we will argue below, this means that blanket prohibitions on quantum research collaboration based solely on researchers' nationality would likely fail this test. Most challengingly, they must be demonstrably necessary for general welfare rather than narrow security interests. A restriction justified primarily by military advantage or economic competition would not meet the "solely for promoting general welfare" standard if its other effects, such as diminishing the rate of scientific progress, outweigh the benefits of restriction for society as a whole. Similarly, intellectual property restrictions on quantum algorithms or hardware must pass this test, as we explore in Sect. 3.2 below. The Committee's emphasis on choosing the least restrictive option means States must continuously evaluate whether their quantum-related restrictions remain justified as the technology and its applications evolve.

6.3 Barriers to Reconciling Quantum Computing with the Human Right to Science

In this section we map the principal barriers that shape today's quantum landscape, trace the roots of their tension with the human right to science, gauge present levels of compliance, and, where the balance tilts too far, offer recalibration measures for

---

[60] Craven (2002).

[61] ICESCR (1966), Art. 4.

[62] United Nations (1987); ICJ (1997).

[63] CESCR (2020), para. 21.

[64] CESCR (2020), para. 22.

scholars and regulators to refine. We focus on five overarching barriers, each of which implicates different legal and policy challenges: (1) geopolitical access controls, (2) concentrated control of quantum infrastructure and technical knowhow, (3) economic exclusion, (4) scientific freedom; and (5) the scope of 'science' and the overemphasis on "STEM" subjects.

6.3.1 *Barrier 1—Geopolitical Access Controls*

The growing strategic value of quantum computing has triggered a re-ordering of scientific space, erecting invisible, algorithmically enforced frontiers—digital "borders"—separating those who may participate in (and benefit from) quantum science and those who may not. These borders result from multiple factors, including export-control schedules,[65] investment-screening regimes,[66] classified-patent procedures,[67] cloud-service terms of use,[68] and university research-compliance protocols.[69] Each of these measures pursues a legitimate security objective, yet in combination they can complicate, and at times constrain, the inclusive ethos that underpins the human right to science.

Quantum processors, unlike their classical forebears, arrive already entangled with national security fears. Three policy rationales have moved export officials to scrutinize core quantum kit (dilution refrigerators, for example)[70] under licensing regimes that increasingly resemble the Cold-War controls once reserved for gas centrifuge.

[65] European Commission (2023a), (2023b), § 1; U.S. BIS (2023a)(2023b).

[66] Regulation (EU) 2021/821, Annex I; European Commission (2025).

[67] In the European Union, every major Member State operates a cognate mechanism: Germany's Patentgesetz § 50 authorizes the Patent Office—on advice from the Defense Ministry—to halt the disclosure of any application embodying a "state secret," while § 52 bars the applicant from filing abroad without written consent (*Patentgesetz* §§ 50, 52). The United Kingdom preserves a similar power in s. 22 of the Patents Act 1977 (*Patents Act* 1977, s. 22.).

[68] E.g., IBM Quantum Platform (2023), § 7(a): "IBM Quantum is unavailable to individuals ordinarily resident in the following countries and You shall not access IBM Quantum from the following countries: Afghanistan, Armenia, Azerbaijan, Belarus, Myanmar (Burma), Cambodia, Central African Republic, People's Republic of China (including Hong Kong), Democratic Republic of the Congo, Cuba, Cyprus, Eritrea, Georgia, Haiti, Iran, Iraq, Kazakhstan, North Korea, Kyrgyzstan, Laos, Lebanon, Libya, Macau, Moldova, Mongolia, Russia, Somalia, South Sudan, Sudan, Syria, Tajikistan, Turkmenistan, Ukraine, Uzbekistan, Venezuela, Vietnam, Yemen, and Zimbabwe."; IBM Cloud (2022): "Qiskit Runtime (beta) is unavailable from the following countries (as of April 2022): Armenia, Azerbaijan, Belarus, Cambodia, China (including Hong Kong S.A.R. of the PRC), Cuba, Georgia, Iraq, Iran, Kazakhstan, Kyrgyzstan, Laos, Libya, Macao S.A.R. of the PRC, Moldova, Mongolia, Myanmar (Burma), North Korea, Russia, Sudan, Syria, Tajikistan, Turkmenistan, Ukraine, Uzbekistan, Venezuela, Vietnam, and Yemen."

[69] E.g., Massachusetts Institute of Technology instructs faculty that letting a non-U.S. person handle restricted source code is legally the same as shipping it abroad, a "deemed export" that can trigger felony liability. MIT Office of the Vice President for Research (n.d.).

[70] U.S. BIS (2024), introducing ECCNs 3A904 and 3B904, the latter covering cryogenic refrigeration equipment capable of reaching $\leq$25 mK, i.e. dilution refrigerators.

First, cryptanalytic risk: a fault-tolerant implementation of Shor's algorithm would collapse public-key encryption, threatening everything from e-commerce receipts to nuclear-command links.[71] Second, non-cryptographic military utility: entanglement-enhanced gravimeters could spot stealth submarines and quantum illumination radar might defeat low-observable aircraft.[72] Third, techno-industrial rivalry: Beijing's Fourteenth Five-Year Plan,[73] Brussels' 2023 Economic Security Strategy[74] and Washington's CHIPS and Science Act[75] all elevate quantum information to "critical" status and funnel strategic subsidies into domestic supply chains. The rational response, from a security point of view, is to slow uncontrolled diffusion of these capabilities.

Yet the present controls— catch-all definitions of "advanced computing,"[76] nationality-based account blocks on public quantum clouds,[77] secrecy orders on patent filings for cryogenic-control assemblies,[78] and even enrolment embargoes imposed by online course providers—capture more than the weaponizable edge. They now reach routine academic use: a doctoral student who needs four logical qubits on a public service to benchmark an error-mitigation routine; a refugee whose only nexus to "countries of concern" is a passport; or an open-source pulse sequence whose sole destination is the arXiv preprint server. Major massive open online course (MOOC) platforms also exclude residents of sanctioned jurisdictions from free quantum computing courses under the U.S. Office of Foreign Assets Control rules. Learners from countries like Iran, Cuba or Syria have been barred from enrolling in free quantum computing courses on platforms such as MITx or edX.[79] In short, broad restrictions aimed at quantum technology can end up excluding legitimate

[71] Shor's algorithm is a quantum method that, on a sufficiently powerful error-corrected computer, can efficiently solve the problems that make today's public-key cryptography hard. Such machines do not exist yet, but because attackers can record traffic now and decrypt it later, standards bodies are migrating to post-quantum cryptography. Shor (1994); NIST (2025).

[72] *Roblin* (2025); Weinberger (2008); Cassens et al. (2025); Post Quantum (2023).

[73] CSET (2021).

[74] European Commission (2023a).

[75] CHIPS and Science Act (2022), § 10,372.

[76] U.S. BIS (2023a); *See* U.S. BIS (2023b) for over-breadth concerns voiced by stakeholders such as the Semiconductor Industry Association, Intel and SIA.

[77] IBM Quantum Platform (2023); Microsoft (n.d.); AWS (n.d.), § 1.25.

[78] E.g., United States (1951) Invention Secrecy Act; USPTO (n.d.) The United States Invention Secrecy Act of 1951 empowers the Pentagon, NSA and other agencies to impose an *ex parte* order on any patent application deemed "detrimental to national security," thereby blocking publication and foreign filing for renewable one-year terms; more than 5700 such orders were in force at the end of 2024, with quantum algorithms and cryogenic-control assemblies now expressly listed in the USPTO's classified technology matrix.

[79] MITxOnline, Computational Data Science in Physics I, "Who can take this course? Because of U.S. Office of Foreign Assets Control (OFAC) restrictions and other U.S. federal regulations, learners residing in one or more of the following countries or regions will not be able to register for this course: Iran, Cuba, Syria, North Korea and the Crimea, Donetsk People's Republic and Luhansk People's Republic regions of Ukraine." MITxOnline (n.d.).

researchers and open science initiatives in direct contravention to the obligations imposed by the right to science.

Under international law, State-imposed limits on the right to "enjoy the benefits of scientific progress" must pass a four-part test: they must be (i) provided by law, (ii) pursue a legitimate aim, (iii) be strictly necessary, and (iv) be proportionate to demonstrate that the least-intrusive means among those reasonably capable of achieving the aim was selected by regulators.[80] Quantum export rules are very likely to satisfy the first two limbs: for example, the EU's dual-use regulation,[81] the U.S. Export Administration Regulations[82] are precise legal instruments, and national security is generally recognized as a legitimate objective under Article 4's 'general welfare' aim. Difficulties arise primarily at stages (iii) and (iv).

Necessity. Because export-control offices lack the staffing, analytic bandwidth, and near-real-time technical insight to decide, experiment-by-experiment, what cryptanalytic work is benign and what is weaponizable, they default to blanket nationality presumptions or technology-wide embargoes rather than case-by-case licensing.[83] Administrative convenience, however, cannot satisfy the "strict necessity" standard when less intrusive means are available. Notably, other dual-use domains such as nuclear physics and synthetic biology have developed finer-grained controls: e.g., tiered general licenses for low-risk research (UK OGELs),[84] EU-style "trusted research" compliance programmes for international labs,[85] or secure compute enclaves that let collaborators run code on encrypted data[86]—that could be applied here by analogy. [87] For example, a standing open general license for low-risk quantum work could let vetted labs run only small test jobs inside secure, audited sandboxes: error-reduction checks go through, while any job that plainly aims to crack encryption is blocked and reviewed.

Proportionality. Consider that a Dutch PhD candidate of Iranian nationality may not run a five-qubit parity check on IBM's public cloud, while the same platform allows paying institutional users to execute encrypted circuits whose contents the provider never sees.[88] If the goal is to curb proliferation of cryptanalytic know-how, the ban on certain users by nationality is over-inclusive; if the goal is deterrence by denial, it is under-inclusive, because well-resourced actors will simply

[80] CESCR (2020), §§ 21–22.

[81] Regulation (EU) 2021/821, Arts 2 & 3.

[82] ECRA (2018) § 4812; EAR, 15 C.F.R. § 774, Supp. No. 1.

[83] A similar phenomenon was observed in crypto controls. See Diffie & Landau (2001).

[84] UK ECJU (2025), Open General Export Licences.

[85] See European Commission (2021).

[86] Such a solution is widely used in genomics and synthetic-biology data analysis. See, e.g., Kavianpour et al. (2022).

[87] European Commission (2021).

[88] IBM Quantum Platform (2023): §7 (a) embargo list; §9 (h)–(i) ban on releasing technology "to nationals, wherever they may be located" of those countries; Huang et al. (2017), demonstrating encrypted quantum circuits executed on IBM cloud without disclosing the algorithm.

migrate to unpoliced back-ends. Either way, the measure fails the least-restrictive-means requirement and, by discriminating on the basis of national origin, also raises concerns under Article 2(2) of the ICESCR (the Covenant's non-discrimination guarantee).

Article 15 imposes tripartite duties on States: to respect, protect, and fulfil, and, in paragraph 4, expressly calls on them to foster the benefits of international scientific cooperation. *Respect* requires States to refrain from arbitrary barriers to scientific collaboration; *protect* obliges them to prevent private actors—cloud vendors, patent offices, defense primes—from doing the same; *fulfil* demands positive steps to cultivate an open quantum ecosystem. The proportionality assessment recognizes the need to strike a delicate balance between many competing interests, but this balance must also include interests listed in Article 15(4) ICESCR that require State Parties to recognize the benefits of international cooperation in scientific fields. To ensure ongoing consistency with human rights obligations, States need not dismantle existing controls; rather, they should consider fine-tuning them so that they meet Article 4 criteria.

Several concrete adjustments could better align quantum controls with human rights standards of necessity and proportionality. For example, clarifying the "basic research" carveout in export law would help: the EU Dual Use Regulation already exempts fundamental research intended for immediate publication, but licensing officers apply this unevenly.[89] An EU-wide interpretative notice could codify a safe harbor for experiments below defined logical qubit or coherence-time thresholds. Authorities could also create quantum specific general licenses: following the U.K.'s Open General Export License model, regulators might issue standing authorizations for intangible technology transfers that stay within pre-set resource limits (e.g., number of two-qubit gates, total runtime, pulse amplitude), much as nuclear regulators distinguish between trivial tracer-level and weaponizable isotopes.[90] Likewise, accrediting "trusted research" labs could facilitate collaboration: the European Commission Recommendation (EU) 2021/1700 already invites universities to adopt compliance programs in lieu of passport vetting.[91] An EU-wide accreditation scheme could permit consortia of mixed nationalities to work under monitored conditions rather than perpetual license limbo. Finally, leveraging secure compute enclaves offers a technical fix: the European Commission's 2024 research security proposal endorses the use of confidential cloud enclaves where foreign users can run code on sensitive quantum hardware without ever downloading the underlying IP,[92] and prototypes such as *QEnclave* and open-source frameworks like *Gramine* show the

---

[89] Regulation (EU) 2021/821, Art. 3(2)(a). Reports by industry associations maintain that member-state authorities apply the EU dual-use exemptions for 'basic scientific research' and information 'in the public domain' differently, owing to the lack of common definitions in Regulation (EU) 2021/821. Bromley et al. (2021), p. 6.

[90] UK Export Control Joint Unit, Department for International Trade and Department for Business and Trade (2023); IAEA (1996).

[91] European Commission (2021), Annex I.

[92] European Commission (2024) COM(2024) 26, § 4.2.

concept is practical.[93] Scaling up that model would preserve scientific collaboration while safeguarding critical know-how.

Each of the above measures has precedents in adjacent regulatory regimes. Transplanting them into quantum control practice would help ensure that any limits on the right to science are strictly necessary and proportionate. In practical terms, such steps would recalibrate export barriers to intrude no further than needed to meet legitimate security aims, provide for periodic review as technologies evolve, and incorporate built-in safety valves for basic scientific research. That, in turn, would help reconcile security imperatives with the demands of the right to science.

The jurisprudence of quantum governance is nascent, and not all measures that have been successfully applied to other technologies will be suitable in the quantum context. We therefore suggest several research agendas to inform future policy. First, compliance audit trails for cloud-based quantum research deserve study. Because quantum states cannot be copied and many quantum jobs execute opaquely on remote hardware, there is no forensic duplicate of the process to seize or inspect. The classical output can be recorded, but it does not reveal which algorithm, qubits, or controls were used, which is what matters for proving an unlawful technology transfer. Developing tamper-evident log architectures, such as Merkle-tree chains of pulse-job metadata with differential privacy guards,[94] could provide auditable records without exposing proprietary code. Empirical tests should examine whether such logs would satisfy courts' authentication standards under rules of evidence in various jurisdictions.

Second, we need impact metrics for scientific diffusion. Article 15 of the ICESCR speaks of "enjoy[ing] the benefits" of scientific progress and its applications but offers no quantitative yardstick. Metrics would be highly desirable as General Comment No. 25 acknowledges that a "balance must be reached between intellectual property and the open access and sharing of scientific knowledge and its applications"[95] and ways of measuring the sharing of scientific progress would facilitate a transparent and fair balance between this and intellectual property rights. Bibliometric and patent-citation analyses, disaggregated by researchers' nationality and licensing status, could reveal whether current quantum borders materially slow diffusion of knowledge to the Global South, to disadvantaged groups and, ultimately, to the wider public. If they do, then any security gains from tight controls would need to be weighed against the human rights cost of delayed benefit sharing.

Third, normative models of risk stratification for quantum research should be developed. Present controls tend to treat all mid-scale quantum processors alike, yet the threat vector of a 100-qubit variational chemistry solver differs from that of a 100-qubit code-breaking rig optimized for Shor's algorithm. Interdisciplinary work linking cryptographers, export-control lawyers, and human-rights scholars could devise a taxonomy of risk tiers matched to tailored licence conditions, reducing overbreadth without undermining deterrence.

---

[93] Ma et al. (2022); Kowalczyk et al. (2024).

[94] Shikarpur (2022); Hu et al. (2021).

[95] CESCR (2020), § 62.

In sum, geopolitical competition has made quantum technology a magnet for precautionary regulation. However, for precautionary regulation to be compatible with human rights, there must be a fine-grained calibration of targeted measures, not the sledgehammer of nationality-wide exclusion. The ICESCR does not forbid export controls; it does require that they intrude no further than necessary to meet a legitimate security aim, that they remain open to periodic review as conditions change, and that they incorporate built-in safety valves for bona fide research. The recalibration tools sketched above—general licenses, trusted-research accreditation, secure enclaves, and evidence-generating audit logs—offer concrete ways to meet security needs while upholding the right to science. They translate the proportionality principle into operational criteria that regulators can test, scholars can scrutinize, and courts can enforce.

6.3.2 *Barrier 2—Concentrated Control of Quantum Infrastructure and Technical Knowhow*

Large platform companies sit at every layer of the emerging quantum stack. They fabricate scarce hardware, write and control the middleware that renders that hardware usable, and capture the user data and application workflows that run across it.[96] Their control over these technical assets means that the policies large firms set on key parameters such as access fees, API terms, and data sharing, can strongly influence how new knowledge circulates through the quantum research ecosystem. One question is how far human rights law, which is directed toward State parties, can play a role in responding to this barrier. It is an exaggeration to hold that human rights law plays no role in regulating the actions of private industry actors. The obligations placed on State parties by human rights law may require them to take positive actions and actively regulate private industry. The obligations to protect and fulfil human rights may thus lead State parties to pass domestic laws that require private industry to align their practices with principles found in human rights law, despite its lack of direct applicability to non-State actors.

International human rights law places primary, legally binding duties on *States*, not on private enterprises. The ICESCR therefore obliges governments, in their protect and fulfil dimensions, to regulate and steer non-State actors.[97] Finally, soft law regulations are increasingly acknowledging the role of corporate behavior so that private exercises of market power do not eclipse the public's right to share in scientific progress. General Comment 24 confirms that this regulatory duty extends to "all business entities," whether publicly traded, privately held, or State-owned.[98] At the same time, the UN Guiding Principles on Business and Human Rights (UNGP)[99]

---

[96] OECD (2025), pp. 11–15.

[97] Churches and Zalnieriute (2020); Davies (2016).

[98] CESCR (2017), paras 10–13.

[99] United Nations Human Rights Council (2011).

assign firms a parallel responsibility—albeit a soft-law one— to respect human rights throughout their operations. New legal obligations are not created and the focus for businesses is ensuring that they respect human rights through avoiding infringements and addressing known adverse human rights impacts. The UNGP also highlight that businesses should not undermine States' abilities to meet their obligations related to operations and value chains, and to conduct ongoing due-diligence assessments of the impacts their IP strategies, cloud terms, or data practices may have on the right to science.[100] The analysis that follows proceeds on this dual footing: States remain the ultimate duty-bearers, but their compliance increasingly depends on how effectively they shape and supervise the conduct of the platform companies that dominate the quantum innovation ecosystem.

A first quantitative glimpse of this proprietary consolidation comes from the patent record. Data show that the five largest quantum platform companies (leading firms in the United States, Europe and Asia) together hold well over 6,500 quantum-related patents granted between 2020 and 2024, and their annual awards have grown at roughly 50% per year, which represents nearly a five-fold rise over the period.[101] The claims concentrate on foundational bottlenecks—qubit read-out, cryogenic wiring and surface-code error correction—identified by the European Patent Office as the fastest-growing quantum-IP sub-sectors and ones that any interoperable quantum device will eventually need.[102] When overlapping portfolios reach this density, the clearance costs of tracing, negotiating and bundling the required rights threaten to delay follow-on research. This is the classic "patent-thicket" problem already familiar from biotechnology and smartphone litigation.[103]

While concerns about the concentration of quantum knowledge and infrastructure—particularly in the hands of a few powerful corporate actors—are justified, recent empirical findings suggest a more nuanced landscape. According to a comprehensive patent landscape analysis,[104] approximately 50% of quantum technology patents are already in the public domain, meaning they are no longer protected or never became enforceable due to non-renewal, expiration, or rejection. This substantial proportion of accessible intellectual property indicates that a significant base of quantum knowledge is legally available for further research, development, and dissemination.

Moreover, the report challenges the common narrative that quantum technologies are dominated by a small oligopoly of multinational tech firms. While certain corporations do hold large patent portfolios, the overall distribution of patent ownership is markedly less concentrated than in classical computing. A wide range of actors—including universities, public research organizations, and smaller companies—are actively participating in quantum innovation. This diversified landscape

[100] United Nations Human Rights Council (2011), Principles 11–24.

[101] Mason (2024).

[102] EPO (2023), p. 11.

[103] A patent thicket is a dense web of overlapping IP rights that innovators must navigate to avoid infringement. Shapiro (2001).

[104] Aboy et al. (2022).

could foster greater competition and openness, particularly if appropriate governance mechanisms are put in place to sustain it.

The study also observes that the "quantum patent thicket" feared by some commentators has not yet materialized at a scale comparable to other high-tech sectors like biotechnology or classical software. Although there is growing activity in patent filings—particularly in areas such as quantum cryptography and quantum sensing—the field remains in a relatively early and dynamic phase. This presents a crucial window of opportunity: policymakers, standard-setting bodies, and multilateral institutions can still shape the norms and infrastructure that will govern access to quantum knowledge.

That said, vigilance remains warranted. Patent landscapes can evolve rapidly, especially as commercially viable quantum applications become clearer. The increasing use of "strategic patenting" by certain actors to build influence in standard-setting processes or block competitors may reintroduce barriers to access and collaboration. In this context, the right to science provides a normative compass: it emphasizes the importance of both access to scientific knowledge and opportunities for participation, alongside respect for scientific freedom and intellectual property rights.

Intellectual property exclusivity in quantum is not confined to patents. Platform providers routinely keep calibration routines, error-mitigation protocols, and qubit-control firmware as trade secrets.[105] Because near-term quantum advantage depends more on error suppression and control software than on raw qubit counts, these undisclosed methods can determine who tops a performance benchmark.[106] As described in Chap. 6 of this volume, the leading firms have adopted a mixed IP strategy: patent the interface-visible elements of their systems, but keep the optimization levers confidential. The approach is lawful and efficient, yet it reduces the amount of information available for peer review or independent validation. From a right to science perspective, opacity at this level risks slowing cumulative progress when researchers must reinvent solutions that have already been achieved behind walls of secrecy.[107]

A further filtering layer appears in the terms of service for cloud-based quantum platforms—the route through which most universities and start-ups now access cutting-edge devices. Providers' terms typically reserve broad compliance levers: they can suspend or disable accounts, condition publication of benchmark data, and block routing techniques that hide a user's true location. Microsoft's Azure Quantum service incorporates the Microsoft Online Subscription Agreement, which allows Microsoft to "suspend your use of the Online Services" whenever it detects activity that violates the Acceptable Use Policy or other term.[108] Amazon's Braket service terms permit benchmarking only if the user discloses all details needed for AWS to

[105] Das et al. (2023).

[106] Hosseinkhani et al. (2025) notes that "the utility of quantum computing hinges not only on increasing qubit counts but also on efficiently mitigating the inherent noise that disrupts computations."

[107] Note the Venice Statement that explicitly identified the tension between IP regimes and the right to science as a key challenge, noting that overly strong IP protection can impede the diffusion of scientific applications. UNESCO (2009), para. 11.

[108] Microsoft (n.d.), Azure Online Subscription Agreement, "Suspension" paragraph.

replicate the test—and they give AWS a reciprocal right to benchmark and publish results on the user's own tools.[109] IBM's end-user agreement bars "masking physical location," a clause that effectively blocks ordinary VPN use even where export law would not.[110] Each of these provisions, in effect, gives a private company veto power over certain scientific communications or collaborations. While often justified on security or business grounds, such private constraints can conflict with the right to science if they are overbroad or not strictly necessary to protect legitimate interests.

The right to science does not object to private forms of exclusivity. Article 15(1)(c) safeguards the "moral and material interests" of authors, but—as the *travaux préparatoires* and Special Rapporteur commentary underline—that clause draws on the civil-law tradition of *droit d'auteur* (recognition, integrity, fair remuneration), not on modern patent or copyright monopolies.[111] The legal problem therefore arises only when patents, trade secrecy, or contract terms impair the parallel entitlement in Article 15(1)(b) to "enjoy the benefits of scientific progress," together with the affirmative duties in Article 15(2) to develop and diffuse science and in Article 15(3) to protect the freedom indispensable for research. General Comment 25 restates the test: a restriction that is lawful and pursues a legitimate aim, such as incentivizing innovation, must still be strictly necessary and proportionate in context. An exclusivity term that outlasts the period reasonably required to recoup R&D costs, or a publication veto that blocks non-confidential benchmarking results, will fail that test if a narrower safeguard—say, a brief publication embargo or a government-vetted redaction—could achieve the same objective instead.

A number of familiar legal and policy mechanisms could help realign incentives toward openness without undermining private investment. Public procurement and grant contracts are one lever. Horizon Europe already mandates open-access publication of peer-reviewed outputs arising from funded projects.[112] Extending similar conditions to instrument development awards would push openness down from articles into firmware APIs and pulse-sequence specifications after a defined embargo. In the United States, the National Quantum Initiative Act gives agencies authority to set "access conditions" at new quantum research centres;[113] those agencies could require that, once a government-supported quantum device moves beyond the prototype stage, its interface specifications be deposited in a public repository. These steps would ensure that core technical knowledge eventually transitions from proprietary silos into the public domain, to the benefit of the broader scientific community.

When dense patent thickets threaten interoperability, patent pools offer another solution. For instance, a Quantum Computing Industry Intellectual Property Alliance, launched in China in 2023, has set up a patent pool that will cover quantum error correction technologies.[114] While its detailed license terms have not yet been

[109] AWS (n.d.), § 1.8.

[110] IBM Quantum Platform (2023), Art. 9(g).

[111] Shaver (2010), p. 154; United Nations General Assembly (2015).

[112] European Union (2021) Reg. 2021/695, Recital 8; Art. 14.

[113] NQIA (2018), §§ 102(b)(6–7), 402.

[114] Chen (2023).

disclosed, China's 2025 patent pool guidelines require FRAND-style conditions.[115] A comparable transatlantic pool would allow researchers and smaller firms to "clear" the use of essential quantum patents under predictable licensing terms, while still returning royalties to the originators.[116] Competition authorities have substantial experience in supervising such pooling arrangements, and indeed EU law provides tools to mandate access if dominant firms refuse licenses. Article 102 of the TFEU prohibits abuse of a dominant position, and the European Commission could invoke it to require participation in a patent pool if a refusal to license key quantum IP would eliminate a downstream market for research and innovation.

Soft law frameworks can also help. The UN Guiding Principles on Business and Human Rights call on companies to assess and address human-rights impacts throughout their operations and value chains. Building on that, a sector-specific quantum due-diligence standard—covering firm's practices on patenting, secrecy, and user agreements—could provide tech companies, auditors and investors with a shared benchmark.[117] Companies would be encouraged to regularly evaluate whether their knowledge governance practices (e.g. patent strategies or cloud terms) align with the right to science, and to make adjustments if they do not. Such an initiative could be led by multi-stakeholder organizations or as part of corporate ESG (environmental, social, governance) reporting frameworks. Regulatory action in this area should be guided by data wherever possible— an injunction that is itself part of aligning with the right to science, whose minimum core obligations include "adopt[ing] mechanisms aimed at aligning government policies and programmes with the best available, generally accepted scientific evidence."[118] For example, patent landscaping studies can quantify how concentrated and overlapping the quantum IP space has become and identify potential chokepoints. Network analysis of cloud service terms could reveal how frequently (and under what circumstances) providers exercise their contractual rights to block publications or suspend users. Longitudinal work could then track whether, once FRAND-oriented patent pools or patent pledges materialize, they correlate with faster replication of experimental results across institutions. Such findings would be directly relevant to ongoing policy evaluations—for instance, the scheduled 2026 review of the EU's Intellectual Property Action Plan and parallel efforts in the U.S. to assess competition in emerging tech.[119] Where such data is not available, efforts should be made to introduce ways and means of collecting data to ensure States comply with their human rights obligations in this area.

None of the measures outlined here would eliminate private firms' incentives to innovate. Experience from earlier technology waves—the Internet, GPS, CRISPR, even the first superconducting qubits[120]—suggests that the riskiest, foundational

[115] Wininger (2025).

[116] As argued by, i.a., Räsänen et al. (2021).

[117] UN HRC (2011), Principles 17–21.

[118] CESCR (2020), para. 52.

[119] European Commission (2020), § 3.3; Executive Office of the President of the United States (2022).

[120] Leiner et al. (1999); Aerospace (n.d.); Fajardo-Ortiz et al. (2022); DARPA (2023).

stages are usually financed with public funds, while private capital joins once technical feasibility is clearer. The safeguards proposed above therefore aim only to keep exclusive rights within the bounds of necessity and proportionality, ensuring that downstream researchers retain viable pathways to build on prior work and that the public, which so often underwrites early research, receives a fair return in shared knowledge and capability. Calibrating grant conditions, fostering collaborative IP mechanisms and mainstreaming human-rights due diligence can preserve the commercial momentum driving quantum engineering while sustaining the open circulation of information on which the right to science ultimately depends.

6.3.3 Barrier 3—Economic Exclusion: "The Global Quantum Divide"

Quantum computing is advancing under a pattern of spatial and economic concentration familiar from earlier technological waves[121] but intensified by the high capital cost and export-sensitivity of key hardware. As of 2024, the vast majority of public spending on quantum R&D (roughly 85–90%) originates in just a handful of jurisdictions (China, the United States, the EU and select larger member states, Japan, Canada, the UK, and Korea).[122] The OECD tallies total government commitments at roughly USD 42 billion; adding up the eight biggest programs in those jurisdictions accounts for ≈ USD 35 billion, i.e. well over four-fifths of the world total.[123] Nearly 90% of operational multi-qubit processors live in those same countries.[124] Universities in, for example, Brazil, South Africa, or Indonesia can (in principle) access some of these devices through cloud platforms, but published tariff schedules show that executing one million two-qubit gates on a cloud quantum computer can cost on the order of USD 2000–5000.[125] Voucher schemes do exist, but they are finite:

[121] Note the pattern of technological gatekeeping that entrenched global inequality in past tech revolutions (like the patent-driven monopolies in medicines or the digital divide in internet access). Trouiller et al. (2002). Also consider that wealthy early movers are not only investing in technology but are also setting standards and norms to suit their own interests, often at the expense of poorer nations. Karanicolas (2024).

[122] OECD (2025), pp. 36–37.

[123] OECD (2025), p. 34.

[124] A December 2024 audit by Quantum Computing Report lists 64 on-premise systems worldwide; 56 of them are in Europe, the United States, Japan, South Korea or Taiwan, leaving only a handful elsewhere. Quantum Computing Report (2024).

[125] *IonQ Forte-1* on qBraid/AWS is priced at USD 0.08 per shot + USD 0.30 per task. A workload that fires 50,000 shots with ~20 two-qubit gates per shot (≈ 1 million two-qubit gates) lands at about USD 4000; *IBM Pay-As-You-Go* starts at USD 96 per minute on Falcon/Eagle-class QPUs; circuits of comparable depth fall in the same window once queueing overheads are included. qBraid (n.d.); IBM Quantum (n.d.), pricing.

access often lapses once the pilot funding ends,[126] recreating for quantum hardware the same cycle of episodic dependence that Global South virology labs experienced when donor-funded gene sequencers arrived without long-term reagent budgets.[127]

Moreover, international research collaborations and talent flows are clustering ever more tightly among high-income States (and a few large emerging economies), leaving many developing regions virtually absent from the global quantum research map.[128] UNESCO has warned that, without proactive intervention, a "global quantum divide" will open between countries that possess quantum knowledge and infrastructure and those that do not, compounding the scientific capacity gaps already visible in fields such as AI and high performance computing.[129] The consequences are far-reaching: countries excluded from the quantum revolution risk losing competitiveness in industries—from pharmaceuticals and advanced materials to cryptography—and becoming dependent on foreign providers for quantum-secured communications or climate-modelling tools. Security analysts likewise caution that first-mover States could monopolise quantum-resistant encryption and spy-proof networks, reinforcing a gate-keeping role that leaves the Global South more vulnerable in terms of cybersecurity, economic sovereignty, and technological autonomy.[130]

A second layer of exclusion operates within high-income economies, where public–private funding models often channel federally financed know-how back to a handful of incumbent firms. However, the strategies jurisdictions deploy to address it vary. In the United States, NSF and DOE quantum centers routinely license the resulting IP to their industrial members on non-exclusive, royalty-free terms, with an option to negotiate exclusivity—an approach that accelerates transfer but can also consolidate advantage.[131] By contrast, Europe's programs are beginning to implement inclusion safeguards into their contracts. The Netherlands' Quantum Delta NL initiative, for example, designates "anchor" firms that supply fabrication runs or specialized tooling and, in return, receive preferred—but not automatically exclusive—access to foreground intellectual property; its guidelines expressly *prefer* non-exclusive licensing and allow exclusivity only when partners make "substantial co-investment".[132] Such guardrails accelerate prototyping without letting publicly funded breakthroughs drift entirely into private hands; where they are absent, collective subsidy is more likely to become a private asset portfolio.[133]

---

[126] IBM's *Quantum Credits* grant free runtime on >100-qubit devices until the quota is exhausted. IBM, Build utility-scale quantum applications with the updated Open Plan and IBM Quantum Credits. IBM (2023), Quantum Credits.

[127] See, e.g., Moyo et al. (2023); Dhawan (2025).

[128] See 2025 Nature Index data which shows all top 10 institutions for quantum physics clustered in China, Europe and the United States (Austin (2025)).

[129] Vermaas & Mans (2024).

[130] Karanicolas and Zornetta (2025).

[131] IUCRC (n.d.), cl. F; CQN (2022), § 13(c)–(d)

[132] Quantum Delta NL (n.d.), §§ 5–7.

[133] This dynamic was seen in the pharmaceutical sector, where drugs developed with public research funds were often patented by corporations and sold at high prices worldwide, leading to calls for a "human rights approach" to innovation that guarantees access. Perehudoff & Sellin (2022).

The right to science frames these distributional asymmetries in normative terms. Article 15(1)(b) ICESCR guarantees the right of "everyone" to enjoy the benefits of scientific progress, while paragraph 4 "recognizes the benefits to be derived from the encouragement and development of international contacts and co-operation." Drafted in 1966 as a largely aspirational clause, Article 15(4) is treated by General Comment No. 25 as a positive duty on States to facilitate cross-border scientific exchange and diffusion.[134] General Comment 25 further calls on governments to secure *equitable* access to scientific benefits both between countries and within their own populations.[135] Where large shares of public R&D effectively underwrite proprietary gains that remain out of reach for most researchers—or where the geography of hardware access hardens into a North-South divide—States risk falling short of their obligation to fulfil the right to science as now understood.

The international intellectual property regime already offers formal tools that could mitigate these divides if necessary. The Agreement on Trade-Related Aspects of Intellectual Property Rights (TRIPS), for example, permits compulsory licensing[136] of patents under certain conditions, including for public non-commercial use (Article 31), and obliges developed countries to encourage technology transfer to least-developed countries (Article 66.2).[137] To date, no government has invoked these provisions for quantum enabling technologies (say, a patent on a qubit control chip or error-correction firmware). Even if a compulsory license *were* issued, it would bring little immediate, practical access. Running today's superconducting- or spin-qubit processors demands gear that remain overwhelmingly concentrated in the world's wealthiest research hubs.[138] Until that core infrastructure diffuses far beyond today's hubs, compulsory licensing and similar IP flexibilities will remain largely symbolic, capable of easing legal barriers but unable to supply the physical capacity needed to exploit a quantum patent.

Financing design can also enhance equity. One novel approach is to tie public grants to public equity stakes or return-on-investment mechanisms. For example, Israel's Innovation Authority recoups its larger R&D grants via conditional royalties of roughly 3–5% of a recipient's sales, and those repayments flow straight back into the Authority's revolving innovation fund to finance the next cohort of start-ups.[139] Adapting that model, one could imagine CHIPS and Science Act or Horizon Europe grants above a certain threshold carrying a small equity-warrant or royalty

[134] See CESCR (2020), paras 3, 24, 42, 45, and 52.

[135] Note that the General Comment also highlights *extraterritorial* obligations, meaning a state like the U.S. should ensure that corporations under its jurisdiction (e.g. IBM, Google—"multinational companies over which they can exercise control") do not violate the right to science of people in other countries, for instance by imposing unfair terms globally or denying access arbitrarily. CESCR (2020), para. 84.

[136] Compulsory license allows a government to authorize the use of a patent without the owner's consent under certain conditions (typically with some royalty payment).

[137] WTO TRIPS (1995), Arts 31, 66.2.

[138] Allied Market Research (2025), showing that North America and Europe dominate current demand, with East Asia a distant third and the rest of the world in single-digit percentages.

[139] World Services Group (2017).

obligation (say) 1–5% with any dividends, royalty streams or exit proceeds funneled into a *global-access fund* that subsidizes quantum cloud time for researchers in under-resourced regions. A precedent for this already exists in biopharmaceuticals: Sanofi agreed to pay the non-profit DNDi a 3% royalty on private-sector sales of the publicly funded malaria therapy ASAQ, and DNDi earmarks that income for further neglected disease R&D instead of treating it as profit.[140]

Building capacity in disadvantaged regions is equally critical, since IP rights are of little help if one lacks the infrastructure to exploit them. Joint international laboratories and training partnerships have shown promise. India and Finland, for example, have launched an *Indo-Finnish Virtual Network Centre on Quantum Computing* that links Indian institutes with Finnish partners for hands-on hardware know-how transfer.[141] Regional pooling mechanisms could scale such models. One might envisage a consortium of ASEAN countries pooling funds to purchase a mid-scale cryogenic quantum platform from a European vendor, with the deal including a clause that idle processor time be made available at marginal cost to affiliated public universities in the region. Similarly, multi-country partnerships could co-finance open-access quantum testbeds, spreading both cost and benefit. One practical step would be an intergovernmental Global Quantum Fund—modelled on CERN's pooled-budget system and UNESCO's SESAME synchrotron[142]—to channel a small share of high-income countries' quantum budgets into regional hubs, training fellowships and the donation of de-commissioned hardware. Such a scheme would give concrete effect not only to the ICESCR duty of international scientific co-operation (arts. 15 (4) and 2 (1)) but also to the companion obligations in arts. 15 (1)(b), 15 (2) and 15 (3) to ensure the enjoyment, diffusion and freedom of scientific progress. It also dovetails with UNESCO's 2025 International Year of Quantum agenda, which highlights the need to bridge the emerging "quantum divide."[143]

Pricing architecture also matters for inclusion. Major cloud providers do offer academic discounts for quantum computing access, but the rates are typically pegged to usage volume and take no account of differing local purchasing power. Adopting a *differential pricing* model—akin to tiered pricing of pharmaceuticals in different income-level markets—could lower barriers for researchers in low-income countries without unduly burdening providers.[144] For example, pricing per quantum "shot" or per device-hour could be indexed to the GDP per capita of the user's country. Providers could argue this would invite arbitrage (resellers from low-price regions selling access to others), but technical mitigations are available, including geofenced login tokens and per-user shot quotas, both of which are already employed to enforce export controls and prevent unauthorized reuse of cloud credits.[145]

[140] Pécoul et al. (2008).

[141] The Hindu (2022).

[142] UNESCO (n.d.), CERN model; UNESCO (n.d.), SESAME.

[143] Innovation News Network (2025).

[144] Tetteh (2009).

[145] IBM Quantum Platform (2023).

Finally, monitoring remains essential. Policymakers could consider mandating transparent reporting on quantum access metrics—for instance, requiring cloud providers to publish annual data on average pricing per user category and country, which would allow regulators and researchers to spot disparities and trends.

Economic exclusion is less visible than an export ban or a corporate non-disclosure clause, but it may prove the more enduring barrier. Hardware will eventually scale, and algorithms will mature, but without intervention, sunk-cost advantages and infrastructure asymmetries tend to lock in early lead positions.[146] Legal and financing tools to counter the imbalance do exist; the challenge for policy is to deploy them early enough, and with sufficient precision, that the distribution of quantum capabilities is guided by the "general welfare in a democratic society" standard (to borrow the language of ICESCR Article 4) rather than by the inertia of first-mover geography. Doing so would not negate private incentives to invest in quantum R&D; it would simply ensure that the public contributions receive a commensurate public return, thereby anchoring the quantum revolution within the inclusive architecture that the right to science envisions.

6.3.4 Barrier 4—Balancing Participation and Freedom in Quantum Science

The right to science unquestionably includes a participatory dimension. From the drafting history[147] to the Venice Statement[148] and the 2012 Shaheed report,[149] from General Comment No. 25[150] to the 2024 Special Rapporteur's report on participation in science,[151] international human rights bodies have consistently affirmed that Article 15(1)(b) encompasses "not only a right to receive the benefits of the applications of scientific progress, but also a right to participate in scientific progress."[152] Since participation in science is needed for scientific progress, and since the freedom to participate in science is an element of scientific freedom more broadly, the participatory element is reinforced by Article 15(2)'s mandate to develop and diffuse science and Article 15(3)'s protection of scientific freedom.

At its core, the right to participate in quantum science means that no one should be excluded from quantum education, the quantum research profession, or quantum citizen science initiatives based on irrelevant characteristics.[153] States violate this

[146] Farrell & Klemperer (2007); Foxon (2002).

[147] Porsdam Mann (2024a,b).

[148] UNESCO (2009), para. 11.

[149] Shaheed (2012), paras 25, 43–44.

[150] CESCR (2020), para. 11.

[151] Xanthaki (2024).

[152] CESCR (2020), para. 11.

[153] Porsdam Mann (2024a,b); CESCR (2020), para. 10; Shaheed (2012), para. 42; UNESCO (2009), para. 13(a); Xanthaki (2024), para. 38.

right when they limit quantum physics education to certain groups, when quantum research positions are inaccessible due to unjust discrimination, when States prevent individuals from joining quantum-related citizen science projects, or when quantum computing infrastructure is reserved for special groups. The right also encompasses access to quantum scientific information—research papers, educational materials, and basic knowledge about quantum phenomena should be broadly available, not locked behind prohibitive paywalls or classified unnecessarily.[154] These are uncontroversial applications of the participatory principle that align with the right to science‘s anti-discrimination and access dimensions.

However, recent scholarship, UN bodies, and special procedures have advanced more expansive interpretations. Some argue that the participatory dimension extends to democratic decision-making over scientific priorities, suggesting that citizens should help determine *inter alia* which quantum research directions receive funding.[155] This interpretation, while well-intentioned, requires careful scrutiny in light of both the drafting history and the instrumental relationship between scientific freedom and scientific progress. Mandatory citizen participation in scientific decision-making or priority-setting is in clear tension with both scientific freedom and the role of scientific expertise.[156] This tension is especially vivid in quantum computing, which is characterized by a high degree of theoretical complexity. Consider what an expansive interpretation of participation would mean in practice for quantum computing. Should citizen panels determine whether research funding flows to ion trap systems versus photonic qubits versus superconducting architectures? Should public votes influence whether researchers prioritize quantum error correction through surface codes or topological approaches? Should democratic assemblies decide whether theoretical work on quantum algorithms merits support over experimental work on qubit coherence times? The epistemic absurdity of such proposals is, we hope, immediately apparent. These decisions require deep understanding of quantum mechanics, materials science, engineering constraints, and the interdependencies and opportunity costs between different research directions. Even within the quantum research community, fierce debates rage over these priorities precisely because they require sophisticated technical judgment.

Yet the scholars and UN bodies advancing participatory interpretations are not naive. They recognize these tensions and are clearly responding to genuine concerns about science’s social accountability. When quantum computing promises to revolutionize cryptography, drug discovery, financial modeling, and artificial intelligence, the public has legitimate interests at stake. When public funds support quantum research, taxpayers reasonably expect some voice in how their resources are used. When quantum technologies may reshape labor markets, threaten privacy, or create

[154] Xanthaki (2024), paras 33–34; CESCR (2020), para. 17.

[155] Besson (2023); Shaheed (2012), para. 43; Xanthaki (2024), para. 93; CESCR (2020), paras 10, 55.

[156] CESCR (2020), para. 55; Xanthaki (2024), para. 54; Besson (2023), p. 517.

new forms of inequality, affected communities deserve input into these transformations. The question is not whether public participation has any role in quantum science, but rather what form that participation should take.

We suggest this apparent tension dissolves when we pay careful attention to the drafting history of Article 15. The delegates who crafted the right to science were remarkably prescient about precisely this issue.[157] Their key insight was to distinguish between two fundamentally different objects of potential public influence: the development of science itself versus the application and use of scientific discoveries. As delegates from Lebanon, Australia, and Greece emphasized, there is a fundamental difference between these two arenas of participation. Azkoul of Lebanon captured this precisely: "it could be argued that limitation and orientation of the use of scientific discoveries was desirable, but that could not apply to the development of pure science."[158] In response to a proposal by the USSR to tie the development of science to certain goals, such as the advancement of democracy, Whitlam of Australia "agreed with other speakers that the reference to the development of science in the interests of progress and democracy in the USSR amendment was undesirable, since that reference did not relate to the application of science, but to science itself."[159] The Greek delegate Rossides elaborated: "[s]cientific progress could be used for peaceful purposes or for the destruction of mankind. To limit the freedom of the individual in his research or study would not alter that situation. It was in the possible application of scientific discoveries that the danger lay".[160]

This distinction has profound implications for quantum computing. The key argument for scientific freedom—that it is necessary to advance scientific progress—applies only to the development of science, not to the subsequent application of the resulting knowledge.[161] Thus, basic quantum research, such as investigations into quantum entanglement, superposition, error correction algorithms, or fundamental quantum mechanics, falls squarely within the realm of scientific development that must remain free from control by the State or the public. Scientists must be free to pursue counterintuitive hypotheses, to investigate phenomena that seem to have no immediate application, to follow the internal logic of their discipline wherever it leads, and not to have to explain themselves unnecessarily to politicians or the wider public. This freedom is not a privilege but an instrumental necessity: scientific breakthroughs have consistently emerged from research directions that would have seemed pointless or impossible to non-specialists.[162]

Consider how public participation might have affected pivotal moments in quantum computing's development. Would citizen panels in the 1980s have approved

---

[157] For much more on the drafting history, see Porsdam Mann (2024a,b); Porsdam Mann et al. (2024).

[158] UNCHR (1952), p. 11.

[159] UNCHR (1952), p. 14.

[160] UNGA (1957), para. 17.

[161] Porsdam Mann (2024a,b).

[162] Braben (2007); Porsdam Mann et al. (2024).

funding for research into quantum entanglement—a phenomenon Einstein dismissively called "spooky action at a distance"? Would democratic decision-making have supported decades of investment in quantum error correction when classical computing was advancing rapidly? The history of science is littered with transformative discoveries that emerged from research programs that seemed arcane, impractical, or even absurd to contemporaries.[163]

This is not to say that public participation has no role in quantum science. Rather, following the drafters' distinction, public involvement becomes appropriate and even essential when we move from quantum science to quantum technology, from the development of knowledge to its application. When decisions must be made about how quantum computers should be deployed, which applications should be prioritized, how quantum advantages should be distributed, or what safeguards should govern quantum technology, public participation is not only permissible but necessary. These are precisely the kinds of decisions about "the use of scientific discoveries" that the drafters recognized as legitimate subjects for democratic input.

The distinction also illuminates why different aspects of quantum computing might properly be subject to different levels of control. The circulation of basic quantum science knowledge, such as research papers on quantum algorithms, theoretical advances in quantum mechanics, mathematical proofs about quantum computation, should face minimal restrictions, as this knowledge represents the development of science itself. By contrast, the circulation of quantum computing applications, viz., actual quantum computers, specific implementations of quantum algorithms for breaking encryption, quantum sensing devices with military applications, may legitimately be subject to export controls, licensing requirements, and other forms of democratic oversight, so long as these meet the limitations criteria discussed above.

Scientific freedom under Article 15(3) is not to be understood as an absolute principle that trumps all other considerations, but as a carefully calibrated protection for the space scientists need to advance knowledge. It protects the quantum researcher's freedom to investigate whatever aspects of quantum mechanics seem promising, to collaborate with colleagues across borders, to publish findings that challenge conventional wisdom. But it does not protect a claimed "freedom" to deploy quantum computers in ways that violate privacy, to monopolize quantum advantages for narrow interests, or to ignore legitimate public concerns about quantum technology's societal impacts.

The challenge for quantum governance is to institutionalize this distinction in practice. Universities and research institutions must fiercely protect the freedom of their quantum researchers to pursue basic science without political, public, or commercial interference. Funding agencies must resist pressure to evaluate quantum research solely by its immediate applications. At the same time, bodies governing quantum technology deployment must create meaningful channels for public participation in decisions about how quantum computing shapes our collective future.

---

163 Braben (2007); Porsdam Mann et al. (2024).

6.3.5 *Barrier 5—The Scope of Science and the STEM Trap*

Recent years have witnessed growing calls for expanded ethical, legal, and societal scholarship on quantum computing. Ten Holter et al.'s embedded study within the UK's Networked Quantum Information Technologies Hub,[164] for instance, explicitly advocates for greater interdisciplinary engagement, arguing that "questions around societal impact" require input from fields beyond physics and engineering. Similar calls have emerged from those examining quantum ethics and legal scholars grappling with quantum's implications for privacy and encryption.[165] Without this kind of scholarship, the implications of QC for individuals and societies cannot be understood, mitigated, enhanced, or regulated appropriately.

These calls raise a question fundamental to any human rights analysis of quantum computing: Which aspects of quantum computing scholarship fall within the scope of the right to science? This is not merely a semantic exercise. The answer determines the reach of all the obligations discussed above. States must ensure availability, accessibility, acceptability, and quality; they must respect, protect, and fulfil; they must implement core obligations immediately and pursue progressive realization; but they are required to do so only for activities that constitute "science" within the meaning of Article 15 ICESCR and Article 27 UDHR.

The stakes of this definitional question become apparent when we examine the emerging consensus definition of science in the right to science scholarship. General Comment No. 25 adopts the definition from the 2017 UNESCO Recommendation on Science and Scientific Researchers, which characterizes science as "the enterprise whereby humankind… makes an organized attempt, by means of the objective study of observed phenomena and its validation through sharing of findings and data and through peer review, to discover and master the chain of causalities, relations or interactions."[166] This definition, with its emphasis on "objective study of observed phenomena," creates an immediate problem in the context of quantum computing.

On its face, this empiricist definition arguably excludes quantum computing itself. Quantum information theory operates in the realm of mathematical abstraction, not empirical observation. The development of quantum algorithms involves formal proofs and logical derivations, not the study of observed phenomena. Even experimental quantum computing often deals with quantum states that cannot be directly observed without destroying the superposition that makes them useful. If the theoretical foundations of quantum computing do not clearly qualify as "science" under the prevailing definition, what hope exists for recognizing the philosophers, ethicists, and social scientists whose work is equally crucial for quantum's responsible development?

This *reductio ad absurdum* is perhaps the strongest argument against the 2017 UNESCO definition, but it is far from the only one. Historical analysis reveals that

---

[164] Ten Holter et al. (2023).

[165] See, e.g., Perrier (2022).

[166] CESCR (2020), para. 4; UNESCO (2017), para. 1(a)(i).

this definition emerged through institutional accident rather than deliberate design—originally crafted as a working definition for a 1960s meeting of European science ministers, it was incorporated into successive UNESCO documents through bureaucratic inertia rather than philosophical rigor.[167] Linguistic analysis shows that the terms used in the other authentic language versions of the human rights instruments—Arabic, Chinese, French, Russian, and Spanish—all encompass broader conceptions than the narrow English term "science".[168] And the limited drafting history that exists points toward an expansive understanding: when asked whether "scientific research" included social sciences, the Chairman of the drafting committee confirmed that "the term applied to every possible branch of research".[169]

These considerations point toward understanding the right to science as protecting a broader notion of systematic intellectual inquiry, regardless of field. Indeed, while English narrowed its definition of 'science' to the natural sciences only in the late 19th or early twentieth century, many languages continue to employ the more expansive concept today.[170] German maintains *Wissenschaft*, Dutch uses *wetenschap*, and the Scandinavian languages employ *vetenskap* (Swedish), *videnskab* (Danish), and *vitenskap* (Norwegian)—all referring to systematic knowledge-seeking across all disciplines. As articulated by the philosopher of science Sven Ove Hansson, what makes an endeavor scientific is not its subject matter but its epistemic warrant: "the sciences and humanities have something important in common: their very *raison d'être* is to provide us with the most epistemically warranted statements that can be made, at the time being, on the subject matter within their respective domains."[171] Under this conception, a historian employing rigorous archival methods to document quantum computing's development, an ethicist applying normative reasoning to quantum's dual-use implications, or a social scientist using formal models to predict quantum's economic impacts all engage in science.

This broader understanding has immediate and practical consequences for quantum computing governance. If the right to science protects *Wissenschaft* as systematic truth-seeking, as we argue, then States' obligations extend equally to supporting the full ecosystem of knowledge necessary to understand and govern quantum computing responsibly.

The right to science, properly understood as protecting *Wissenschaft*, thus breaks down the disciplinary barriers that would otherwise limit quantum computing to a purely technical endeavor. Just as States must ensure quantum research facilities are available, quantum knowledge is accessible, quantum applications meet quality standards, and quantum benefits reach all members of society, so too must they ensure these conditions for the broader scholarly ecosystem—including the philosophical, ethical, legal, and social inquiry that responsible quantum computing requires.

167 Porsdam Mann (2024b).

168 Porsdam Mann (2024a,b).

169 Porsdam Mann (2024a,b).

170 Phillips (2015).

171 Hansson (2013).

6.4 Discussion: Challenges & Opportunities for the Future

Quantum computing is a powerful general-purpose technology that will, at some point in the not-so-distant future, likely have a significant impact on individual rights and collective well-being. To date, however, governance initiatives and the scholarship informing them have focused narrowly on national security, economic competitiveness, and technical standard-setting. This leaves unaddressed many of the bigger-picture concerns about equity, access, participation, and the fair distribution of benefits that human rights law is designed to secure. In this paper, we have argued that no existing legal framework better encapsulates these issues than the human right to science, despite its long history of relative neglect.

Applying the right to science framework to quantum computing can, we believe, be mutually beneficial. As we hope to have shown, the normative standards of the right, including the AAAQ framework, the tripartite state obligations, and the strict criteria for any limitations, are directly applicable to many of the most pressing governance challenges in the quantum domain. Conversely, quantum computing serves as a crucial test case for the right to science itself. As a powerful, emerging technology still in a formative stage of regulation, it provides an ideal arena for applying and refining our understanding of the right. As right to science scholarship matures, it must be applied to real-world scientific and technological challenges, and quantum computing is an obvious and important candidate for this work.

In applying this framework, our analysis identified and addressed five principal barriers where the right to science can provide a critical normative perspective. We argued that: (1) Geopolitical access controls, often implemented as blanket restrictions, must be rigorously tested against the human rights principles of necessity and proportionality. (2) The concentration of infrastructure, know-how, and trade secrecy must be balanced against the concurrent State obligations under the right to science to protect scientific freedom and ensure the development and broad diffusion of scientific knowledge. (3) The profound economic exclusion creating a "global quantum divide"runs counter to the right's provisions for equitable benefit-sharing and international scientific cooperation. (4) Debates over public participation can be clarified by adhering to the drafters' distinction between the near-absolute freedom required for the *development* of science and the legitimate public interest in governing its *applications.* (5) The very scope of "science" protected by the right must be understood broadly as *Wissenschaft* (systematic, truth-seeking inquiry in all fields), with the consequence that the ethical, legal, and social scholarship necessary for responsible quantum development is also supported and protected.

Building on this analysis, several pathways toward a more rights-fulfilling quantum future emerge. An integrated approach is key, as the solutions to these barriers are mutually reinforcing. For example, calibrating export controls to be less restrictive not only respects the rights of individual researchers but also furthers the international collaboration needed to counter the global quantum divide.

These pathways require action from all major actors in the quantum ecosystem. States bear the primary duty to respect, protect, and fulfill the right to science, which means embedding its principles in their funding, regulatory, and foreign policies. The private sector, which drives much of quantum innovation, nevertheless has a responsibility, in line with the UN Guiding Principles on Business and Human Rights, to conduct due diligence on how their commercial practices impact the right to science. The research community, in turn, must not only advocate for scientific freedom but also actively contribute the empirical and normative analysis needed to inform rights-based governance.

At the same time, the right to science does not exist in isolation. States also carry duties to protect other fundamental rights, including the right to life, security, and dignity, as well as the rights of those beyond their borders. This raises the possibility that opening quantum technologies too widely or too quickly could create tensions with these parallel obligations—for example, where diffusion of cryptanalytic or surveillance capacities could enable authoritarian repression or large-scale human rights violations. International human rights law has long recognized such collisions between rights and duties, and courts have developed balancing principles to address them. The German constitutional doctrine of *praktische Konkordanz* ('practical concordance'), which has influenced human rights reasoning more broadly, is one influential example: it seeks to reconcile competing rights by ensuring that each is given the greatest possible effect, without sacrificing one entirely to the other. Applied to quantum computing, this suggests that barriers to access should not be absolute, but designed as proportionate, conditional, and, where possible, time-limited.

From this perspective, the challenge is not to deny access wholesale, but to calibrate restrictions so that they intrude no further than necessary to protect against real risks. Our earlier discussions of proportionality criteria provide one guide: States should favor semi-permeable arrangements—such as narrowly tailored export controls, monitored research collaborations, or tiered licensing schemes—over blanket exclusions. While such restrictions may be justified in principle, in practice they must be continuously scrutinized against the standards of necessity and proportionality, given the strong human rights claims that favor openness and diffusion. In short, practical concordance offers a framework for reconciling security-related duties with the imperative of broad scientific access, but it places a heavy burden on regulators to demonstrate that limitations remain narrowly crafted and temporary rather than entrenched.

To support both innovation and equity in the quantum ecosystem, policymakers should adopt governance strategies that align with the right to science while enabling agile, entrepreneurial market-driven development. Public R&D funding should include incentives for open standards, interoperable platforms, and shared infrastructure, which can reduce entry barriers for startups and academic labs. In parallel, regulatory sandboxes, public-private partnerships, and mission-driven innovation challenges can provide early-stage quantum ventures with the flexibility to develop socially beneficial applications without being prematurely constrained by heavy compliance burdens. These innovation-friendly mechanisms should be designed to uphold the core elements of the right to science—accessibility, participation, and scientific freedom—while encouraging entrepreneurship and diversification in the quantum sector.

At the international level, right to science-aligned quantum governance should emphasize inclusive standard-setting, responsible technology transfer, and equitable access to talent and infrastructure. Multilateral efforts—through organizations such as WIPO, ISO, IEC, and regional alliances—can help ensure that norms around intellectual property, international standards, export controls, and interoperability support open innovation and do not entrench early technological advantages. Startups and small and medium-sized enterprises, particularly in emerging markets, should be systematically included in global governance dialogues to avoid a two-tiered innovation landscape. By embedding right to science principles into both domestic and international policy frameworks, governments can help shape a quantum future that is not only competitive and secure, but also just, inclusive, and globally beneficial.

6.5 Conclusions

Quantum computing presents an inflection point not only for technological capability but for rethinking how global society governs emerging scientific frontiers. This chapter has argued that the right to science, grounded in international law, offers a valuable and underused framework for shaping the development and governance of quantum technologies in ways that promote equity, participation, and accountability.

Drawing on the AAAQ framework and the tripartite model of State obligations, we explored how right to science principles can illuminate structural barriers—ranging from geopolitical restrictions and uneven economic access to tensions between openness and scientific autonomy. We also examined the role of public and private actors, showing that while concerns about concentrated control are valid, empirical evidence (such as the patent landscape in quantum technologies) reveals a more open and pluralistic innovation environment than often assumed. Approximately half of existing quantum patents are in the public domain, and the field is currently less concentrated than classical computing, offering a critical window for proactive and inclusive governance.[172]

The right to science not only supports individual entitlements to access and benefit from scientific progress; it also guides collective decisions about whose voices are included in shaping scientific agendas, what norms govern participation, and how benefits are distributed. In the context of quantum computing—a field often framed in terms of national prestige or commercial competition—the right to science reorients the discussion toward human dignity, transnational justice, and long-term public interest.

This chapter calls for quantum governance strategies to integrate the legal and ethical obligations embedded in the right to science. Doing so would not only expand the legitimacy and inclusiveness of quantum technology development but also affirm the continuing relevance of international human rights law in navigating complex scientific futures. Quantum computing should not be treated solely as a strategic

[172] Aboy et al. (2022)

asset or commercial race; it must also be seen as a test of our global commitment to ensuring that science serves all of humanity.

To that end, policymakers should translate right to science principles into practical governance measures that also promote innovation. Public R&D investments should incentivize open standards and shared infrastructure to lower entry barriers for startups, while regulatory sandboxes and public-private partnerships can provide early-stage ventures with the flexibility to innovate responsibly. At the international level, standard-setting processes through bodies including WIPO, ISO, and IEC must ensure that standards, interoperability, IP rules, and export controls support a competitive yet inclusive quantum ecosystem. By embedding the right to science into both national strategies and multilateral coordination, governments can help steer quantum computing toward outcomes that are not only scientifically and technically groundbreaking, but also socially just and globally beneficial.

Ultimately, applying the standards of the right to science to quantum computing presents a key opportunity to advance two important frontiers simultaneously. It offers a principled, coherent, and legally grounded framework to guide the responsible development and governance of a transformative technology. At the same time, it gives concrete expression and immediate relevance to a fundamental human right which, much like quantum computing itself, will only grow in its power and importance in the coming decades.

Acknowledgments This work was made possible through the generous support of the Novo Nordisk Foundation (NNF) via a grant for the scientifically independent Collaborative Research Program in Bioscience Innovation Law (Inter-CeBIL Program—Grant No. NNF23SA0087056). Any use of AI in this manuscript adheres to ethical guidelines for use and acknowledgement of AI in academic research. Each author has made a substantial contribution to the work, which has been thoroughly vetted for accuracy, and assumes responsibility for the integrity of their contributions in accordance with the ethical guidance on AI use and disclosure set out by Porsdam Mann et al.[173]

References

Aboy, M., Minssen, T. and Kop, M., (2022). Mapping the patent landscape of quantum technologies: patenting trends, innovation and policy implications. IIC-International Review of Intellectual Property and Competition Law, 53(6), pp.853-882.

Aerospace (n.d.) A brief history of GPS. Available at: https://aerospace.org/article/brief-history-gps.

Allied Market Research (2025) *Dilution Refrigerators: 6.8% CAGR Growth Outlook 2025–2033.* 10 Jun 2025.

Amazon Web Services (n.d.) AWS Service Terms. Available at: https://aws.amazon.com/service-terms.

Austin, A. (2025) The world's top 10 institutions for quantum physics, *Nature Index*, 10.07.2025. Available at: https://www.nature.com/nature-index/news/ten-best-countries-for-quantum-physics-research.

[173] Porsdam Mann et al. (2024).

Beiter, K.D. (2019) Where have all the scientific and academic freedoms gone? And what is "adequate for science"? The right to enjoy the benefits of scientific progress and its applications. *Israel Law Review* 52:233.

Besson, S. (2023a) The "human right to science" qua right to participate in science. *The International Journal of Human Rights*, 28, 497

Besson, S. (2023b) Anticipation under the human right to science: concepts, stakes and specificities. *SSRN Working Paper*. Available at: https://papers.ssrn.com/abstract=4431685. Accessed 13 Dec 2023.

Bishop, L. (2021) Foreword. In: Porsdam, H., Porsdam Mann, S. (eds) *The Right to Science: Then and Now*. (Cambridge University Press, Cambridge), p. xi.

Boggio, A. (2021) The right to participate in and enjoy the benefits of scientific progress and its applications: a conceptual map. *New York International Law Review* 44:43.

Braben, D.W. (2007) *Scientific Freedom: The Elixir of Civilization*. (John Wiley & Sons, Chichester).

Bromley, M., Brockmann, K. (2021) Implementing the 2021 recast of the EU Dual-use Regulation: challenges and opportunities. *SIPRI Non-Proliferation and Disarmament Papers* No. 77 (Sept 2021).

Cassens, C. et al. (2025) Entanglement enhanced atomic gravimeter. *Physical Review X* 15, 011029.

Center for Quantum Networks (2022) Industrial Partners Program, § 13(c)–(d). Available at: https://cqn-erc.org/wp-content/uploads/2022/09/CQN-Industrial-Partners-Program-IPP-May2022.pdf.

Centre for Security and Emerging Technology (2021) Outline of the People's Republic of China 14th Five-Year Plan for National Economic and Social Development and Long-Range Objectives for 2035. Xinhua News Agency, 12 Mar 2021. Translation available at: https://cset.georgetown.edu/wp-content/uploads/t0284_14th_Five_Year_Plan_EN.pdf.

Chapman, A. (1998) A human rights perspective on intellectual property. In: *Intellectual Property and Human Rights: Proceedings of a Panel Discussion held by the World Intellectual Property Organization in collaboration with the Office of the United Nations High Commissioner for Human Rights, 9 November 1998*. WIPO, Geneva, pp. 126–168.

Chen, G. (2023) China's first Intellectual Property Alliance for Quantum Computing Industry is set up in Beijing. *JW Insights*, 28 Mar 2023. Available at: https://jw.ijiwei.com/n/854240.

Churches, G., Zalnieriute, M. (2020) "Contracting Out" human rights in international law: *Schrems II* and the fundamental flaws of U.S. surveillance law. 14 Aug 2020. Available at: https://journals.law.harvard.edu/ilj/2020/08/contracting-out-human-rights-in-international-law-schrems-ii-and-the-fundamental-flaws-of-u-s-surveillance-law/. Accessed 16 Jun 2025.

Clark, D. (1988) The design philosophy of the DARPA internet protocols. *SIGCOMM Computer Communication Review* 18:106. doi:https://doi.org/10.1145/52325.52336

Committee on Economic, Social and Cultural Rights (2017) General Comment No. 24 on State obligations under the ICESCR in the context of business activities. UN Doc. E/C.12/GC/24.

Committee on Economic, Social and Cultural Rights (CESCR) (1991) General Comment No. 3: The nature of States parties' obligations (Art. 2, para. 1, of the Covenant). UN Doc. E/1991/23.

Committee on Economic, Social and Cultural Rights (CESCR) (1999) General Comment No. 13: The right to education (Art. 13 of the Covenant). UN Doc. E/C.12/1999/10.

Committee on Economic, Social and Cultural Rights (CESCR) (2000) General Comment No. 14: The right to the highest attainable standard of health (Art. 12). UN Doc. E/C.12/2000/4.

Committee on Economic, Social and Cultural Rights (CESCR) (2009) General Comment No. 21: The right of everyone to take part in cultural life (Art. 15, para. 1(a)). UN Doc. E/C.12/GC/21.

Committee on Economic, Social and Cultural Rights (CESCR) (2020) General Comment No. 25 on science and economic, social and cultural rights. UN Doc. E/C.12/GC/25.

Craven, M.C.R. (2002) *The International Covenant on Economic, Social and Cultural Rights: A Perspective on Its Development*. (Clarendon Press, Oxford).

DARPA (2023) DARPA-funded research leads to quantum computing breakthrough. Available at: https://www.darpa.mil/news/2023/quantum-computing-breakthrough.

Das, S., Chatterjee, A., Ghosh, S. (2023) SoK: A first order survey of quantum supply dynamics and threat landscapes. In: *Proceedings of the 12th International Workshop on Hardware and Architectural Support for Security and Privacy (HASP '23).* (Association for Computing Machinery, New York), 82.

Davies, A.C.L. (2016) Judicial review and Human Rights Act review in contracted-out public services: options for litigation in English law. In: Kahana, T., Scolnicov, A., (eds) *Boundaries of State, Boundaries of Rights: Human Rights, Private Actors, and Positive Obligations.* (Cambridge University Press, Cambridge). Available at: https://www.cambridge.org/core/books/boundaries-of-state-boundaries-of-rights/judicial-review-and-human-rights-act-review-in-contractedout-public-services/A4998B432E84874F7E854904E082FF56. Accessed 16 Jun 2025.

Dhawan, S. (2025) Covid genome sequencers lying defunct at two Rohtak institutes. *The Tribune India*, 5 Jun 2025. Available at: https://www.tribuneindia.com/news/haryana/covid-genome-sequencers-lying-defunct-at-two-rohtak-institutes.

Diffie, W., Landau, S. (2001) The export of cryptography in the 20th century and the 21st. In: Treichel, J., Holzer, M. (eds) *Sun Microsystems Laboratories: The First Ten Years 1991–2001*, Sun Labs Perspectives Essay Series, pp. 410–415. Available at: https://privacyink.org/pdf/export_control.pdf.

Donders, Y., Plozza, M. (2023) Look before you leap: states' prevention and anticipation duties under the right to science. *The International Journal of Human Rights* 28, 354.

DukeSpace (n.d.) *The Bermuda Principles.* Available at: https://hdl.handle.net/10161/7407.

Eide, A. (1987) Report on the right to adequate food as a human right. UN Doc. E/CN.4/Sub.2/1987/23.

European Commission (2020) Making the Most of the EU's Innovative Potential—An Intellectual Property Action Plan to support the EU's Recovery and Resilience. COM(2020) 760.

European Commission (2021) Commission Recommendation (EU) 2021/1700 of 15 September 2021 on internal compliance programmes for controls of research involving dual-use items under Regulation (EU) 2021/821 of the European Parliament and of the Council setting up a Union regime for the control of exports, brokering, technical assistance, transit and transfer of dual-use items, OJ L 338, 23.9.2021, pp. 1–52.

European Commission (2023a) Joint Communication to the European Parliament, the European Council and the Council on "Economic Security Strategy". JOIN(2023) 20 final, 20 Jun 2023.

European Commission (2023b) Recommendation on critical technology areas for the EU's economic security for further risk assessment with Member States, C(2023) 6689 final, 3 Oct 2023.

European Commission (2024) Proposal for a Council Recommendation on enhancing research security. COM(2024) 26. Available at: https://research-and-innovation.ec.europa.eu/document/download/e82a2fd9-ac12-488a-a948-87639eef10d4_en.

European Commission (2025) Commission Delegated Regulation (EU) 2021/2126 of 29 September 2021 amending the Annex to Regulation (EU) 2019/452 of the European Parliament and of the Council establishing a framework for the screening of foreign direct investments into the Union, OJ L 432, 3.12.2021, pp. 1–6.

European Patent Office (2023) *Quantum computing: Insight report.* Munich: European Patent Office. Available at: https://link.epo.org/web/epo_patent_insight_report-quantum_computing_en.pdf.

European Union (2021a) Regulation (EU) 2021/695 of the European Parliament and of the Council of 28 April 2021 establishing Horizon Europe—the Framework Programme for Research and Innovation, laying down its rules for participation and dissemination, and repealing Regulations (EU) No 1290/2013 and (EU) No 1291/2013. OJ L 170, 12.5.2021, pp. 1–68.

European Union (2021b) Regulation (EU) 2021/821 of the European Parliament and of the Council of 20 May 2021 setting up a Union regime for the control of exports, brokering, technical assistance, transfer and transit of dual-use items, OJ L 206 11.6.2021.

Executive Office of the President of the United States (2022) National Strategy for Advanced Manufacturing. Available at: https://www.energy.gov/sites/default/files/2024-03/National-Strategy-for-Advanced-Manufacturing-10072022.pdf.

Fajardo-Ortiz, D., Hornbostel, S., Montenegro de Wit, M., Shattuck, A. (2022) Funding CRISPR: understanding the role of government and philanthropic institutions in supporting academic research within the CRISPR innovation system. *Quantitative Science Studies* 3:443.

Farrell, J., Klemperer, P. (2007) Coordination and lock-in: competition with switching costs and network effects. In: Armstrong, M., Porter, R. (eds) *Handbook of Industrial Organization*, Vol. 3. (North-Holland, Amsterdam), 1967.

Foxon, T.J. (2002) Technological and institutional 'lock-in' as a barrier to sustainable innovation. ICCEPT Working Paper, November 2002. Available at: https://www.imperial.ac.uk/media/imperial-college/research-centres-and-groups/icept/7294726.PDF.

Germany (2009) Patent Act (*Patentgesetz*), as amended to 17 Dec 2008. Available at: https://www.wipo.int/wipolex/en/text/462033.

Green, M. (2000) Drafting history of Article 15(1)(c) of the International Covenant on Economic, Social and Cultural Rights. UN Doc. E/C.12/2000/15.

Hansson, S.O. (2013) Defining pseudoscience and science. In: Pigliucci, M., Boudry, M. (eds) *Philosophy of Pseudoscience*. (University of Chicago Press, Chicago).

Haugen, H.M. (2025) A human right to science: inadequate without participation in science? Human rights as a governance tool in scientific fields. *Nordic Journal of Human Rights* 43:1.

Hosseinkhani, S., et al. (2025) Noise-robust estimation of quantum observables in noisy hardware. *arXiv* 2503.06695.

Hu, Y., et al. (2021) Merkle^2: a low-latency transparency log system. *IACR ePrint* 2021/453.

Huang, H.-L., et al. (2017) Homomorphic encryption experiments on IBM's cloud quantum computing platform. *Frontiers of Physics* 12:120305.

IBM (2023) Build utility-scale quantum applications with the updated Open Plan and IBM Quantum Credits. Available at: https://www.ibm.com/quantum/blog/utility-scale-quantum-credits.

IBM Cloud (2022) FAQs for IBM Cloud Qiskit Runtime, 14 Apr 2022. Available at: https://cloud.ibm.com/docs/quantum-computing?topic=quantum-computing-qiskit-runtime-faqs.

IBM Quantum Platform (2023) IBM Quantum End User Agreement, 2 Dec 2023. Available at: https://quantum.ibm.com/terms.

Innovation News Network (2025) UNESCO launches the International Year of Quantum Science and Technology. 6 Feb 2025. Available at: https://www.innovationnewsnetwork.com/unesco-launches-the-international-year-of-quantum-science-and-technology/55248.

International Atomic Energy Agency (1996) *Clearance levels for radionuclides in solid materials: application of exemption principles*. Interim report for comment, IAEA-TECDOC-855. Available at: https://www-pub.iaea.org/MTCD/Publications/PDF/te_855_web.pdf.

International Commission of Jurists (1997) Maastricht Guidelines on Violations of Economic, Social and Cultural Rights. Available at: https://www.refworld.org/policy/legalguidance/icjurists/1997/en/63964.

Internet Society (1997) A brief history of the Internet. B.M. Leiner, et al. Available at: https://www.internetsociety.org/wp-content/uploads/2017/09/ISOC-History-of-the-Internet_1997.pdf.

IUCRC (n.d.) Membership Agreement, cl. F. Available at: https://iucrc.nsf.gov/industry/joining-a-center/membership-agreement/.

Karanicolas, M. (2024) Challenging minority rule: developing AI standards that serve the majority world. *U.C.L.A. Law Review* (online), 21 May 2024. Available at: https://www.uclalawreview.org/challenging-minority-rule-developing-ai-standards-that-serve-the-majority-world/.

Karanicolas, M., Zornetta, A. (2025) The digital divide meets the quantum divide. *Just Security*, 1 May 2025. Available at: https://www.justsecurity.org/111035/digital-divide-meets-quantum-divide.

Kavianpour, S., Sutherland, J., Mansouri-Benssassi, E., Coull, N., Jefferson, E. (2022) Next-generation capabilities in Trusted Research Environments: interview study. *Journal of Medical Internet Research* 24(9):e33720.

Kowalczyk, M., et al. (2024) Rapid deployment of confidential cloud applications with Gramine. *ACSAC 2024*, Artifacts Competition and Impact Award. Available at: https://www.acsac.org/2024/program/artifacts_competition.

Leiner B.M. et al., (1999) A Brief History of the Internet, arXiv:cs/9901011.

Ma, Y., Kashefi, E., Arapinis, M., et al. (2022) QEnclave: a practical solution for secure quantum cloud computing. *npj Quantum Information* 8:128. doi:https://doi.org/10.1038/s41534-022-00612-5.

Mancisidor, M. (2021) The dawning of a right: science and the Universal Declaration of Human Rights (1941–1948). In: Porsdam, H., Porsdam Mann, S. (eds) *The Right to Science: Then and Now*. (Cambridge University Press, Cambridge), pp. 17–32.

Mason, E.J. (2024) State of quantum industry innovation: what patents tell us. *QED-C Blog*, 11 Dec 2024. Available at: https://quantumconsortium.org/publication/state-of-quantum-industry-innovation-what-patents-tell-us.

Massachusetts Institute of Technology, Office of the Vice President for Research (n.d.) Using restricted material at MIT. Available at: https://research.mit.edu/security-integrity-and-compliance/export-control/scholarly-activities/using-restricted-material-mit.

Massimi, M. (2025) Local knowledges and the right to participate in science. *Philosophy of Science* [early view]:1.

Mazibrada, A. (2022) Is there a right to be protected from the adverse effects of scientific progress and its applications? *EJIL:Talk!* Available at: https://www.ejiltalk.org/is-there-a-right-to-be-protected-from-the-adverse-effects-of-scientific-progress-and-its-applications/. Accessed 15 Jun 2023.

Mazibrada, A., Plozza, M., Porsdam Mann, S. (2023) Innovating in uncharted terrain: on interpretation and normative legitimacy in the CESCR's General Comment No. 25 on the right to science. *The International Journal of Human Rights* 28:148.

Microsoft (n.d.-a) Azure Preview Supplemental Terms. Available at: https://azure.microsoft.com/en-us/support/legal/preview-supplemental-terms.

Microsoft (n.d.-b) Azure Online Subscription Agreement. Available at: https://azure.microsoft.com/en-us/support/legal/subscription-agreement/

MITxOnline (n.d.) *Computational Data Science in Physics I*—"Who can take this course?" Available at: https://mitxonline.mit.edu/courses/course-v1:MITxT+8.S50.1x.

Moyo, E., Moyo, P., Mashe, T., Dzobo, M., Chitungo, I., Dzinamarira, T. (2023) Implementation of public health genomics in Africa: lessons from the COVID-19 pandemic, challenges, and recommendations. *Journal of Medical Virology* 95(1):e28295.

Müller, A. (2010) Remarks on the Venice Statement on the right to enjoy the benefits of scientific progress and its applications (Article 15(1)(b) ICESCR). *Human Rights Law Review* 10: 765.

National Institute of Standards and Technology (2025) Post-Quantum Cryptography FAQ. Available at: https://csrc.nist.gov/projects/post-quantum-cryptography/faqs. Accessed 9 Jun 2025.

OECD (2025) *A quantum technologies policy primer*. *OECD Digital Economy Papers* No. 371´. https://doi.org/10.1787/fd1153c3-en.

Pécoul, B., Sevcsik, A.M., Amuasi, J., Diap, G., Kiechel, J.R. (2008) The story of ASAQ: the first antimalarial product development partnership success. In: Matlin, S.A., de Francisco, A., Sundaram, L., Faich, H.S., Gehner, M. (eds) *Health Partnerships Review*. (Global Forum for Health Research, Geneva), 77.

Perehudoff K, Sellin J. (2022) The Right to Science as a Guidepost for Fair Access to COVID-19 Vaccines: Investigating the Interpretive Role of the United Nations Committee on Economic, Social and Cultural Rights. Health Hum Rights 24: 191.

Perrier, E. (2022) Ethical quantum computing: a roadmap. *arXiv* (20 Apr 2022). Available at: http://arxiv.org/abs/2102.00759. Accessed 15 Jun 2025.

Phillips, D. (2015) Francis Bacon and the Germans: stories from when "science" meant "Wissenschaft". *History of Science* 53: 378.

Plomer, A. (2021) IP rights and human rights: what history tells us and why it matters. In: Porsdam, H., Porsdam Mann, S. (eds) *The Right to Science: Then and Now*. (Cambridge University Press, Cambridge).
Porsdam, H. (2022) *Science as a Cultural Human Right*. (University of Pennsylvania Press, Philadelphia).
Porsdam, H., Porsdam Mann, S. (eds) (2021) *The Right to Science: Then and Now*. (Cambridge University Press, Cambridge).
Porsdam Mann, S. (2024a) The right to science or to *Wissenschaft*? Five lessons from the *travaux préparatoires*. *Netherlands Quarterly of Human Rights* 42: 153.
Porsdam Mann, S. (2024b) *The Orphan of Time: A History and Theory of the Human Right to Science*. D.Phil. thesis, University of Oxford.
Porsdam Mann, S., Porsdam, H., Donders, Y. (2020) "Sleeping Beauty": The Right to Science as a Global Ethical Discourse. *Human Rights Quarterly* 42: 332.
Porsdam Mann, S., Vazirani, A. A., Aboy, M., Earp, B. D., Minssen, T., Cohen, I. G., Savulescu, J. (2024b). Guidelines for ethical use and acknowledgement of large language models in academic writing. *Nature Machine Intelligence* 6: 1272.
Porsdam Mann, S., et al. (2018) Advocating for science progress as a human right. *Proceedings of the National Academy of Sciences* 115: 10820.
Porsdam Mann, S., et al. (2024a) *Scientific Freedom: The Heart of the Right to Science*. (Rowman & Littlefield, Lanham, MD).
qBraid (n.d.) Pricing for IonQ Forte-1 on AWS/qBraid. Available at: https://www.qbraid.com/pricing.
Quantum Computing Report (2024) Not New, Now Booming: On-premise quantum computing. Dec 2024. Available at: https://quantumcomputingreport.com/not-new-now-booming-on-premise-quantum-computing/.
Quantum Delta NL (n.d.) *IP Guidelines*. Available at: https://assets.quantum-delta.prod.verveagency.com/assets/qdnl-ip-guidelines.pdf.
Post Quantum (2023) Quantum radar: the next frontier of stealth detection and beyond, 15 Feb. 2023. Available at: https://postquantum.com/quantum-sensing/quantum-radar/.
Räsänen, M., Mäkynen, H., Möttönen, M., Goetz, J. (2021) Path to European quantum unicorns. *EPJ Quantum Technology* 8:5. https://doi.org/10.1140/epjqt/s40507-021-00095-x.
Riedel, E. (2012) Sleeping Beauty or Let Sleeping Dogs Lie? The Right of Everyone to Enjoy the Benefits of Scientific Progress and Its Applications (REBSPA). In: Hestermeyer, H. et al. (eds) *Coexistence, Cooperation and Solidarity* (2 vols.). (Brill/Nijhoff, Leiden/Boston).
Roblin, S. (2025) Quantum Sensors' Could Make America's Billion-Dollar Submarines Obsolete. *Popular Mechanics*, 30 Jan 2025. Available at: https://www.popularmechanics.com/military/navy-ships/a63382376/quantum-sensors-submarines/.
Romano, C., Boggio, A. (2024) *The Human Right to Science: History, Development, and Normative Content*. 1st ed. (Oxford University Press, Oxford).
Schabas, W.A. (2024) Codifying the human right to science. *The International Journal of Human Rights* 28: 313.
Shaheed, F. (2012) The right to enjoy the benefits of scientific progress and its applications. UN Doc. A/HRC/20/26.
Shapiro, C. (2001) Navigating the Patent Thicket: Cross Licenses, Patent Pools, and Standard Setting. Innovation Policy and the Economy. *Innovation Policy and the Economy* 1: 119.
Shaver, L. (2010) The right to science and culture. *Wisconsin Law Review* 2010:121.
Shikarpur, P. (2022) A TamperProof logging implementation. *Pangea Cloud* blog, 15 Jun 2022.
Shor, P.W. (1994) Algorithms for quantum computation: discrete logarithms and factoring. In: *Proceedings 35th Annual Symposium on Foundations of Computer Science 1994*, pp. 124.
Shue, H. (2020) *Basic Rights: Subsistence, Affluence, and U.S. Foreign Policy*. 40th Anniversary Edition. (Princeton University Press, Princeton). Available at: http://www.jstor.org/stable/10.2307/j.ctvqsdnkw. Accessed 6 Jun 2025.

Ten Holter, C., Inglesant, P., Jirotka, M. (2023) Reading the road: challenges and opportunities on the path to responsible innovation in quantum computing. *Technology Analysis & Strategic Management* 35: 844.

Tetteh, E.K. (2009) Implementing differential pricing for essential medicines via country-specific bilateral negotiated discounts. *Applied Health Economics and Health Policy* 7:71. https://doi.org/10.1007/BF03256143

The Hindu (2022) India, Finland to establish Virtual Network Centre on Quantum Computing. 19 Apr 2022. Available at: https://www.thehindu.com/sci-tech/technology/india-finland-to-establish-virtual-network-centre-on-quantum-computing/article65335313.ece.

Tomasevski, K. (1999) Preliminary report of the Special Rapporteur on the right to education, submitted in accordance with Commission on Human Rights Resolution 1998/33.

Trouiller, P. et al. (2002) Drug Development for Neglected Diseases: A Deficient Market and a Public Health Policy Failure, The Lancet 359, 2188.

UK Export Control Joint Unit, Department for International Trade and Department for Business and Trade (2025) Open General Export Licences (updated 13 Oct 2025). Available at: https://www.gov.uk/government/collections/open-general-export-licences-ogels.

UN Commission on Human Rights (1952) 'Summary Record of the Two Hundred and Ninety-Second Meeting [of the Commission on Human Rights], 27 May 1952, UN Doc E/CN.4/SR.292

UNESCO (1974) Recommendation on the Status of Scientific Researchers. 18 C/Resolutions.

UNESCO (2009) Venice Statement on the right to enjoy the benefits of scientific progress and its applications. UN Doc. SHS/RSP/HRS-GED/2009/PI/H/1.

UNESCO (2017) *Recommendation on Science and Scientific Researchers*. SHS/BIO/PI/2017/3.

UNESCO (n.d.-a) Addressing global challenges through science diplomacy and scientific excellence: the CERN model. Available at: https://www.unesco.org/en/articles/addressing-global-challenges-though-science-diplomacy-and-scientific-excellence-cern-model.

UNESCO (n.d.-b) SESAME: scientific excellence in the Middle East. Available at: https://courier.unesco.org/en/articles/sesame-scientific-excellence-middle-east.

United Kingdom (1977) *Patents Act 1977*.

United Nations (1987) The Limburg Principles on the Implementation of the International Covenant on Economic, Social and Cultural Rights. UN Doc. E/CN.4/1987/17.

United Nations (2011) *Guiding Principles on Business and Human Rights: Implementing the United Nations "Protect, Respect and Remedy" Framework*. (United Nations, New York). Available at: https://www.ohchr.org/sites/default/files/Documents/Publications/GuidingPrinciplesBusinessHR_EN.pdf. Accessed 16 Jun 2025.

United Nations Framework Convention on Climate Change (UNFCCC) (n.d.) *Technology Mechanism*. Available at: https://unfccc.int/ttclear/support/technology-mechanism.html.

United Nations General Assembly (1948) Universal Declaration of Human Rights. Resolution 217 A (III), 10 December 1948.

United Nations General Assembly (1957) Summary record of the 796th meeting of the Third Committee (31 Oct 1957). UN Doc. A/C.3/SR.796.

United Nations General Assembly (1966a) International Covenant on Civil and Political Rights (ICCPR). Resolution 2200A (XXI), adopted 16 December 1966, entered into force 23 March 1976.

United Nations General Assembly (1966b) International Covenant on Economic, Social and Cultural Rights (ICESCR). Resolution 2200A (XXI), adopted 16 December 1966, entered into force 3 January 1976.

United Nations General Assembly (2015) Report on patent policy and the right to science and culture. A/70/279.

United Nations Human Rights Council (2009) Resolution 10/23: Independent Expert in the field of cultural rights. UN Doc. A/HRC/RES/10/23.

United Nations Human Rights Council (2011) Guiding Principles on Business and Human Rights. UN Doc. A/HRC/17/31.

United Nations Human Rights Council (2012) Resolution 19/6: Special Rapporteur in the field of cultural rights. UN Doc. A/HRC/RES/19/6.
United Nations Human Rights Council, Special Rapporteur in the field of cultural rights (Xanthaki, A.) (2024) *Right to Participate in Science.* UN Doc. A/HRC/55/44.
United States (n.d.) Export Administration Regulations, 15 C.F.R. § 774, Supplement No. 1 (Commerce Control List).
United States Bureau of Industry and Security (2023a) Implementation of Additional Export Controls: Certain Advanced Computing Items; Supercomputer and Semiconductor End Use; Updates and Corrections, *Federal Register* 88:73458 (25 Oct 2023).
United States Bureau of Industry and Security (2023b) Public comments on "Implementation of Additional Export Controls: Certain Advanced Computing and Semiconductor Manufacturing Items; Supercomputer and Semiconductor End Use; Entity List Modification," Docket BIS-2022-0025-0052. Available at: https://www.regulations.gov/document/BIS-2022-0025-0052.
United States Bureau of Industry and Security (2024) Commerce Control List additions and revisions; implementation of controls on advanced technologies consistent with controls implemented by international partners. *Federal Register* 89:72926, (6 Sep 2024).
United States Congress (1951) Invention Secrecy Act of 1951, Pub. L. 82-256.
United States Congress (2018a) National Quantum Initiative Act, Pub. L. 115-368.
United States Congress (2018b) Export Control Reform Act of 2018, 50 U.S.C.
United States Congress (2022) CHIPS and Science Act of 2022, Pub. L. 117-167.
United States Patent and Trademark Office (n.d.) 120 Secrecy Orders [R-07.2022].
Van Daalen, O. (2024) Developing a Human Rights Compatible Governance Framework for Quantum Computing. Research Directions: Quantum Technologies 2, e1.
Van Daalen, O. (2025) From Encryption to Quantum Computing—The Governance of Information Security and Human Rights. Vol. 38. (TMC Asser Press, The Hague). Available at: https://link.springer.com/10.1007/978-94-6265-635-2_1. Accessed 6 Jun 2025.
Vermaas, P., Mans, U. (2024) Quantum technologies and their global impact: discussion paper. UNESCO, CI/DIT/2024/QP/01. Available at: https://unesdoc.unesco.org/ark:/48223/pf0000388955.
Weinberger, S. (2008) Lockheed's "Spooky Radar" gets U.S. patent. *Wired*, 22 May 2008.
Wininger, A. (2025) China's National Intellectual Property Administration releases Guidelines for the Construction and Operation of Patent Pools. *China IP Law Update* blog, 15 May 2025. Available at: https://www.chinaiplawupdate.com/2025/05/chinas-national-intellectual-property-administration-releases-guidelines-for-the-construction-and-operation-of-patent-pools/.
World Services Group (2017) New rules published by the Israeli Innovation Authority. Available at: https://www.worldservicesgroup.com/publications.asp?action=article&artid=8603.
World Trade Organization (1995) *Agreement on Trade-Related Aspects of Intellectual Property Rights (TRIPS).*
World Trade Organization (2022) TRIPS Council welcomes MC12 TRIPS waiver decision, discusses possible extension. 6 Jul 2022. Available at: https://www.wto.org/english/news_e/news22_e/trip_08jul22_e.htm.

Index

M. Aboy et al. (eds.), *Quantum Technology Governance II*, Perspectives in Law, Business and Innovation, https://doi.org/10.1007/978-981-92-3768-5